APPROACHES TO ANCIENT JUDAISM

BROWN UNIVERSITY
BROWN JUDAIC STUDIES

edited by

Jacob Neusner

Ernest S. Frerichs

Richard S. Sarason

Wendell S. Dietrich

Number 1

APPROACHES TO ANCIENT JUDAISM:
Theory and Practice

edited by
William Scott Green

SCHOLARS PRESS
Missoula, Montana

APPROACHES TO ANCIENT JUDAISM:

Theory and Practice

edited
by
William Scott Green

Published by
SCHOLARS PRESS
for
Brown University

Distributed by

SCHOLARS PRESS
Missoula, Montana 59806

APPROACHES TO ANCIENT JUDAISM:

Theory and Practice
edited
by
William Scott Green

Library of Congress Cataloging in Publication Data

Main entry under title:

Approaches to ancient Judaism.

   (Brown Judaic Studies ; no. 1)
   Includes bibliographical references and index.
   1. Judaism—History—Post exilic period, 586 B.C.-
210 A.D.—Addresses, essays, lectures. 2. Rabbinical
literature—History and criticism—Addresses, essays,
lectures. 3. Jewish studies—Addresses, essays, lectures. I. Green, William Scott. II. Title.
BM173.A66   296'.09   76-57656
ISBN 0-89130-130-5

Printed in the United States of America
1 2 3 4 5

Edwards Brothers, Inc.
Ann Arbor, Michigan 48104

For

Harmon R. Holcomb

The publication of this volume was made possible through funds provided by the Jewish Community Federation of Rochester, New York, Irving Ruderman, President, Darrell D. Friedman, Executive Director.

1, 2, 5, 9

TABLE OF CONTENTS

PREFACE

My teacher, Jacob Neusner, encouraged the preparation of this volume and generously gave his time to discuss its form and content. His continued interest and support helped to make this project a reality and are acknowledged with deep appreciation. This anthology takes its place among the inaugural volumes of *Brown Judaic Studies* and will, I hope, constitute a useful beginning to an important new venture in American scholarship on Judaism.

It is a pleasure to record my gratitude to the Jewish Community Federation of Rochester, New York for its support of the publication of this volume. The desire of the Federation generously to commit its resources, both human and financial, to the scholarly study of Judaism illustrates a recognition of the value of learning which is utterly exceptional among Federations nationally but wholly typical of the Jewish Community of Rochester. My profound thanks go to the Federation, its President, Mr. Irving Ruderman, and its Executive Director, Mr. Darrell D. Friedman.

Thanks also are due to my student, Paul V. Flesher, who assisted with the proofreading and compiled the index, and to Michael Sullivan and Joanna Alexander, whose preliminary rendering of Renée Bloch's "Note methodologique pour l'étude de la litterature rabbinique" formed the basis for parts of the present translation.

I have tried throughout the volume to maintain consistency in abbreviations and in the transliteration of Hebrew and Aramaic terms. Certain of the latter, however, because of frequent use, are treated by some authors as English words. This and the choice of footnote style were left to the various authors, as was the English spelling of vocalized Hebrew.

Geza Vermes' essay, "The Impact of the Dead Sea Scrolls on Jewish Studies during the last Twenty-Five Years," initially appeared in the *Journal of Jewish Studies*, XXVI (1975), pp. 1-14, and is reprinted by permission. The two articles of Renée Bloch originally appeared in French as follows: "Midrash" in *Supplément au Dictionnaire de la Bible*, Vol. V (Paris, 1957), col. 1263-1281, and "Note methodologique pour l'étude de la litterature rabbinique," *Recherches de Science Religieuse*, XLIII (1955), pp. 194-227. They are offered here for the first time in English translation.

In addition, my thanks go to my student, Marjory Aronson, for her help with the page-proofs and to Professors James Rieger, University of Rochester, and Richard Sarason, Brown University, for assistance in correcting some inaccurate renderings in Chapter III. A final word of special gratitude goes to Professor Robert Funk, Director of Scholars Press, and Ms. Carol Denison, Production Manager. Their professionalism, commitment to quality and patience with a rather protracted editorial process made working on this book both a pleasure and an education.

This anthology is dedicated to a colleague and a friend who, because of his extraordinary and acute intellect and his remarkable and responsive humanity, has created an environment at the University of Rochester in which the academic study of religion not only exists, but thrives.

                                                                          W. S. G.

Rochester, New York
October 8, 1976
ᶜErev Sukkot, 5737

ABBREVIATIONS

b.	=	Babylonian Talmud
B.B.	=	Bava Batra
B.M.	=	Bava Meṣiᶜaᵓ
Ber.	=	Berakot
CBQ	=	*Catholic Biblical Quarterly*
Chron.	=	Chronicles
Cor.	=	Corinthians
Dan.	=	Daniel
D.B.S.	=	*Dictionnaire de la Bible Supplement*
Deut.	=	Deuteronomy
Eccles.	=	Ecclesiastes
ᶜEd.	=	ᶜEduyot
Esth.	=	Esther
Ex.	=	Exodus
Gal.	=	Galatians
Gen.	=	Genesis
Giṭ.	=	Giṭṭin
Heb.	=	Hebrews
Hos.	=	Hosea
HTR	=	*Harvard Theological Review*
HUCA	=	*Hebrew Union College Annual*
Is.	=	Isaiah
JJS	=	*Journal of Jewish Studies*
JQR	=	*Jewish Quarterly Review*
Jer.	=	Jeremiah
Kel.	=	Kelim
Ket.	=	Ketuvot
Kip.	=	Kippurim
Lam.	=	Lamentations
Lev.	=	Leviticus
Lk.	=	Luke
M.	=	Mishnah
Matt.	=	Matthew
M.Q.	=	Moᶜed Qaṭan
Maksh.	=	Makshirin
Mekhilta	=	Mekhilta de Rabbi Ishmael
MGWJ	=	*Monatschrift für Geschichte und Wissenschaft des Judenthums*
Miq.	=	Miqvaᶜot
Mk.	=	Mark
Ned.	=	Nedarim
Neh.	=	Nehemiah
Nid.	=	Niddah
Num.	=	Numbers
Num. R.	=	Numbers Rabbah
PAAJR	=	*Proceedings of the American Academy of Jewish Research*

Par.	=	Parah
Pes.	=	Pesaḥim
Pesh.	=	Peshitto
Pes. R.	=	Pesiqta Rabbati
Prov.	=	Proverbs
Ps.	=	Psalms
Qid.	=	Qiddushin
RB	=	*Revue Biblique*
RecSR	=	*Recherches de Science Religieuse*
REJ	=	*Revue des Etudes Juives*
Rom.	=	Romans
Sanh.	=	Sanhedrin
Shab.	=	Shabbat

Shevu.	=	Shevuᶜot
Sheq.	=	Sheqalim
Song	=	Song of Songs
Suk.	=	Sukkah
Ta.	=	Taᶜanit
Ter.	=	Terumot
TgJ	=	Jerusalem Targum
Toh.	=	Tohorot
Tos.	=	Tosefta
VT	=	*Vetus Testamentum*
y.	=	Palestinian Talmud
Yev.	=	Yevamot
Zach.	=	Zachariah

TRANSLITERATIONS

א	=	ʾ	מ ם	=	m
ב	=	b	נ ן	=	n
ג	=	g	ס	=	s
ד	=	d	ע	=	ʿ
ה	=	h	פ ף	=	p
ו	=	w	צ ץ	=	ṣ
ז	=	z	ק	=	q
ח	=	ḥ	ר	=	r
ט	=	ṭ	שׁ	=	š
י	=	y	שׂ	=	ś
כ ך	=	k	ת	=	t
ל	=	l			

Introduction

WILLIAM SCOTT GREEN

UNIVERSITY OF ROCHESTER

Although it begins with artifacts and documents of the past, historical investigation ultimately is the product of the historian's curiosity, imagination and mode of argumentation. These three elemental features, and the interplay among them, generate the problems the historian tries to solve, transform neutral data into revealing, even probative evidence, and, in general, make the writing of history into something more than aimless antiquarian jottings. As Hayden White observes, "Before the historian can bring to bear upon the data of the historical field the conceptual apparatus he will use to represent and explain it, he must first *pre*figure the field—that is to say, constitute it as an object of mental perception."[1] This suggests that it is the approach adopted by the investigator which determines the scope and depth of the inquiry as well as the viability and durability of its results. White further specifies that ". . . before a given domain can be interpreted, it must first be construed as a ground inhabited by discernible figures. The figures, in turn, must be conceived to be classifiable as distinctive orders, classes, genera, and species of phenomena. Moreover, they must be conceived to bear certain kinds of relationships to one another, the transformation of which will constitute the 'problems' to be solved by the 'explanations' provided on the levels of emplotment and argument in the [historian's] narrative."[2] In any given case, then, the sort of analysis or history which is produced is a function not only of the primary materials which constitute the object of research, but also of the way those materials are characterized and portrayed, the questions which are then brought to them, and the procedures which are employed to answer those questions.

These observations may strike some readers as commonplace, but because they evidently have played a minor role in its past, they bear a particular pertinence to the study of ancient Judaism and therefore merit repetition. The data about ancient Judaism include literature of diverse sorts produced by different groups of Jews at various periods of time, archaeological relict and the reports of outside, sometimes hostile observers. These variegated materials offer dissimilar pictures of the phenomena which constitute ancient Judaism, and we certainly cannot suppose that they provide a comprehensive testimony. Following White, our ability to penetrate the complex religious systems of ancient Judaism depends on the techniques we use to distinguish and classify these different kinds of data and on the processes of reasoning with which we evaluate and integrate the various perspectives they offer. The failure to assess the nature of the data before determining their implications and the inattention to a range of legitimate hermeneutical options, both characteristic of past research, yield a monolithic depiction of evidence and a consequent description of ancient Judaism which is unbalanced, if not altogether arbitrary.

The papers contained in this volume were selected neither because they treat a common problem nor because they address a common theme, but because they illustrate the attitude which informs the remarks above. Either by argument or example, they represent different approaches to the critical study of ancient Judaism. Some selections are primarily conceptual; they attempt to identify a problem to be studied, to unravel its internal logic and expose its dynamic. Others focus on particular materials from ancient, principally rabbinic, Judaism (exegetical or liturgical literature, for instance) and construct, defend or demonstrate a technique for analyzing them. The several papers highlight the dialectical relationship between fixed data and scholarly imagination either by showing how new methods enrich our understanding of familiar materials or by indicating how new materials necessitate the rethinking and reformulation of old questions. Despite their varied perspectives, they uniformly exhibit a posture which is authentically critical. The purpose of this volume, then, is heuristic. It is intended to indicate something of the variety of materials which testify about ancient Judaism, to underscore the legitimate application to those materials of new investigative and hermeneutical approaches and to stress that the critical study of ancient Judaism must begin with deliberate and self-conscious attention to matters of method and procedure.

For a volume with these aims, Jonathan Z. Smith's "redescription" of the category canon is an ideal beginning. The canon, the authoritative, fixed collection of scripture, of "holy books," which constitutes the foundation of a religion and guides the lives of its adherents, is a category fundamental to Judaism, Christianity and other literate religious traditions of the West. Using the techniques of the History of Religions, Smith constructs a theoretical typology of canon and delineates its essential features. He skillfully employs the example of food (the limited number of items consumed) and cuisine (the almost limitless number of ways to prepare those items) to show that, as a phenomenon, canon is "one form of a basic cultural process of limitation and the overcoming of that limitation through ingenuity." In his view, canon may be construed as a sub-type of the genre list, but it differs from a list or a catalogue (a list exhibiting "relatively clear principles of order") because it is closed and immutable. One of its inherent features, therefore, is the presence of a hermeneute or of some technique of translation or interpretation. Smith acutely characterizes the thinking which generates canon and its exegesis as an example of *Listenwissenschaft,* "a science, a prime intellectual activity that produces and reflects on lists, catalogues and classifications, which progresses by establishing precedents, by observing patterns, similarities and conjunctions, by noting repetitions." Drawing on ethnographic materials of non-literate peoples, he supplies evidence of the existence of canon in those cultures and also distinguishes various modes of the exegetical process.

With these arguments, Smith begins to establish effective criteria for the analysis of canon, and he constructs a convincing case against those theorists who locate the essence of religion in some primal, ontic experience and portray routinization or "concretization" in religion as intrinsically degenerate. He places the problematic of the canon and its interpretation high on the agendum of the History of Religions, and his suggestion that "the study of comparative systematics and exegesis ought to be a major preoccupation of the historian of religions" signals an important new direction for that discipline. His contribution therefore not only demonstrates how the History of Religions can instruct and refine the critical study of ancient Judaism, it also shows how the basic features of Judaism and other Western religions can serve to "modulate" the categories and shape the program of an important approach to the study of religion.

The two articles of Renée Bloch also take up the problem of canon and exegesis, but the approach they illustrate is quite different from that of Jonathan Smith. Bloch's subject is midrash, the Jewish, particularly rabbinic, interpretation of the Hebrew scriptures, and her pioneering work, along with that of Geza Vermes, has played a decisive role in formulating the agendum of the modern critical study of midrashic materials. In the first of her articles presented here, Bloch offers a definition of midrash; in the second, she outlines a method for its investigation.

Broadly construing it as a genre of literature, Bloch defines midrash as a "reflection, a meditation on the sacred texts, a 'searching' of scripture." She describes it as a popular, homiletical genre, characterized by careful scrutiny of the biblical text, whose "practical" goal is to "reinterpret scripture, to 'actualize' it" to serve contemporary needs. Because it "presupposes faith in the revelation which is recorded in the holy books, " Bloch regards midrash as a genre "peculiar to Israel, like prophecy, but perhaps even more unique." She locates the origins of midrash in post-exilic times and points to examples of it in scripture itself. Bloch's approach to the study of midrash, unlike those of her predecessors, is historical, not synthetic. In her words, her goal is "to determine, by a careful work of historical and above all of literary criticism, as well as by comparative study, the development and the respective antiquity of traditions, the formulation, the historical situation and the interdependence of rabbinic writings." The comparative method she proposes begins with a biblical text, examines the various treatments of that text as they appear in different rabbinic and non-rabbinic documents, determines their chronological relationship, and then attempts to trace and explain the development of that single line of interpretation. Its focus, then, is on the evolution of themes or traditions, and implicit in its operation is the assumption that the history of a particular midrashic theme provides the key to its full understanding.

It is important to clarify that while Bloch's approach to the study of midrash is historical, it is not contextual. That is, she considers the various midrashic passages not within the framework provided by the documents in which they appear, but rather in terms of their relationship to the biblical text. Her purpose is to identify the stages in the evolution of a single interpretation, to explain the reasons for change and thereby to chart its development through time. Under this rubric, regardless of their author, context, style or date, all texts which treat the same verse of scripture or address and elaborate a common biblical theme are regarded as representative of a single tradition and therefore legitimately may be compared to one another. This perspective, according to which the Hebrew bible almost appears to unfold organically in antiquity, certainly is consistent with, if not informed and justified by, Bloch's view of the centrality of the biblical canon in Judaism and her conviction about the uniqueness of midrash to the Judaic enterprise.

Jonathan Smith's argument that

> the radical and arbitrary reduction represented by the notion of canon and the ingenuity represented by the rule-governed exegetical enterprise to apply the canon to every dimension of human life is that most characteristic, persistent and obsessive religious activity . . . [and,] at the same time, the most profoundly cultural. . . .

serves as an important corrective to Bloch's work. It certainly makes clear that Bloch's claim for the uniqueness of the midrashic genre must be discarded and that the critical study of midrash can benefit from comparative exercises which examine it alongside other systems of canon and exegesis. More important, Smith's discussion also forces a reconsideration of the role in midrashic research of the sort of historical study Bloch proposes. If, as he shows, canon-making and exegesis represent a basic cultural activity, then preliminary to any study of the history of midrash is an analysis of the phenomenon of midrash. An approach, therefore, which delineates the modes, styles and techniques of rabbinic biblical interpretation, which elucidates the systematics of midrash and which identifies the important traits of the various midrashic documents is a definite desideratum.[3]

These observations ought not to diminish the significance of Bloch's work. She was among the first to insist that midrashic literaure be examined critically and systematically and to devise a method for doing so. Although the critical study of midrash has made some progress since she wrote these articles in the fifties, Renée Bloch's formative influence on the entire field of midrashic research should not be underestimated.[4]

The papers of Smith and Bloch treat the same topic in dissimilar ways, and the contrast between their approaches therefore serves to emphasize the importance in any scholarly inquiry of a plausible and clearly defined problematic. My own contribution attempts to delimit such a problematic for another line of research into ancient Judaism, the biographical study of rabbinic figures. Rabbinic literature contains passages which attribute opinions to and describe the activities of individual masters, and scholars routinely (and uncritically) have used such materials to produce biographies or portraits of important rabbinic figures. These depictions, in turn, often are employed as evidence with which to reconstruct the history of rabbinism. The central task of biography is to recover an individual life, to expose the persona who stands behind the sources. Its agendum therefore is extrinsic to any given set of materials and is determined by the investigator's curiosity, interests, and notions about human psychology and personality. My paper asks if the materials which testify about rabbinic masters are appropriate objects for the legitimate concerns of biography. I try to show that the construction of rabbinic documents and the quality of the materials they contain make it unlikely that studies which focus on the traditions of a single master will yield results of a genuinely biographical character. Such studies, however, can help us to understand the processes and dynamics of rabbinic tradition. My essay thus attempts to demonstrate the methodological principle that the problematic of any inquiry, regardless of the origin of that inquiry, must be shaped, conditioned and limited by the nature of the primary sources if it is to produce worthwhile conclusions.

This same principle is at the core of Richard Sarason's survey of the methodological techniques employed in the modern study of Jewish liturgy. Sarason's aim is to evaluate the approaches of various scholars, and he states his principles of judgment at the outset. He argues that "the results of any scholarly inquiry are only so good as the basic assumptions and types of inference with and upon which they are constructed. A method . . . must be judged by the plausibility of its assumptions and by their applicability to the data under examination. . . . The final court of appeal for any method is the nature of the data in question." Sarason applies these criteria to the work of a number of researchers, and it will be helpful to highlight some of his conclusions. The majority of scholars, including such figures as Zunz, Elbogen, Kohler, and Finkelstein, adopted some form of the "historical-philological" approach to the study of Jewish liturgy. The goal of this approach is to uncover the original version of the prayers, and the actual existence of a single original text of each of the statutory prayers, an *Urtext,* therefore is an axiom of research, not a conclusion deduced from evidence. This approach, moreover, produces an inevitably schematic representation of the history of Jewish prayer marked by the following features: prayers were instituted by the rabbis; the simplest version of a prayer is the earliest; Jewish liturgy experienced a sequential, monolinear development from unity and simplicity to diversity and complexity. Sarason repeatedly shows how commitment to this model led scholars to ask artificial and misleading questions and to propose arbitrary, sometimes ridiculous solutions.

Presaged by the work of Arthur Spanier, Joseph Heinemann's *Hatefillah bitequfat hatanna²im weha²amora²im* (*Prayer in the Period of the* Tanna²im *and the* ²Amora²im) substantially altered the presuppositions and analytical techniques of Jewish liturgical research. Rejecting the view of most of his predecessors, Heinemann suggests that Jewish prayers are the popular products of the synagogue and not the creations of the rabbinical elite. Working inductively and employing the insights and procedures of biblical form-criticism, he denies the axiom of an *Urtext* with the argument that unless internal evidence suggests textual manipulation or corruption, there is no reason to suppose that several extant versions of a prayer are variants of a single, original text. Liturgical formulae initially were not standardized, and similar versions of the same prayer can have existed simultaneously. Evidence from the Cairo Geniza supports this conclusion. Heinemann's model, as Sarason notes, is "decentralized" and "flexible"; despite some deficiencies, it generally is persuasive because of its abilities to respond to the vagaries of the evidence. Sarason's essay palpably demonstrates the significance of the issues which motivated the creation of this volume, and it constitutes a significant contribution to the study of Jewish liturgy.

While Sarason describes the theory behind form-criticism and the role of this procedure in Heinemann's liturgical research, Gary G. Porton shows how a version of this technique can be applied to other types of rabbinic literature. Porton locates a literary form unique to the Palestinian Talmud, explains its operation and function, and convincingly identifies the circle of sages responsible for its creation. Although Porton's approach focuses on the analysis of literary forms, the method he employs differs from biblical form-criticism. Porton does not suggest that the form he isolates is the product of oral transmission, nor does he deduce the historical locus of the form from its function. By using the analysis of forms as an exegetical technique, he shows that Talmudic texts are constructed of small, sometimes nearly incomprehensible units of tradition which have been combined, recast and shaped by tradents and editors. He thereby underscores the redacted character of rabbinic literature and demonstrates that attention to the formal characteristics of rabbinic materials can assist in the reconstruction of the history of rabbinic documents.

Porton's analysis also makes clear that the study of forms can help specify distinctive substantive traits of rabbinic Judaism. The form he isolates and identifies juxtaposes traditions of Aqiba and Ishmael which are of unequal reliability. The difference between the two traditions generally is not a point of law, but a mode of argumentation. The form itself thus demonstrates the tendency of rabbinic authorities to group independent traditions around points of consensus. It also illustrates the intellectual character of rabbinism. The mode or style of argumentation is hardly a concern of ordinary people, but it is a matter of practical importance for people whose principal activity is thinking. Porton's essay thus elucidates both the basic characteristics of the form-analytical approach and the fundamental role of this procedure in the study of rabbinic literature.

Dean Miller's essay does not center on a problem which either derives from or specifically pertains to the study of ancient Judaism. Rather, it uses ancient Jewish materials to help define and delimit the image of a social type known to all cultures, the slave. Rejecting economic or political explanations of slavery as deficient, Miller explores what he terms the "'deep' dimension" in the archaic perception of the slave. He asks, ". . . what is 'the slave'? What indelible mark is set upon him—upon the unfree—in the archaic mind, or is there such a mark?" Drawing on the theoretical work of Victor Turner, Mary Douglas and E. R. Leach, Miller identifies the slave as a liminal being, "the *tertium quid,* between man and non-man," who, on account of his ambiguous state, is apprehended as the possessor of unusual potency. He explains, "The slave is not and cannot be perceived as a full or normal human being, because he is less than subordinate, he is owned. . . . He is part of the homologic *Gestalt* which includes so many 'powerful ones' in the archaic perceptive field, and his powers: dangerous, negative, contaminative—dark in most senses of that word—explain much about societal patterns of behavior and definition concerning the slave." Miller suggests that the biblical ritual of boring the slave's ear reflects the liminal image he describes, and he compares the biblical case with that of other ancient Near Eastern cultures. He then identifies this same perception in a rabbinic aggadic pericope. Miller's approach thus directly confronts the imaginal realm and attempts to mark off its contours. By incorporating them in a comparativist framework, Miller shows how ancient Jewish materials can help solve the problems of the "general" historian. Analyses of the sort he offers are rare enough in the study of ancient Judaism, and his demonstration suggests their potential.

Geza Vermes' review of a quarter-century of research on the Dead Sea Scrolls provides an overview of scholarship on ancient Judaism from Zunz and Geiger to the present as it shows how the discovery of the Scrolls and the analysis of their contents have undermined old hypotheses, raised new questions and thereby helped sharpen critical scholarly attitudes. Vermes describes, for instance, the effect of the evidence of the Scrolls on the scholarly understanding of the transmission of the Hebrew biblical text.

> In brief, Qumran has disclosed that even in the field of the transmission of the Biblical text itself we have to reckon not with a single chain of tradition, but with a multiplicity of parallel sources. If fully substantiated, this finding will mark a major breakthrough not only in textual criticism, but also in Jewish intellectual and religious history.

In addition, he demonstrates how the materials found at Qumran, notably the apocryphal and pseudepigraphic writings, document the fluid character of pre-70 Judaism and how works such as the Damascus Document and the Temple Scroll might revise some perspectives of rabbinism. In his concluding observations about the character of non-legal biblical exegesis in the Qumran literary corpus, Vermes illustrates, with an example, that the Scrolls cannot adequately be analysed or evaluated apart from other materials of ancient Judaism, particularly the Targums and rabbinic literature. His essay thus indicates the importance of considering the perspectives of a variety of ancient Jewish sources, and it shows how the sober and realistic assessment of new data can raise issues, specify problems and thereby shape the agendum for future research.

While Vermes indicates the Scrolls' potential for the historical reconstruction of first-century Palestinian Judaism, Jacob Neusner seeks to delimit the legitimate use of rabbinic literature for that same purpose, with particular reference to Pharisaism. Rabbinic materials now routinely figure in descriptions of the Judaism of first-century Palestine, but Neusner points out that the questions brought to those materials, with the consent and participation of scholars of rabbinic literature, too often derive from or conform to the agendum of New Testament studies, with unfortunate results.

> When scholarship of the New Testament and scholarship of the rabbinic literature agreed that the latter would be asked to contribute to the work of the former, the study of rabbinic literature paid a heavy price. For attitudes of mind and questions of investigation came to be imposed on the historical study of rabbinic sources which are wholly congruent neither to the character of those sources nor to their principal concerns.

Unwarranted preoccupation with the question of the veracity of words assigned to, or stories told about, rabbinic masters and excessive attention to sectarianism and messianism at the expense of other, equally pertinent matters are two prominent features of this approach; Neusner documents their incongruence to rabbinic materials and, in important ways, to the Dead Sea Scrolls as well. The desire to construct the Judaism of Jesus' time out of rabbinic sources, moreover, has led many rabbinic scholars incorrectly to depict those sources as full and accurate representations of first-century Pharisaism and to portray that particular version of Judaism as the one which dominated Jewish life in Palestine. Neusner dissects this consensus and exposes the error and caprice of its basic assertions.

He argues that the "later rabbinic evidence for the study of first-century Pharisaism cannot be dealt with item by item atomistically . . . ," nor can it adequately be treated monolithically, ". . . as if the evidence derived wholly from a single source, period, set of tradents, or group of redactors." To the contrary, he insists, the historical study of rabbinic sources must take account of the integrity and diversity of rabbinic documents and reflect the concerns which motivate and direct the literature itself. He presents a program of investigation guided by those considerations and offers a description of first-century Pharisaism composed on its basis. Fundamental to the picture of Pharisaism projected by rabbinic sources is an ". . . ontological conviction that regularity, recurrence, and perpetual activity define what is normal and delimit life from non-life,'" a conviction which finds expression in a system of piety whose central metaphor is the Temple cult. This ontology contrasts with that of the Gospels, ". . . which centers on a profoundly disruptive historical event, one which has shattered all that has been regular and orderly." Neusner concludes that

> . . . the two kinds of piety, the one with its effort to replicate eternity and perpetual order, the other with its interest in the end of an old order and the beginning of a new age of history, scarcely come into contact with one another.

Neusner's essay thus constitutes a careful and effective objection to the faulty, uniform classification of heterogeneous evidence. If allowed its integrity, the rabbinic evidence for Pharisaism hardly is apt to animate the exegesis and historical study of New Testament texts. But, as Neusner indicates, with the application of the tools and perspectives of the History of Religions, the comparative study of these two forms of piety portends a significant and bounteous yield.

The several approaches represented by the papers collected here by no means exhaust the possible methodologies which may be applied to the materials of ancient Judaism. But if this volume calls attention to the importance of methodological questions in the study of ancient Judaism, it will have served a constructive purpose.

NOTES

[1] Hayden White, *Metahistory*, Baltimore and London, 1973, p. 30.

[2] *Ibid.*

[3] Geza Vermes, *Scripture and Tradition in Judaism*, Leiden, 1961, p. 8.

[4] See Gary G. Porton, "Midrash: The Jews and the Hebrew Bible in the Greco-Roman Period" in the forthcoming volume on religion of *Aufstieg und Nedergang der römischen Welt*, deGruyter, makes an important advance in this direction. The bibliography to Bloch's article, "Midrash" (below, Chapter II), is dated and has not been reproduced. Current and more comprehensive bibliographies are supplied by Porton in the article referred to above and by Merill P. Miller in the *Journal for the Study of Judaism*, 2, 1971, pp. 36–78.

[5] See the preliminary remarks of James A. Sanders, "From Isaiah 61 to Luke 4," in J. Neusner, ed., *Christianity, Judaism and Other Greco-Roman Cults: Studies for Morton Smith at 60*, Leiden, 1975, *Part I*, pp. 75-106.

I

Sacred Persistence:
Towards a Redescription of Canon

JONATHAN Z. SMITH

UNIVERSITY OF CHICAGO

Some ten years ago, in a pioneering article entitled "Judaism in the History of Religions," Jacob Neusner argued that not only must the issues and methods of History of Religions be applied to Judaism but also that "the particular, Jewish data might modulate the categories characteristically employed by the historian of religions."[1] That is to say, Neusner laid down a challenge to achieve reciprocity. Judaism should "look different" when interpreted from the perspective of the History of Religions; the History of Religions should be altered by the act of interpreting Jewish data. A decade later I may report that some modest progress has been made on the first item on Neusner's agenda. There are an increasing number of historians of religion turning their attention to the study of Judaism and other major Western religious traditions; there are a significant number of scholars working with these materials from other perspectives who are familiar with, and at times employ, the kinds of categories and methods associated with History of Religions. But little progress can be reported on Neusner's second item— which is, for me as an historian of religion, by far the most important. The characteristic categories remain more or less intact. The old ones have not been "modulated," new ones have not been proposed. In this paper I should like to make a modest beginning at accepting Neusner's challenge.

In the prolonged discussions in recent times on the nature and status of models in the sciences, a most important contribution has been made by Max Black and Mary Hesse with their notion that models bear close structural similarities to metaphors, that both invite us to construe one thing in terms of another (most usually, that which is problematic in terms of that which is relatively better understood) so that we may see things in a new and frequently unexpected light. A model, in short, is a "redescription."[2] I should like to propose that the historian of religions is in a splendid position to offer a redescription of certain categories of religious experience and expression which we associate primarily with the West, in particular, with Western theological traditions. To do so will require a reversal of ordinary scientific procedure—i.e., he should attempt to describe that which is familiar in terms of the exotic, that which is relatively well known in terms of materials which are more or less unknown. In this paper I should like to address a topic which has often been held to be a major difference between the major Western religious traditions and archaic religions—the canon and its authority—and subject it to a preliminary redescription.

In part, my attention was drawn to the particular tack I wish to take by being invited to give yet another lecture on "The Persistence of the Sacred." This is a commonplace, a phrase that often occurs in the writings of historians of religion, sociologists and anthropologists of various persuasions. And yet, a few moments of reflection should drive one to the same conclusion I reached: it is really no topic at all. If the Sacred, the Holy, the Divine, or what have you, is really all that it is alleged to be, one of its more frequent characterizations is that it is eternal, enduring or timeless. That the Sacred persists is no novel thesis; it is a tautology. Even if one assumes that the phrase implies the other, at times pejorative sense of persistence, the history of religions (especially of theology if it is to be any kind of theology at all) testifies to a belief that the Sacred stubbornly persists in having traffic with man and the cosmos, even at the risk of becoming somewhat bothersome.

But such uses are clearly not what those who employ such a phrase have in mind. They appeal to more of an anthropological or quasi-biological notion—though one whose cogency I equally doubt—that the Sacred, now understood anthropologically as Religion (or, in less fortunate though more contemporary terms, as a religious response, perspective, dimension or world-view) is one of the enduring, species-specific definitions of man. Man is (or is, among other things) *Homo religiosus*. For example, the eminent British anthropologist Raymond Firth:

> religion is universal in human societies. This is an empirical generalization, an aggregate of a multitude of specific observations.[3]

Such a formulation is widespread and often serves as a kind of demonstration of the truth of religion in a manner reminiscent of earlier attempts to establish "Natural Religion," but it is no more successful. Any enumeration of the persistent features of man (from opposed thumbs to erect posture), or even of the persistent and allegedly unique features of man (e.g. symbol, speech, laughter, religion) must record a set of traits so numerous and diverse as to result in a motley list rather than a persuasive demonstration of truth or of an essence. Such an approach has proven incapable of supplying a satisfactory definition of either man or religion. Nor have there been any satisfying criteria established to enable us to isolate any one of these "persistences" as being more revealing of human nature than another. But the most serious objection is procedural. We need to recall Karl Popper's caution against using quasi-historical enumerative arguments to establish certainty.

> It is far from obvious, from a logical point of view, that we are justified in inferring universal statements from singular ones, no matter how numerous; for any conclusion drawn in this manner may always turn out to be false: no matter how many instances of white swans we have observed this does not justify the conclusion that *all* swans are white.[4]

To translate this into our terms: no matter how many instances of human religiosity we have observed, this does not justify the conclusion that man is religious. And besides, to quote Mel Spiro:

> Does the study of religion become any the less significant or fascinating if, in terms of a consensual, ostensive definition it was discovered that one or six or sixteen societies did not possess religion?[5]

Nor can the notion of persistence be rescued by turning to another anthropological or quasi-biological commonplace understanding: the propensity of religion to "survive," to persist in what is, at times, perceived as a hostile or indifferent environment. That it (whatever "it" is) persists in a "modern" or "secular" age (whatever that is) says nothing in itself. I know of no *heilsgeschichtliche* hymn to the vermiform appendix!

But thinking through this issue had one positive result. If we invert the topic and think about *sacred persistence,* we touch a theme that seems quite pervasive but little explored.

I take some assurance in this strategy from the fact that one of the oldest classical definitions of religion (Cicero) and one of the most creative modern interpretations (Freud) both take *their* point of departure from the *observation* of the phenomenon of sacred persistence.

In his dialogue *De natura deorum,* written about 45 B.C.E., Cicero placed in the mouth of the Stoic Balbo an etymology of the adjective *religious* as being derived from *relegere* meaning: to gather together, to collect, to go over again, to mentally review, to repeat. Balbo proposes that

> those who carefully reviewed and went over again all that pertained to the rituals of the gods were called *religious* from *relegere.*[6]

His argument requires that this exegetical activity be understood as a constant preoccupation. Although the etymology is most likely false, it remains a shrewd insight, based on observation, of a significant (perhaps even distinctive) characteristic of religious thought.[7]

Almost two thousand years later, in 1907, working from a similar grounding in observation but from radically different pre-suppositions, Freud, in his brief essay "Obsessive Acts and Religious Practices" [*Zwangshandlungen und Religionsübungen*], proposed his famous analogy between "what are called obsessive acts in neurotics and those of religious observances by means of which the faithful give expression to their piety." While there is much in Freud's subsequent genetic account that is problematic, his original description of the obsessiveness common to both neurosis and religion as:

> *little* preoccupations, performances restrictions and arrangements in certain activities
> of everyday life . . . elaborated by *petty* modifications . . . [and] *little* details . . .
> [the] tendency to displacement . . . [which] turns apparently *trivial* matters into
> those of great and urgent importance . . .[8]

remains, for me, the most telling description of a significant (perhaps even
distinctive) characteristic of religious activity that I have seen.

I should like, for the remainder of this presentation, to focus on the issue
of sacred persistence: the rethinking of each little detail in a text (Cicero), the
obsession with the significance and perfection of each little action (Freud).[9]

Allow me to take a somewhat roundabout route to my topic. Almost the
first thing observed by any traveler, be he professional or amateur, is the wide
diversity between peoples as to food, both with respect to things they will eat
and things they will not eat. From Herodotus to the present day, anecdotal
instances of variation in diet have provided one of the immediate, all but
intuitive, demonstrations of the notion of cultural relativism. One needs only
think of the instinctive horror aroused in us by the grisly enumeration of the
ingredients which make up the witches' brew in *Macbeth* and then reflect on
the fact that, deprived of imaginary substances ("scale of dragon"),
indigestible condiments ("tooth of wolf") and cannibalistic tidbits ("liver of
blaspheming Jew . . . nose of Turk and Tartar's lips") all of the other items—
from toads to baboons—are part of some other peoples' quite ordinary diet.
And even those items just excised are eaten or believed of others to be eaten on
extraordinary occasions.

Despite the ingenuity that has been brought to the subject by scholars of
every persuasion, the old tag, quoted by Herodotus from Pindar, "custom is
king over all," remains the common relativistic explanation.[10] This or that
food or avoidance of food can be accounted for, but, aside from the obvious
rule that it ought not to be poisonous, no general principle has been found.

There appears, on the one hand, to be virtually no limits to what people
can and do eat if looked at globally. There appears, on the other hand, to be
the most stringent limits on what any particular group of people can and will
eat and a most intense reluctance to alter these boundaries. Only rarely, and
under unusual circumstances, has a culture adopted a new food as its staple
diet (Ireland and the potato is the most familiar, but highly specialized,
exception). New foods have largely been the hallmark of the counter-cultural
group or individual—a means of expressing distance from, hostility to, or
transcendence of one's culture.

But a rehearsal of these well known facts obscures what is, for me, a more
important observation. Granted that food is best understood as a cultural
rather than a natural category, the dynamics of its limitation and variation are
more complex than a simple relativism would suggest.

A given foodstuff represents a radical, almost arbitrary, selection out of the incredible number of potential sources of nutriment that are at hand; but, once the selection is made, the most extraordinary attention is given to the variety of its preparation. That is to say, *if food is a phenomenon character-ized by limitation, cuisine is a phenomenon characterized by variegation.* This most important and suggestive rule may be simply tested. Make a list of the basic foodstuffs which you regularly eat. It will be a short one. Then make a list of the modes of preparation, the names of specific dishes that you know. Whether you are thinking of bread, pasta, wine, cheese, beef, potatoes or chicken, your list will stagger the ingenuity of a Linnaeus!

To take but one example. We think almost exclusively of wine as being made from a single species of grape (*Vitis vinifera*) despite what we may know of the (to us) "quaint" British dedication to dandelions or rhubarb or the equally "quaint" dedication of some of our grandparents to elderberries. But, having so sharply limited the almost infinite potential of the vegetable kingdom (almost any fruit, flower or root can be made into wine) most of us could, with a little thought, reproduce the "classification designed for the average consumer" in the new edition of *The Encyclopaedia Britannica* which contains over one hundred generic and varietal names,[11] not to speak of the other systems which are simultaneously employed: that of the vintage years and rules of etiquette (to whom, when, how, at what temperature, in what and with what to serve the various kinds of wine). In addition to these systems which are in common use, there are also the specialized systems employed by the *connoisseur, sommelier* and vintner: the classifications by *chateux* and growths, the laws of the *Appelations d'Origine,* etc.

The same sort of process may be observed with respect to every important human phenomenon and has received growing attention in recent studies of language, law and taxonomy. An almost limitless horizon of possibilities that are at hand (natural?) is arbitrarily reduced (cultural?) to a set of basic elements (in terms of the example—food). This initial arbitrariness is, at times, overcome by secondary explanations which account for the reduction (e.g. pork causes trichinosis). Then a most intense ingenuity is exercised to overcome the reduction (in terms of the example—cuisine), to introduce interest and variety. This ingenuity is usually accompanied by a complex set of rules.

Without attempting a full discussion, I will note that in cognate fields where such processes have been studied, much of the debate, in recent years, has focused on the status of the reduction and, especially, on the status of the exercise of ingenuity. For some, the emphasis has been on the "givenness" of the basic elements as primordial and the secondary (indeed, at times, degen-erative) character of the ingenuity. For others, the basic elements are funda-mentally arbitrary (although such scholars usually prescind from questions of origin and truth with respect to the reduction) and ingenuity is understood as either work (world-construction or the like) or play.

It is at this point in our reflections, as one thinks of the possibilities for applying this general model of cultural activity to religious phenomena, that one finds oneself both helped and left unsatisfied by the studies of the historians of religion. It has been the special contribution of the historian of religions to insist on the all but infinite nature of the *plenum* which confronts man in his religiousness while, at the same time, pointing to the reduction of this *plenum* by the various historical-cultural units they study. That is to say, to return to the previous analogy, historians of religion have pointed to the innumerable varieties of species of plants and animals that are at hand and have focused some attention on the reduction of these "natural" possibilities to food. For example, the revolutionary (and it is difficult at this late date to appreciate just how revolutionary) words of Mircea Eliade in the introduction to his major morphological treatise:

> We must get used to the idea of recognizing hierophanies absolutely every-where. . . . Indeed we cannot be sure that there is *anything* . . . that has not at some time in human history been somewhere transformed into a hierophany . . . it is quite certain that anything man has ever handled, come in contact with or loved *can* become a hierophany. . . . It is unlikely that there is any animal or any important species of plant in the world that has *never* had a place in religion. In the same way too, every trade, art, industry, and technical skill either began as something holy, or has, over the years, been invested with religious value. This list could be carried on to include man's everyday movements (getting up, walking, running), his various employments (hunting, fishing, agriculture), all his physiological activities (nutrition, sexual life, etc.). . . . But somewhere, at a given time, each human society chose for itself a certain number of things, animals, plants, gestures and so on and turned them into hierophanies; and, as this has been going on for tens of thousands of years of religious life, it seems improbable that there remains anything that has not at some time been so transfigured.[12]

At the same time, the historian of religions has been less convincing in explicating the second moment in our model: that of ingenuity, of cuisine. In part this is because the historians of religion have traditionally resisted the anthropological as the cost of preserving the theological, what they believe (I think wrongly) to be the irreducible, *sui generis* nature of religious phenomena. They have therefore tended to opt for what I have described as the first interpretation of our model: that which has insisted on the givenness of the basic elements as primordial and the secondary, degenerative character of ingenuity. Thus ingenuity is either displaced as mere routinization or swallowed up by postulating some ontic primordium which manifests itself in a variety of forms apparently independent of human agency. Both degrade the anthropological dimension in a way that I find inexcusable, the former by robbing it of significance, the latter by denying its existence.

To take but one example—the characteristic and influential argument of Adolf Jensen building on the work of Leo Frobenius and the Frankfort *Paideuma-Schule.* All truth, meaning and value is located in what Jensen describes as a primal, creative moment of ontic "seizure," a "revelation," a "direct cognition of the essence of living reality." Myth, he argues, "always begins with a condition antecedent to concretization, when the creative idea is already in existence and finally manifests itself through the mythic event." The first "concretization," the first "formulation" is an "intuitive spontaneous experiencing" which Jensen terms "expression." Expression is, for Jensen, an essentially passive experience roughly equivalent to the religious term, inspiration. All subsequent "formulations" and "concretizations" are reinterpretations of this primal experience and are termed by Jensen "applications," a pejorative word in his lexicon. "Application" over time leads ultimately to "mere survivals" of the original, authentic, "seizure" and first "expression." All "application" for Jensen is under the sway of the iron "law of degeneration" or "semantic depletion" and results in the original "spontaneity" becoming a "fixed but no longer understood routine"—a statement, on Jensen's part, of the traditional Protestant bugaboos of "habit," "dogma" and "magic" which has resulted in the vast majority of religious phenomena remaining unintelligible to most Western scholarship. Jensen insists that:

> According to the inescapable law, anything that culture has created must grow more distant from the [original] content of the creative idea; finally it will be only a pale reflection of its 'original expression' . . . [according to] the process of gradual semantic depletion along the way from 'expression' to 'application.'

Or, need I translate, from authentic prophecy to Pharisaism! The history of religions, Jensen claims, is littered with examples

> of the transformation from meaningful belief to absurdity, where the nuclear thought has been lost in historical changes, but the externals are reverently preserved and brought into harmony with new concepts.

Even though such applications and reinterpretations might be judged, from some perspectives, to have been "successful elaborations," Jensen sharply disagrees: "weighed ideologically, the 'successful developments' constitute pauperization and semantic depletion."[13]

I find Jensen's argument extremely dubious in many respects, not the least of which is the fact that, as has been characteristic of many historians of religion, he has attempted a theological apologetic without a theology—if by the latter term one understands, at the very least, a community's self-reflection. Shorn of this necessary communal and, hence, traditional dimension, one is left with the impossible generic abstraction of *Homo religiosus* responding to religion in general and, paradoxically, religion becomes, as it does in Jensen and most historians of religion, an essentially inhuman activity.

I have come to believe that a prime object of study for the historian of religions ought to be what I would call, taking the term in its widest sense, theological tradition—in particular those dimensions of the theological endeavor that are concerned with canon and its exegesis. That is to say,

bracketing any presuppositions as to its character as revelation (and from this
the historian of religions must abstain), the radical and arbitrary reduction
represented by the notion of canon and the ingenuity represented by the rule-
governed exegetical enterprise to apply the canon to every dimension of
human life is that most characteristic, persistent and obsessive religious
activity. It is, at the same time, the most profoundly cultural (as I sought to
argue with my food/cuisine analogy) and hence the most illuminating for
what ought to be the essentially anthropological viewpoint of the historian of
religions and a concern for religion as human labor. The task of application as
well as the judgement of the relative adequacy of particular applications to a
community's life situation remains the indigenous theologian's task; but the
study of the process, particularly the study of comparative systematics and
exegesis, ought to be a major preoccupation of the historian of religions.

This has a number of consequences. It would mean that the historian of
religions might find as his most congenial colleagues those concerned with
Scripture and with Law rather than his present romantic preoccupation with
the "primitive" or the "archaic"—a term which for him has largely meant
simple or primordial in the sense of uninterpreted which has given him
license for the ultimate act of imperialism, the removal of all right to interpretation from the native and the granting of all such rights to himself. It
would mean that the historian of religions might redirect his attention from
his present equally romantic fixation with multivalent and condensed
phenomena such as symbols, which have more often served as eloquent testimony to the exegetical ingenuity of the researcher than of the community
that has bound itself to them, and should rather become concerned with prosaic discourse. It implies that the historian of religions will not lose his freedom to study the all but limitless horizons of human religiosity and objects
of religious concern, but that he will take as a prime comparative task the
understanding of the surrender of that freedom by the communities he
studies and the rediscovery of that freedom through the exercise of ingenuity
within their self-imposed limits.

I do not want, in this paper, to dwell on the implications for my own
discipline; that will have to be undertaken in another forum. Rather, I
should like to further reflect on the notion of canon as a way of exploring
the proposition that sacrality persists insofar as there are communities which
are persistent in applying their limited deposit of tradition; that sacred
persistence, in terms that are congruent with both Cicero and Freud, is
primarily exegesis; that, if there is anything distinctive about religion as a
human activity it is a matter of degree not of kind, what might be described
as the extremity of its enterprise of exegetical totalization. To do so I must
undertake, for the remainder of this presentation, a redescription of the
category canon.

I know of no comparative study of our topic and therefore I must invite
you into the historian of religion's workroom in order that you may observe

and evaluate some of the preliminary typologies that might be developed and a sample of the kinds of data such a study might employ. I have largely drawn my materials from non-literate peoples in order to further the enterprise of redescription. Such societies would seem, at first glance, to be those for whom the category of canon would be most difficult to establish, as I am aware that the notion of canon, in ordinary use, is primarily associated with the Western "Peoples of the Book" (Judaism, Christianity, Islam, Manichaeism and other Iranian traditions) and that it appears to be a relatively rare and, with the possible exception of Islam, a secondary or tertiary phenomenon in the history of religions, even among literate groups. But I want to insist that canon, broadly understood as the arbitrary fixing of a limited number of "texts" as immutable and authoritative, is far from unusual. At the same time I want to give full due to the necessary concomitant of exegetical ingenuity which ought to prevent our applying terms such as "closed" or "cool" to such societies.

To begin the task of redescription. Canon, looked at from one perspective, is a subtype of the genre *list*, list being perhaps the most archaic and pervasive of genres, but one which has received surprisingly little scholarly attention. Most lists, whether in simple enumerative or nominal form, or in complex forms such as lexica or encyclopaedias, are open-ended. That is to say, they have neither a necessary beginning nor end save that provided by the duration of the attention of their compiler or the use to which the list is to be put. There is no necessary order; everything may appear to be quite arbitrary. Hugh Kenner has argued that lists are characterized by the notion of the "isolated fact," the "fragmentation of reality," the "nearly surrealistic discontinuity of the final product." "Nothing," he maintains, "except where a cross-reference is provided, connects with anything else . . . or affords perspective on anything else."[14] Indeed, not even the cross-reference guarantees much. One is reminded of the fact that in the French Enlightenment *Encyclopédie* more than half of the cross-references are to non-existent articles! Other forms of ordering lists appear equally arbitrary: the utterly artificial device of alphabetizing; the topical list (exemplified for me by the popular medieval encyclopaedia of Bartholomew of Glanville [*De proprietatibus rerum*] which began with a discussion of God and concluded, twelve hundred and thirty chapters later, with an alphabetical list of thirty-six eggs —from *Aspis* to *Vultur*—the Paris edition of 1574 added a treatise on bees!) or the grouping and arrangement of items according to external appearance (e.g. the scribal tradition, required by the scroll and continued, shorn of necessity, in the codex listing texts in order of decreasing length as in the epistles of Paul or the *suras* in the Qur°an). At times, the sheerly arbitrary principles of ordering swallow up the content of the list. For example, while the Jewish, Roman Catholic, Lutheran and Reformed traditions divide them differently, there are always Ten Commandments; while almost none of the lists agree as to names, and while some lists enumerate ten or eleven or thirteen, there are always Twelve Tribes of Israel and Twelve Disciples of Jesus. In other instances, a secondary elaboration of lists occurs. The Biblical traditions remained content with the simple enumeration of either seven pairs of clean animals and one pair of unclean animals brought on Noah's ark or one pair of every kind—depending on what source is followed. It remained for the subsequent ingenuity of exegetes, such as Benedictus Pererius, to attempt to name them all, eighteen pages of names, including that of the "unknown animal that Cardan saw in Pavia."[15]

When lists exhibit relatively clear principles of order, we may begin to properly term them *catalogues,* a sub-type whose major function (analogous to modern libraries) is information retrieval. It makes little difference whether we are dealing with oral or literary materials with mnemonic devices or codes of classification. The items in a catalogue may remain heterogeneous, the catalogue in principle is open; but an account can be given, transmitted and learned as to why they have been brought together.

For example, it is one thing to find in History of Religions manuals the principle that the beginning or first time is pristine, precious and requires celebration; it is quite another thing to encounter a list of first times from an Iatmul informant in New Guinea and attempt to appreciate the application of this principle. The same ceremony (*naven*), undertaken by mother's brother, will be performed for the male:

> the first time a boy kills an enemy or foreigner or victim bought for the purpose . . .
> the [first] killing of any of the following animals: birds, fish, eel, tortoise, flying fox;
> [the first] planting of any of the following plants: yams, tobacco, coconut, areca,
> betal, sago, sugar cane. . . .

.Is this an open or a closed list? Only these animals or plants, or are the species enumerated to be taken as *exempli gratia,* i.e. the rule is any important animal or plant?

> the [first] spotting of an opossum in the bush; the [first] felling of a sago palm,
> opening or beating sago; [the first] using of a spear thrower; [the first] using a
> throwing stick to kill a bird; [the first] using an axe; [the first] sharpening of a fish
> spear; [the first] cutting a paddle; [the first] making a canoe; [the first] making a
> digging stick; [the first] making a spear thrower; [the first] incising patterns on a
> lime gourd; [the first] plaiting of an arm band; [the first] making of a shell girdle;
> [the first] beating a hand drum, beating a slit drum, blowing a trumpet, playing a
> flute, beating the secret slit gongs; [the first] travelling to another village and
> returning; [the first] acquiring of shell valuables; [the first] buying of an axe, knife,
> mirror or other trade goods; [the first] buying of an areca nut; [the first] killing of a
> pig and sponsoring of a feast.[16]

Note that these last items are an excellent example of native exegetical labor. Traditional articles of value and exchange (shells, areca nuts, pigs) have been extended by analogy and the application of a principle to the novel, post-colonial purchase of foreign, manufactured objects (axe, knife, mirror) and that this list is the only portion of our text left explicitly open ("or other trade goods") to allow for novelty and innovation not in the natives' control.

The Iatmul enumeration is, at one level, a simple catalogue which organizes a heterogenous group of material around the single principle: the first performance of a cultural activity is to be celebrated. But the schema according to which the various items are listed and grouped is more complex. It does not just testify to the centrality of the notion of "beginning," but represents a map of a particular culture's selection out of the multitude of elements which make up their common life, those which are capable of bearing obsession, those which are understood as significant. Properly interpreted, it is a diagram of the characteristic preoccupations of this people. I do not intend a full analysis of this catalogue, or, what would be of more importance, a correlation of such an analysis with other elements in the ethnography of the Iatmul, but I would note that the enumeration is organized around the rubric: relations with strangers. The catalogue has two sections: the first begins with killing an enemy, foreigner or victim; the second with journeying to another village and returning (safely). The first begins with negative relations; the second, with positive. Once these fundamental headings have been established, the rest is generated by association. To simplify:

[Negative relations]	[Positive relations]
Killing humans	
Killing animals for food	
Preparation of plant foods	
The use and manufacture of tools for killing and agriculture	
The use and manufacture of ceremonial objects	
The use of ceremonial instruments	Travelling to foreign places
	Acquiring foreign goods
	Inviting others to feast

Please note that in this case I have supplied the explicit statements of the principle that governs the catalogue and the rules by which it was organized. In many societies, there is a native meditation on these principles which may be called, to use Albrecht Alt's useful term, *Listenwissenschaft*.[17] This is a science, a prime intellectual activity that produces and reflects on lists, catalogues and classifications, which progresses by establishing precedents, by observing patterns, similarities and conjunctions, by noting repetitions. Such a science has been particularly noticed in omen and legal materials, perhaps with most clarity in Near Eastern literature from the extensive Babylonian omen series to the quite parallel Talmudic enterprise. But *Listenwissenschaft* is an all but universal phenomenon.

To provide but one, complex example (taken from Claude Lévi-Strauss, *The Elementary Structures of Kinship*):

> For several very primitive peoples of the Malay Archipelago, the supreme sin, unleashing storm and tempest, comprises a series of superficially incongruous acts which informants list higgledy-piggledy as follows: marriage with a near kin; father and daughter or mother and son sleeping too close to one another; incorrect speech between kin; ill-considered conversation; for children, noisy play; for adults, demonstrative happiness shown at social reunions; imitating the calls of certain insects or birds [particularly the cicada]; laughing at one's own face in the mirror; and, finally, teasing animals and, in particular, dressing a monkey as a man and making fun of him.

Lévi-Strauss goes on to ask the obvious question:

> What possible connection could there between such a bizarre collection of acts? . . . Why does native thought group them under one heading? Either native thought must be accused of being incoherent or . . . [there must be a] common characteristic which . . . makes these apparently heterogenous acts express an identical situation. A native remark puts us on the track. The Pygmies of the Malay Peninsula consider it a sin to laugh at one's own face in the mirror, but they add that it is not a sin to ridicule a real human being [to his face] since he can defend himself. This interpretation obviously also applies to the dressed up monkey which is treated as a human being when it is teased and looks like a human being (just as does the face in the mirror), although it is really not one. This interpretation can be extended to the imitation of certain insects or birds. . . . By imitating them, one is treating an emission of sound which 'sounds' like a word as a human manifestation when it is not. Thus we find [in the list] two categories of acts definable as an immoderate use of language: the first, from a quantitative point of view, to play noisily, to laugh too loudly or to make an excessive show of one's feelings; the second, from a qualitative point of view, to answer sounds which are not words, or to converse with something (mirror or monkey) which is human only in appearance. These prohibitions are all thus reduced to a single denominator: they all constitute a misuse of language.

I shall break off the quotation at this point and not follow the relationship that is posited between "misuse of language" and the incestuous acts in the catalogue nor the extension of these principles to the complex set of actions forbidden by the Malaysian Dyaks under the rubric that it is forbidden to give "a man or animal a name that is not his or its . . . or to say something about him [or it] that is contrary to his nature."[18] I have dwelt on this example at some length only as revelatory of the quest for a unifying principle behind the most diverse list of items that is the essence of *Listenwissenschaft*.

Indeed, a number of processes are involved in generating such a catalogue, the ensemble of which constitutes *Listenwissenschaft*. First, the empirical collection of data—in the example, what happened in the village at the same time a thunderstorm occurred; the remembering or recording of such co-occurrences over a period of time; then the discovery of a pattern to the synchronisms; and, finally, the determination of a common principle that underlies the pattern, one that may be used predictively (omen) or generalized proscriptively (law or taboo) as well as retrospectively (history).

The only formal element that is lacking to transform a catalogue into a *canon* is the element of closure: that the list is held to be complete. And this formal requirement generates a corollary. Where there is a canon we can predict the necessary occurrence of a hermeneute, of an interpreter whose task it is to continually extend the domain of the closed canon over everything that is known or everything that is. It is with the canon and its hermeneute that we encounter the necessary obsession with exegetical totalization. (It is worth noting that in my comparative studies of canons I have been struck with the number of hypothetical instances that are generated by exegesis in order to complete the canon's range of applicability to the realm of the possible as well as the actual.)

It is difficult to demonstrate the existence of canon in non-literate societies if one thinks of a canon as solely a corpus of written texts. It is clear from the presence of multiple, ever-changing versions as well as from evidence for native debate over what version is to be authoritative for a particular recitation,[19] that one may not simply turn to oral material such as myths. Regardless of the mnemonics, a corpus of myth is rarely held to be closed.

One possibility is to examine the widespread evidence for the use of a totalizing and complete system of signs or icons which serve as functional equivalents to a written, canonical corpus.

At its simplest level, such a canon may be illustrated from the Walbiri of Central Australia as reported by Nancy Munn.[20] A set of less than two hundred and fifty designs, capable of being reduced to a small set of basic elements which are extended through combination, is used to accompany and encapsulate every narrative from a story of everyday activity to the report of a novel dream, to the transmission of esoteric ancestral traditions. Each element bears a wide range of meanings (quite arbitrary with respect to its visual form) but is unambiguous in context. It may be drawn in the sand as a woman tells a story (much like a doodle), taught to children as a "language system" or painted on the body of a male during initiation ceremonies. But in each instance, although the lexicon is complete and public, the presence of a hermeneute is lacking—although his role is to some degree substituted for by the narrator. That is to say, in this most simple system, we find no clear evidence for the process of interpretation, but rather a process of translation of the verbal into the visual or, perhaps more accurately, of the simultaneous and parallel expression of both. However, it would be an error to think of the designs as mere illustration of the narrative: they are the result of ratiocination, an example of *Listenwissenschaft*. When a given design can synonymously (although not simultaneously) denote a variety of things, there is a principle by which these referents are perceived both as similar and as reducible to the geometric form that calls them to mind. At the same time, the system is capable of extension so as to include novelties without the need for adding any new designs.

Similar systems, more complex, show forth the interpreter's role. For example, the set of fifty-eight figurines of human and animal forms presented to novices in fixed order with oral interpretation at the initiation rites of the Senufo, as described by Bochet, which correspond to the basic classes of cosmic, human and social relations: an "inventory," to quote Bochet, that "constitutes a sort of lexicon of symbols and different possible ways of using them."[21] Or the even more complicated, totalistic, theosophical system of two hundred and sixty-six signs, capable of being "read" in four different ways depending upon one's stage of initiation, among the Dogon, which is still being deciphered by the French team associated with Marcel Griaule.[22]

There is a double value in examining this sort of corpus of non-literate canonical materials. It reveals that a canon cannot exist without a tradition and an interpreter, without the public lexicon (*langue*) and explicit engagement in application (*parole*) or the closure of canon would be impossible. Secondly, in each instance the basic strategy appears the same. The process of limitation (the food of the earlier analogy) and of overcoming limitation through ingenuity (cuisine) will recur. As the pressure is intensified through extension and through novelty, because of the notion of canonical completeness, it will be the task of the hermeneute to develop exegetical procedures that will allow the canon to be applied without alteration—or, at least, without admitting to alteration (what Henry Maine has analyzed as the "legal fiction").[23] And, in some complex situations, there may be a further need to develop parallel secondary traditions that will recover the essentially open character of the list or catalogue.

A preliminary comparative survey of a wider range of materials than I can present in this paper reveals that the canonical-interpretive enterprise comes to the fore in five situations: that of divination, law, legitimation, classification and speculation. While these may be further reduced, or made more complex, cross-cultural study has convinced me that the primary *Sitz* of canon is divination. At the very least, it is in divinatory procedures that we may observe with particular clarity the relationship between canon and hermeneute, and therefore I will draw my final examples from African divination, from Victor Turner's study of the Ndembu and Bascom's study of the Yoruba.[24]

Among the Ndembu there are two features of the divinitory situation that are crucial to our concern: the diviner's basket and his process of interrogating his client.

The chief mode of divination consists of shaking a basket in which some twenty-four fixed objects are deposited (a cock's claw, a piece of hoof, a bit of grooved wood, a black withered fruit, etc.). These are shaken in order to winnow out "truth from falsehood" in such a way that few of the objects end up on top of the heap. These are "read" by the diviner both with respect to their individual meanings and their combinations with other objects and the configurations that result. The client's situation is likewise taken into account in arriving at an interpretation. Thus, to invoke the categories of classical linguistics, there is a semantic, syntactic and pragmatic dimension to the "reading." Each object is publicly known and has a fixed range of meanings. Although some debate is possible among the diviners as to this or that possibility, the broad semantic field is never violated. The total collection of twenty-four objects is held to be complete and capable of illuminating every situation. Nothing new may be added to the basket, although the objects themselves may be subjected to a variety of manipulations. What enables the canon to be applied to every situation or question is *not* the number of objects (as in all canons, the number is relatively small) nor the breadth of their range of meanings. Rather it is that, prior to performing the divination, the diviner has rigorously questioned his client in order to determine his situation with precision. The diviner functions with respect to his client much as the successful preacher functions with respect to his congregation. Application, in this sense, is not a generalized systematic process but a homiletic endeavor, a quite specific attempt to make the "text" speak to a quite particular situation. While, at one level, the lists of divinitory objects and their general public meanings as printed in Turner (the lexicon, the *langue*) is reminiscent of those lists which disfigure Bibles in motel rooms across the country: If depressed, read . . . ; if sick, read . . . ; if lonely, read . . . etc., at another level, the objects as applied after the interrogation quite clearly function as *parole,* as unique and individualized sentences addressed to an unduplicatible audience. It is the genius of the interpreter to match a public set of meanings with a commonly known set of facts (so and so is sick; so and so's relative died, etc.) in order to produce a quite particular plausibility structure which speaks directly to his client's condition, which mediates between that which is public knowledge and the client's private perception of his unique situation.

The opposite extreme is represented by the Yoruba procedure. Here the central rule is that the diviner knows nothing of his client's situation, not even his question. Rather the diviner serves as a mediator, making available the canonical resources to the client but leaving the interpretation entirely in the latter's hands.

The basis of Yoruba divination is a large repertoire of poems. These are correlated with a set of two hundred and fifty-six divination figures. The diviner selects one of these figures by a simple process. While shaking sixteen palm nuts in his loosely clasped hands, he abruptly tries to lift all of the nuts out of his left hand with his right. Because of the size of the nuts it is virtually impossible to hold all sixteen of them in one hand; one or two will remain in the left hand. If one nut remains, the diviner draws parallel lines; if two nuts, one line. He makes repeated casts and records his results until he completes a figure consisting of two parallel columns of four marks each. This is one divination figure. Each column has 4 x 4 or 16 possible combinations of marks, the two columns combined have 16 x 16 or 256 possible combinations. Once the figure is drawn and named, the diviner recites the poems associated with it. A novice diviner should know at least four poems for each figure (a total of 1024 poems) each consisting of five to fifty lines that have been memorized. The experienced diviner knows as many as eight for each figure. After hearing the full set of poems, the client chooses the one which seems most relevant to his problem. Not knowing the client's question, the diviner has no way of manipulating his client's interpretation and choice of verse. It is rather a purely private relationship between and individual and his own destiny.[25]

In this instance, strikingly similar in many ways to the Chinese *I Ching,* it is not so much the text of the poems that constitutes the canon, but rather the mathematically fixed number of possible divination figures. These give access to a possible set of interpretations (the poems) which vary in number according to the skill of the tradent. But it is the individual—much as in a "chain-reference Bible"—who must ultimately decide which one is the most plausible. It is the individual who serves as his own hermeneute.

As one examines the great varieties of such canons and divinitory situations, he will be struck by the differences in exegetical techniques and skills. But the essential structure of limitation and exegetical ingenuity remains constant and provides a suggestive base for a redescription of the category canon.

Other work remains to be done. An examination of the rules which govern the sharp debates between rival exegetes and exegetical systems attempting to manipulate the closed canon for their own ends. There is need for a careful study of individuals who may be termed tribal theologians, whose systematic endeavors, exegetical totalizations and cabalistic interpretations of their culture's canon makes them worthy of comparison with an Aquinas, Barth or Maimonides. I have in mind here figures such as Muchona the Hornet, Ogotemmeli, Antonio Guzman and, perhaps, Castaneda's ubiquitous don Juan Matus. I look forward to the day when courses and monographs will exist in both comparative exegesis and comparative theology, comparing not so much conclusions as strategies as they seek to interpret and translate their received tradition to their contemporaries. But it is time to bring this exercise to a close.

I have attempted a redescription of the category canon from the comparative and generalizing perspective of an historian of religions. I have attempted to argue that canon is one form of a basic cultural process of limitation and the overcoming of that limitation through ingenuity. I have proposed some basic distinctions between list, catalogue and canon (by the way, an interesting test case of the utility of these distinctions in which I am now engaged is to attempt to study the Hesiodic theogonic tradition and attempt to determine what portions are lists, catalogues and canons). I have suggested for non-literate peoples that canon is most clearly to be perceived in divinitory situations and briefly sketched a range from the hermeneute as homiletician to self-interpretation.

By such a redescription, I hope to have suggested how the categories used by historians of religion might be "modulated" by taking seriously structures characteristic of Western religious traditions and thinking through their logic on a comparative basis.

Notes

[1]J. Neusner, "Judaism in the History of Religions," in J. Helfer, ed., *On Method in the History of Religions* (Middlebury, 1968), esp. pp. 38f.

[2]M. Black, *Models and Metaphors* (Ithaca, 1962), esp. pp. 236-38; M. B. Hesse, *Models and Analogies in Science* (Notre Dame, 1966), esp. pp. 164f.

[3]R. Firth, *Elements of Social Organization,* 3rd ed. (London, 1962), p. 216.

[4]K. Popper, *The Logic of Scientific Discovery,* rev. ed. (New York, 1965), p. 27.

[5]M. E. Spiro, "Religion: Problems of Definition and Explanation," in M. Banton, ed., *Anthropological Approaches to the Study of Religion* (London, 1966), p. 89.

[6]Cicero, *De natura deorum* II. 72.

[7]The familiar alternative definition, based on a derivation from *religare,* "to bind," in Lactantius, *Divinae Institutiones* IV.28 is likewise suspect. See J. B. Kätzler, "*Religio:* Versuch einer Worterklärung," 20. *Jahresbericht des Bischöflichen Gymnasiums Paulinum in Schwaz* (1952-53), 2-18 for a review of the present state of the discussion and an argument for a derivation from the root *lig-* "to pay attention to, to take care to."

[8]S. Freud, "Obsessive Acts and Religious Practices," in J. Strachey, ed., *The Standard Edition of the Complete Psychological Works of Sigmund Freud* (London, 1959), Vol. IX, pp. 117-27. Also available in the Collier edition of *The Collected Papers of Sigmund Freud* edited by Philip Rieff in the volume entitled, *Character and Culture* (New York, 1963), pp. 17-26. In this latter edition, the passages quoted occur on pp. 17, 18, 19 and 25 with emphasis added.

[9]In this paper I focus on the exegetical; see the companion piece, "No Need to Travel to the Indies: Towards a Redescription of Ritual" for the other dimension forthcoming.

[10]Herodotus III.38 = Pindar, fragment 169.

[11]M. A. Amerine, "Wine Making," *The Encyclopaedia Britannica,* 15th ed., (Chicago, 1974), Vol. 9, pp. 877f.

[12]M. Eliade, *Patterns in Comparative Religion* (New York, 1958), pp. 11f.

[13]I have taken these quotations from A. E. Jensen, *Myth and Cult Among Primitive Peoples* (Chicago, 1963), pp. 5, 6, 66, 171, 174, 176, 194.

[14]H. Kenner, *Flaubert, Joyce and Beckett: The Stoic Comedians* (Boston, 1962), pp. xiii, xviii-xix, 1-4. I may note that this is one of the rare works of literary criticism to reflect on the aesthetics of the list.

[15]Benedictus Pererius, *Commentarii et disputationes in Genesim* (Lyons, 1607-10), Vol. II, pp. 187-205.

[16]G. Bateson, *Naven,* 2nd ed. (Stanford, 1968), pp. 6f.

[17]A. Alt, "Die Weisheit Salomos," *Theologische Literaturzeitung,* LXXVI (1951), 139-44.

[18]C. Lévi-Strauss, *Elementary Structures of Kinship* (Boston, 1969), pp. 494f. and 495, n. 2.

[19]E.g. K. Burridge, *Tangu Traditions* (Oxford, 1969), pp. 198f.

[20]N. D. Munn, *Walbiri Iconography* (Ithaca, 1973).

[21]G. Bochet, "Le Poro des Dieli," *Bulletin de l'Institut français d'Afrique noire,* XXI (1959), 76.

[22]See, especially, M. Griaule-G. Dieterlen, *Signes graphiques soudanais* (Paris, 1951) and G. Calame-Griaule, *Ethnologie et langage: La parole chez les Dogon* (Paris, 1965).

[23]H. Maine, *Ancient Law* (London, 1917), chapter II. Compare the excellent review of this notion by L. L. Fuller, *Legal Fictions* (Stanford, 1967).

[24]V. Turner, *Ndembu Divination* (Manchester, 1961); W. Bascom, *Ifa Divination* (Bloomington, 1969).

[25]I have summarized the summary in B. Ray, *African Religions* (Englewood Cliffs, 1976), pp. 107f.

II

Midrash

RENÉE BLOCH

Translated by
MARY HOWARD CALLAWAY*
FORDHAM UNIVERSITY

I. THE MEANING OF THE TERM

It is important to give the word midrash its true meaning. It is often taken as a synonym for fable or moral legend. Actually, it designates an edifying and explanatory genre closely tied to Scripture, in which the role of amplification is real but secondary and always remains subordinate to the primary religious end, which is to show the full import of the work of God, the Word of God. The pejorative sense which is often given to the word midrash occasions, among other things, an unfortunate misunderstanding of the antecedents of this genre in biblical literature. However, as Dom G. M. Camps writes, "the fact that the book of Wisdom from chapter 10 to the end is a typical midrash proves that this genre is not unworthy of divine inspiration" (*Midraš Sobre la Historia de les Plagues*, in *Miscellenea biblica B. Ubach*, Monteserrat, 1953, p. 97).

In any case, philology as well as history opposes the misinterpretation noted above. Though the root *drš* has several different nuances in the Bible, it assumes a precise sense already in the later biblical writings. And as early as the Tannaitic age this root, and especially the substantive *mdrš* which is derived from it, took on a technical meaning which it has kept to this day in Judaism. Inadequate information about Judaism usually accounts for much of the misunderstanding of the midrashic genre, although this genre was already completely formed at the time of the birth of Christianity.

1. The Hebrew Bible. The word *mdrš* is mentioned only two times: in II Chron. 13:22 and 24:27, and it designates the non-canonical sources used by the author. The Hebrew text of Sirach 51:23 uses the expression *bbyt mdršy* (Greek ἐν οἴκῳ παιδείας). On the other hand, the verb *drš* occurs very

*With the assistance of Professor James A. Sanders, Claremont School of Theology.

frequently. In all its uses, secular or religious, it evokes the idea of a directed search, such as determining the identity of a person (II Sam. 11:3), searching for that which is lost (Deut. 22:2) or examining the guilt of a man (Job 10:6). Most often, however, the term is used in a religious sense. It means to frequent a cultic place, to seek God, to seek the response of God in worship and in personal prayer (Amos 5:5; II Chron.1:5; Deut. 12:5; Ps. 34:5; 69:33; 105:4, etc.). But it is especially in the Scriptures that one seeks him. This meaning is common in the post-exilic age: it is to Scripture that one turns to find the responses of God. *drš* designates, then, the study of Torah (in the broad sense, that is, the whole divine revelation, conceived of as the standard of life; cf. A. Robert, "Le sens du mot Loi dans le ps. CXIX," in *Revue Biblique*, 1937, p. 205-206): Ps. 119:45, 94, 155; I Chron. 28:8; or the study of the mighty interventions of God in the history of Israel: Ps. 111:2: "Great are the works of the Lord, studied (*drwšym*) by all those who have pleasure in them." Is. 34:16, a post-exilic text (cf. art. Isaie, in *D.B.S.*, IV, 678-679), is significant in this respect; it is an invitation to seek in the book of the Lord—*dršw m^cl spr yhwh*—the prophecies about Edom in order to compare the prediction with the fulfillment.

Those who were filled with thoughts drawn from contemplation of the sacred texts, like Ezra (7:10), or the author of Ps. 111 (cf. vs. 1) and Ben Sira (Sirach 24:23-24, Greek) did not keep them to themselves: diligent study of texts ended in a doctrinal and edifying statement.

Since the meaning of the root *daraš* was fixed during the post-exilic age, we should not pause over the meaning of the word *midraš* in the biblical passages mentioned. The nature of the writings which served as sources for the Chronicler remain somewhat mysterious for us, but since the meaning of the root is clear, it is likely that when the Chronicler used the term *midraš* he was alluding to the historical works which glossed Scripture for the purpose of instruction and edification. As for the "house of midrash" of which Ben Sira speaks, it was probably already a place where Scripture was studied and interpreted. The book of Sirach itself is a typical product of this activity.

2. In the Rabbinic Literature. Rabbinic Hebrew adds nothing, essentially, to the meaning of the verb *daraš*. It always means careful study of a biblical passage. The practical concern for teaching and edification is evident whether the verb or its derivative *deraša^ɔ* appears.

Deraša^ɔ is a "doctrinal statement or a sermon": its purpose is not only to explicate Scripture, but also to make its meaning known in public, "to preach." The *daršan* is the one who publicly expounds Scripture, the "preacher." (The documents from the Judean desert also mention the office of the interpreter of the Law, *doreš ha-Torah*: he should dedicate himself exclusively to study: Rule of the Community of Qumran, VI, 6-7; cf. also the Damascus Document, VI, 7; VII, 18.)

In rabbinic literature midrash has the general sense of "search," with the double nuance of *study* (e.g. M. Avot 1:17: "It is not study [*midraš*] which is essential, but practice"; in this case midrash is often synonymous to *talmud*: y. Pes. 30b, etc.) and explanation (M. Ket. 4:6: "R. Eleazar ben Azariah has presented this explanation [*midraš*] before the court of Yavneh . . ."; M. Sheq. 6:6, etc.). But it is especially in reference to Scripture (y. Yoma, 40c; b. Qid., 49a, 49b; Genesis Rabba 42, 1 [Theodor, 398, 6]: "He explained [*doreš*] the following verse . . ."; Gen. R. 42, 3 [Theodor, 399-400, 1] etc.). From this comes the common usage of *Bet ha-Midraš* (cf. Sirach 51:22), the "house of study," in the sense of a place where one was dedicated to the study of Scripture (M. Shab. 16:1; b. Meg. 27a, etc.). As opposed to the literal explanation, called *pešaṭ*, the term midrash designates an exegesis which moves beyond the simple and literal sense in order to penetrate into the spirit of Scripture; to scrutinize the text more deeply and draw from it interpretations which are not always immediately obvious (the opinion given by Rabba in b. Yev. 24a proves the midrash and *pešat* were clearly distinguished).

In a more special sense midrash (plural: *midrašim*) designates something written for the purpose of interpreting the Bible, usually homiletical, like the Midrash Rabbah, which is a commentary on the Pentateuch (and the five Megillot).

In summary, in the rabbinic literature the term has taken on a "technical" meaning: midrash is always in rapport with Scripture, in the sense of searching, trying to understand the meaning and content of the biblical text in order to reveal and explain publicly the meaning of Scripture.

II. THE CHARACTERISTICS OF RABBINIC MIDRASH

We cannot enter into the details of rabbinic midrash or midrashic literature here. Our purpose is only to try to define and to make clear the essential and fundamental characteristics of midrash.

1. Its Point of Departure is Scripture. This is its fundamental characteristic, which already excludes any possibility of finding parallels to this literary genre outside of Israel. Midrash is therefore a genre which is peculiar to Israel, like prophecy, but perhaps even more unique. Midrash cannot occur outside of Israel because it presupposes faith in the revelation which is recorded in the holy books. It is a reflection, a meditation on the sacred texts, a "searching" of Scripture.

2. It is Homiletical. Those who "search" the Scriptures are not "ivory tower" scholars. Midrash is not a genre of the academy; it is rather a popular genre, and above all it is homiletical. Its origin is certainly to be sought for the most part in the liturgical reading of the Torah for Sabbaths and Feasts. And

the Palestinian Targum, which is functionally midrashic, must not be thought of independently of the lectionary reading of Scripture; it very probably reflects the homilies which followed the Scriptural reading in the synagogues.

3. It is a Study Which is Attentive to the Text. This is a natural corollary. Since the sacred text was read in the synagogue and had to be commented upon in a homily relating to it, attempts were made to understand it better. Because of this it was studied diligently, that it might be understood and its obscurities made clear. This concern of the rabbis meant that they often began their inquiry by asking the question: why?—*mpny mh* is an expression frequently used by the rabbis in their interpretation (cf. Bacher, *Die exegetische Terminologie*, I, 113). Thus, for example, they explained and tried to give the precise meaning of rare or difficult terms: *ᵓyn* . . . *ᵓlᵓ*, "this is nothing other than," "this is the same as." An obscure word was often explained by a similar term belonging to a foreign language related to Hebrew, with the remark that the word given is *lšwn knᶜny*, Phoenician (Sifre, II, 306; ed. Finkelstein, p. 336, 12 and notes, ibid.); or *lšwn mṣry*, Coptic (Pesiqta de Rab Kahana, 109b); or *lšwn swrsy*, Syriac (Mekhilta; ed. Lauterbach, I, 28); or derived from still other languages. Naturally these philological explanations are no longer satisfactory to us; on the other hand, the interpretation itself is often quite pertinent. The principal method by which the rabbis clarify the sacred text and probe its depths is by recourse to parallel passages. The Bible forms a unit; it comes from God in all of its parts and it therefore offers a broad context to which one should always return. Since they knew the Scriptures by heart they were constantly explaining the Bible by the Bible—*twrh mtwk twrh*—which is clearly an excellent principle. The recourse to Scripture took on various forms: the author could refer to isolated passages taken from different places, but he usually used a motif. Ordinarily only a few sources were used, and one senses among the midrashists a tendency to be selective. There are, however, cases in which the author uses a single text.

4. Adaptation to the Present. If midrashic exegesis consists primarily in an attentive study of the texts, it does not stop there. Its aim is not purely theoretical. Its goal is primarily practical: to define the lessons for faith and for the religious way of life contained in the biblical text. The practical aspect was probably not in the foreground in the biblical midrash, for this midrash related to an age in which the need for adaptation was not felt to the same extent as toward the end of the biblical age. But it had already assumed a place in certain apocryphal writings, such as Jubilees, the Damascus Document and the Rule of the Community of Qumran, and was to take on a much more obvious importance in the rabbinic *midrašim*. This practical concern led midrash to reinterpret Scripture, to "actualize" it. This characteristic—among others which we cannot discuss here—along with the close relation and

constant reference to Scripture, is the essence of midrash. These two characteristics, which are constant, are the very soul of the midrashic method.

This tendency to actualization corresponds to the way in which Israel—and later the Church—has always understood Scripture as the word of God. It always involves a living Word addressed personally to the people of God and to each of its members, a Word which makes clear the divine wishes and demands and calls for a response, never theoretical, and a commitment: the fidelity of a people and each of its members to the demands which the Word makes manifest. Revealed at a specific point in history, this Word is nevertheless addressed to men of all times. Thus it ought to remain open indefinitely to all new understandings of the message, all legitimate adaptations and all new situations. These things are the foundation and the *raison d'etre* of midrash. So long as there is a people of God who regard the Bible as the living Word of God, there will be midrash; only the name might change. Nothing is more characteristic in this regard than the use of the OT in the NT: it always involves midrashic actualization. The newness resides in the actualization itself, in the present situation to which the ancient texts are applied and adapted.

5. *Aggadah* and *halakah.*—As we have already noted, liturgical reading of the Scriptures held the place of honor in the synagogues. This reading provided the material for the sermon, which followed it immediately and was generally a commentary on the Scripture lesson in the form of *aggadah*. In the schools, which often adjoined the synagogue, this same biblical text was used for instruction; it was studied and commented on and a rule of life or *halakah* was drawn from it. Hence the Law became the subject matter for daily instruction and tradition.

We therefore can distinguish two kinds of *midrašim*, based on the nature of the part of the Torah which is studied and the purpose of the study. The first deals primarily with the legal parts of the Torah, seeking therein to define the laws and to discover in them the fundamental principles by which new laws for resolving new problems might be derived, as well as arguments for justifying certain customs which already were traditional. This sort of midrash is designated by the term *midraš halakah* (the basic sense of this term is "walk, step, way", from which the meaning "law, precept", standard of human behavior is derived) or halakhic interpretation of the Torah. The other, which relates particularly to the narrative parts of the Torah and seeks to define the meaning of the stories and the events of history, is designated by the name *midraš aggadah*.

This intense activity of study and "practical" interpretation of the Torah, pursued for many centuries, has given rise to a collection of explanations and commentaries which, having been transmitted orally by scholars from generation to generation were finally redacted to form a whole body of halakhic commentaries, the *Tannaitic midrašim*. These midrashim contain very ancient materials and have for the most part preserved the simple methods of interpretation of the ancient scholars, who limited themselves to a very literal explanation of the biblical text.

Aggadah, which is very rich and of great religious value, has given rise to a vast literature, which included homilies and commentaries following the biblical books. (These "commentaries" are very different from the writings to which this name is given today, which are, rather, expositions that take the text as a point of departure, like certain patristic commentaries or "treatises".)

Aggadah is above all a means of popular instruction, in which the biblical text sometimes serves as a springboard for rising to the level of meditation of the mysteries of God.

III. THE BIBLICAL ORIGINS OF MIDRASH

1. The historical setting of the birth of the midrashic process. (1.) The exile.—We have established that at a certain point the terms *daraš* and *midraš* acquired a precise meaning which refers consistently and almost exclusively to Scripture, and suggests an activity consisting of studying, searching, "pondering" and explaining Scripture, particularly in the form of a homily. This evolution corresponds to a specific situation and reflects a particularly important period of the history of the people of God. It coincides with the doctrinal and literary development which placed the Law at the center of the life of Israel. Historically it is hardly debatable that the Torah acquired this central place as early as the Exile, particularly during the Restoration and the Persian period. Though we know very little about the material life of Israel during the Exile, we are better informed (for example, by the book of Ezekiel and chapters 40-55 of Isaiah) about its spiritual evolution during this long trial, which R. P. Grollenberg, O. P. (in *Atlas de la Bible*, Paris, Elsevier, 1955, p. 98), terms the "years of introspection and hope," when Israel "meditated upon all the previous action of Yahweh; read and re-read what remained of the traditions of Moses and of the great prophets (*ibid.*, p. 100). Israel reflected, in some manner, on her destiny. For though her national patrimony had been lost, in this "return" to Yahweh—*tešuvah*—an idea which took shape with the prophets and of which they never ceased to preach, the people turned to the only patrimony which remained, tradition, composed essentially of narrative traditions about the history of the people of God and of legislative traditions, of which the exiles were the principal trustees. And when the hope of a return to the land of the fathers was raised, the exiles no doubt carefully collected all that remained of the precious patrimony, which linked the present to the past and at the same time served as a program for restoration, provided that it be adapted to the new radically changed circumstances. The prophetic visions of the future, far from excluding the past, were based on the memory of it: thus chapters 40-48 of Ezekiel, which established the liturgical rubric for the new community (a description of the Temple to be constructed,

the functions of the priestly descendants of Zadok, the ritual for the feasts, the partition of Palestine), depend to a great extent on Deuteronomy and the Holiness Code, as Mgr. G. Ricciotti has rightly noted (*Hist. d'Israel*, II, Paris, Picard, 1948, p. 95): "It seems undeniable that Ezekiel worked, as it were, on the fabric of preceding legislation, especially that of Deuteronomy: this would explain the parallelism of the laws; but at the same time the sacred writer was not content with a mere transcription: it was his intention to change the ancient law which he adapted to the future nation. . . ."

(2.) The Persian age.—(a) The canonization of Scripture.—The Persian age, with the decree of Cyrus and the return of the Jews to Palestine, began a new period which was to become especially important since that was when the entire life of Israel was reorganized around Scripture, which began to be codified into a canon of sacred Scripture. The most remarkable activity of this period, which conditioned the whole future and the entire structure of the religious life of Judaism, was in fact that which gave the Pentateuch, after a slow redactional process, its definitive form as a sacred text having the value of law, or canon, for the whole community. This extensive work, of which many elements date very far back into the past, came to gain authority very quickly and to create a "milieu" favoring the exclusion of many other writings of the OT. R. P. Grollenberg (*op. cit.*, 100) described this period with these words: "During the centuries which elapsed between the completion of the Temple and the Maccabean revolt the Jewish people remained, with their priests, gathered around the altar of Yahweh, more than ever a 'people of God,' separated from the pagan world and outside of the great political arena. *It was in the midst of this silent withdrawal that the OT received its present form.* The Jews reflected on the past with a broken heart and they completed the great recital of the saving acts of God on the one hand and of the constant infidelity of his people on the other. The Pentateuch took the form in which we know it; the series of 'former prophets' was edited in a definitive way, and the oracles of the 'later prophets' were reworked and ordered. Many of the Writings date back to this time, and it can be said that they expressed the response of Israel to the revelation of God. We see the people praying in the Psalms, weeping in Lamentations, contending in Job, loving in the Song of Songs. The prophets have now been replaced by the wise men who incorporated the wisdom of the ancient Near East into the heritage of Israel. . . ."

The canonizing of Scripture was of the greatest importance for the genesis of the midrashic genre. From that point on there was a "canonical" text on which the people reflected, with which they prayed and which came to be the object of study, transmission, teaching and preaching.

(b) The role of the Law in life and in the cult.—The sacred text transmitted by tradition, designated by the name of Law, Torah, *became the authority and regulated the life of the community in all its details*. At the same time the reading and the knowledge of Torah became an essential obligation

of piety. It was in this period that the reading and teaching of the Law entered
the public life, on the fringe of the sacrificial cult. It was then that the new form
of divine service appeared, which in the Hellenistic period would become the
synagogue service properly speaking. The center of this service was the public
reading and commentary on the passages of the Torah according to the
Sabbaths and the Feast Days.

Insofar as the written word became the guide of the nation after the exile,
the smallest details of the text took on importance; hence the elaborate study
of the Torah whose goal was to understand the meaning of each word and to
penetrate into the spirit of the text in order to draw out the deeper meaning
and its practical application. This study came to be called midrash, or more
precisely midrash Torah, which might be freely interpreted as "study of the
meaning of the Torah."

The Torah was the Law of God which inspired all of life, and midrash
involved the whole Torah, the narrative as well as the legal parts. There was as
much zeal for studying the meaning of the events of the past as for
investigating the precise content and all the implications of the laws and
commandments contained in the legal parts of the Torah. Nothing warrants
the assertion that the scribes, and later the rabbis, preferred to study the legal
texts, as is often thought; only the urgency of the practical needs accounts for
the fact that this study usually occupied the greatest part of their discussions.

With the authority of the Torah came also the authority of the priests,
designated by the Torah as the official scholars and authorized interpreters
(Deut. 17:8-13); it was from them that knowledge of Torah was sought (Hag.
2:11; Mal. 2:7; cf. Jer. 18:18; Ezek. 44:15-24). After the reconstruction of the
Temple and the restoration of the sacrificial cult they became the religious
heads of the people, with the double task of offering the sacrifices and
teaching the Law of God. New circumstances, however, gave rise to a new
ruling class, at first within the priestly circle itself, then more and more
alongside it: the *Soferim*, who gradually gained authority with the people.
Their work consisted especially in transmitting and studying the Law and
seeing that it was enforced.

The beginning of this essential activity of study and interpretation of the
Torah is traditionally ascribed to Ezra. Begun in the time of Ezra, *scribe
skilled in the Law of Moses (Sofer mahir be-Torat Mošeh)* (Ezra 7:6; cf. 7:11;
Neh. 8:1,4,13; 12:26,36), and his colleagues the *soferim*, it would have been
continued by their successors, the scholars of following generations. This
activity was therefore founded entirely on Scripture. Ezra, *the priest, the
scribe, learned in matters of the commandments of the Lord and his statutes
for Israel. . . , had set his heart to study (lidroš) the Law of the Lord, and to
do it, and to teach his statutes and ordinances in Israel* (Ezra 7:1-10). It is in
this same sense that tradition has understood the solemn reading of the Law,
made before the people at the time of the assembly which Ezra brought
together in the seventh month, when the Levites *read from the book, from the*

law of God, clearly; and they explained the meaning so the people understood the reading (Neh. 8:7-8).

It is clear, therefore, that the book of Nehemiah (8:1-9; 18:3, 9) sets the public reading and explanation of the Law, a sort of preaching, in the time of Ezra by making use of expressions which belonged to an age when public reading, thorough study and homiletical explanation of the Law had already become a sacred institution.

2. The evolution of the literary genres.—We see, then, that the origin of the midrashic genre is inseparable from the formation and the life of the holy Books. The first midrashic development arose from searching the Bible itself and the related literature: the versions and apocrypha (see below). The later literature, of a purely midrashic character, remained in continuity with the Bible and constituted an organic link between the Bible and the rabbinic literature.

When we recall the significance of the sacred Book in the life of the people of God we find this development very normal. At every stage in their progressive formation, and especially in the post-exilic community, the Scriptures were a part of the life of the community. They were constantly read and re-read, they were the sole object of teaching, and they nourished reflection and prayer. The people constantly inquired of them to find responses—divine responses—to the many problems which life posed. It is this life of the Scriptures in the heart of the community which is expressed in the *midrašim*, which were likewise constantly conditioned not only by the ideas and the religious doctrines of the period and the milieu, but more especially by the practical goal to which they responded. Nothing could be more wrong than the idea that midrash is a late creation of rabbinic Judaism. This is what we propose to do, too summarily, by pointing out the beginnings of midrashic tendency within the inspired Scriptures themselves.

The general tendency of the biblical writers to ground themselves in their predecessors is well known: Isaiah referred to Amos; Jeremiah shows the influence of Hosea as well as of Isaiah; Ezekiel, in addition to his relation to the Holiness Code, made use of Amos, Hosea, Isaiah and especially Jeremiah. This tendency is noticeably increased in the post-exilic literature. The inspired writers of this period, like their contemporaries, had a thorough knowledge of the former Scriptures and especially of the Torah, which was at the center of the life of the community. The people faced the problems of the present in light of the Scriptures and they thought and wrote in terms of them; they relied on them for everything. It was during this period that the oral tradition was fixed in the "Writings," which in turn would be studied and reflected upon. The post-exilic books are almost always dependent upon the older inspired writings and they often refer to them, whether by verbatim quotations, free citations, or simple allusions. If the Writings in general were composed in this way, the procedure is nonetheless especially characteristic of the wisdom books.

For example, the first nine chapters of Proverbs are based on Deuteronomy, Jeremiah and Isaiah (56-66), but they integrate this material to give the impression of being an entirely new work (cf. A. Robert, "Les attaches litteraires bibliques de Prov. I-IX", in *RB* 1935, p. 344-65). The work of Ben Sira, who calls his school *the house of midrash* (Eccles. 51:23) is a web of citations (especially Eccles. 44-50). It in turn reuses certain parts of Proverbs, but these parts often take on a more developed meaning. Wisdom, in spite of its Greek veneer, relies on the whole Jewish tradition. In this regard it presents a model of midrashic exegesis (for example chapters 10-12 and 16-19; cf. E. Osty, "Le livre de la Sagesse" in *La Ste. Bible*, Paris, Ed. du Cerf, 1950, p. 19-22). Characteristic examples of the anthological style are also found in the Psalms of Thanksgiving (*Hodayot*) recently discovered in the Judean desert. The Rule of the Community of Qumran and the Damascus Document also frequently cite and comment on the Law and the prophets.

This procedure, which has been termed anthological, consists in "reusing, literally or equivalently, the words or expressions of the former Scriptures" (A. Robert, LITTERAIRES (Genres), in *D.B.S.* V, 411; this procedure has been well defined by the same author in "Le genre littéraire du Cantique des cantiques," in *Vivre et penser*, 1943-44, p. 192-213). It is obviously used extensively in the post-exilic literature.

But the post-exilic writers were not content to reproduce and reuse the texts by simply espousing the thought which they expressed. The reflection of the new authors was a response to the texts which they used; it developed, enriched and transposed the original message. Then, in the movement which in the history of the people of God caused knowledge of revelation to mature and improve, the more recent writers often did not even take account of the fact that the meaning which they gave to the writings of their predecessors was different from the original meaning. They used their sources very freely, with a concern to respond to the needs and problems of their times, and they did not hesitate to give new meaning, by adaptation, to the old texts.

Some examples taken from biblical books of different genres and periods, which for lack of space will be given a very summary treatment below, are only samples and mere indications. The convergent witness of these different biblical passages, in which the characteristics of midrash are manifest to different degrees, testifies that in the post-exilic age the midrashic genre was a widespread phenomenon of which exegesis must take account.

IV. SOME EXAMPLES FROM THE BIBLE

1. In the historical genre.—The most obvious examples of these midrashic methods in the Bible are given by the priestly literature—beginning with the priestly writings integrated into the Pentateuch—and especially

by the books of Chronicles. Their principal sources are the Pentateuch and the books of Samuel and Kings, especially P. The literary dependence of the Chronicler on the priestly document is quite appreciable, for example in the genealogies (with the frequent use of the term *toledot*, characteristic of P). As in the priestly history, these genealogies bring out the central motif of election. The historical books Samuel and Kings are no less already a commentary on the facts of history in the light of prophetic pronouncements. But in the Chronicler concern with the facts of history is even more obscure. It is an oriented history, or rather a meditation on history, giving the past a relevance to the concerns of the moment. At the center of the history of Israel the Chronicler put the reign of David, to whom he attributed the entire organization of the service of the sanctuary, and he gave him the place which Moses had in the community described in the priestly texts of the Pentateuch (for example in the texts which speak of the Covenant). This transposition of history demonstrates the development of religious ideas and at the same time it reveals the immediate goal of the sacred writer, which was to legitimize the privilege of the Levites. It is from this very point of view that the Chronicler takes up the ancient materials and reworks them according to his theological conceptions and his own apologetic aims. These are typically midrashic traits.

2. In the prophetic genre. (1.) Ezekiel 16.—In this chapter, which is from the beginning of the exile, we clearly have an allegory; verses 3, 28, 29, not to mention 27, present us immediately with historical allusion. The general theme is the care of God for Israel, his unfaithful wife; it is taken from Hosea and Jeremiah. A study of the vocabulary shows a number of contacts with Deuteronomy and Jeremiah. There are also contacts with the priestly Code, but these signify little more than a common milieu. From all evidence we are dealing with an essentially biblical composition. A detailed analysis of the literary ties, in vocabulary as well as thought, produces a twofold result.

First, the biblical sources have furnished Ezekiel not only with his general doctrinal theme, but also with the details of his allegory. It is presented as a historical allegory. Here, moreover, Ezekiel guards against fabrication; his narrative follows the events of the holy history with a curious accuracy, such that they are related in the sequence Genesis–Kings (verse 3: the sojourn of the patriarchs in Palestine; 6: the covenant with Abraham; 7-8: the covenant with Moses, etc.).

At first sight this chapter might appear to be very original. But a careful literary analysis shows that most of it was composed by reusing and bringing into play literary elements which already existed in the biblical tradition, the motifs themselves as much as the style. Such a use of the traditions indicates a profound knowledge of and familiarity with them. The writer used them for his parenetic and didactic ends with consummate skill, continually and intentionally blending the memories of the past with the problems of the present into poetic allegory. To give a supreme and solemn warning to

Jerusalem (and to "explain" the catastrophe which had fallen on the city) he used the great motif of the Covenant under the image of an allegorical marriage, by relating the whole history of Israel in its religious significance to the present situation.

All the essential methods of midrash occur in this text: the reuse of transmitted sacred texts with a religious reflection on their content, the past to which they witness, with the contemporization which relates them for a practical end—here it is exhortation—to the present situation. In this case the prophet tries to make the people understand that the cause of the catastrophe which they are experiencing is to be found in the faithlessness of the people. At the same time, in light of the events the theological thinking has been deepened and improved: in our case it is the central idea of the Covenant which, being in line with Deuteronomy and Jeremiah, appears here under a clearly more stable and more developed form.

(2.) Is. 60-62.—This literary unit, which has clearly been taken from another context, is generally considered to belong to the time of Haggai and Zachariah. From a literary standpoint it is related to chapters 40-55 (including the Servant poems) by the number of borrowed elements, while differing in its doctrinal perspective and historical background. In the Servant poems the savior of Israel assumes the identity of a teacher of truth who delivers a universal message, undergoes persecution and death, makes expiation and intercession for the people and triumphs over suffering and death. In chapters 60-62, however, we have a more strictly national perspective, where the universalism remains firmly centered on Jerusalem, the beloved of Yahweh, haloed by a divine ray in the darkness, whom the leaders of the past have come to help rebuild. The scope of the magnificent picture of the caravans which march to the holy city remains limited: these are foreigners who carry their precious gifts and who bring back the captive sons of Israel. The latter form as it were a priestly nobility whose servants are the foreigners. This vivid messianic picture is in sharp contrast to the sufferings of the present and the uncertainty of the future; the Scriptures therefore were searched for enlightenment, consolation and hope, especially Is. 40-55 and the messianic promises of the Law (60:15 = Gen. 12:3; 60:22 = Gen. 17:26, 28:3, etc.).

(3.) The Servant poems.—The fundamental question of the relation of these poems to their context, which has been the object of so much discussion, would doubtless be illuminated by a careful study of their literary genre. The resemblance between these pieces and their context is possibly the result of the work of a later author who adapted and rethought the ancient text in a new age by transposing it and deepening its meaning (cf. Renée Bloch, "Quelques aspects de la figure de Moïse dans la tradition rabbinique" in *Moïse, l'homme de l'Alliance*, special issue of *Cahiers Sioniens*, 1954; and Paris, *Desclée*, 1955, p. 153-154).

3. In the wisdom genre.—(1.) Prov. 1-9.—The redactor of the first collection of Proverbs, like the later author of Wisdom, undertook a re-evaluation of traditional teaching. Using the old motifs he made a new synthesis, and he was the one who first placed the idea of divine Wisdom at the center of this synthesis. He "transposed" the idea of Torah into Wisdom. This transposition corresponded to a new historical context, but it was not done without careful consideration, which enabled it to end in a coherent synthesis.

Since A. Robert has made a detailed study of the vocabulary of this anthology in five *Revue Biblique* articles (1934-35) we will not dwell on Prov. 1-9 here. We will only recall that the vocabulary of these chapters was taken from just three writings; Deuteronomy, Jeremiah and Isaiah (especially 40-66), but has been uniformly inflected with the meaning of the doctrine of Wisdom. Wisdom assumes the messianic role traditionally reserved for an elect descendent of David (chap. 8). Even the Temple of Jerusalem is "transposed" into the Temple of Wisdom.

Prov. 1-9 is a literary and theological construction based on a method of adaptation and profound reflection on Scripture which is already definitely midrashic.

(2.) The Song of Songs.—If the exegesis of the Song of Songs has been greatly debated and its allegorical significance, based on prophetic teaching confronted by contemporary history, has often been misunderstood, it is because the study of its genre and its literary structure has too often been neglected.

The vocabulary of the poem is directly and consistently biblical. The most classical themes are used: king, shepherd, flock, vineyard, garden, Lebanon, blossoming springtime, night, awakening; all with eschatological significance and grouped around the central motif, already developed by Hosea, Jeremiah, and III Isaiah: the unfaithful wife (Israel) taken back by her husband (Yahweh) as though he had just married her. The constant reference to the biblical motifs and the dramatization and reinterpretation of the events and aspirations of the period after Nehemiah indicate that this is pure midrash.

(3.) Eccles. 24.—The entire chapter is full of biblical reminiscences, but it is particularly related to Prov. 8:22-33. The imagination of the author, however, gives a new form to the ancient motif. Wisdom is personified as coming forth from the mouth of the Most High, singing her own praise to the heavens, searching the earth for a dwelling place, settling in Israel, fulfilling the liturgical offices of the Temple and finally revealing that she is identical with the Law of Moses. This figure originates entirely from meditation on Scripture. The personality of the author is asserted in the presentation rather than in the content or the material used. The apparent newness of the identification of Wisdom with the Law is actually only the elucidation of a motif constantly presupposed in the sources used.

(4.) Eccles. 44:1-50:24: The eulogy of the fathers.—The activity of Wisdom in Israel is described in detail in this eulogy of the fathers. It is a series of portraits of the great figures of biblical history, touched up with some traits taken from different biblical books. A number of details show that the author's goal was edification. The insistence in the passages which relate to the cult (45:6-26; 50:1-21) and the succession of the high priests (45:24-26), etc. clearly corresponds to contemporary affairs which concerned the author: the disaffection with the ceremonies of the Temple and the intrigues surrounding the succession of the high priest. Here again the two principal characteristics of midrash can be seen: the use of biblical texts for the purpose of edification, in the service of contemporary needs. This important unit can therefore be considered aggadic midrash, in accordance with the allusion of 51:23.

(5.) The Book of Wisdom.—Confronted with the seductions and the assaults of Greek paganism, the author of this book sought to revive the faith of his countrymen. To strengthen them he emphasized the reward of the just by contrasting it to the punishment of the wicked. He insistently reminded them that God had given the Torah to Israel, a gift more precious than the most alluring inventions of Greek civilization. He repeated classical biblical teaching to them in a way which demonstrated its relevance as well as its transcendence, with which the Hellenistic culture could not compete. The idea of Wisdom, which was found already in the biblical tradition, enabled him to regroup the elements of the traditional doctrine under a philosophical form which lent itself particularly well to a confrontation with Greek wisdom. At the same time it made an appeal to pagans, by denouncing the delusion of idolatry and by presenting to them the glories of divine Wisdom. In this whole effort the author makes extensive use of the language, ideas and culture of the Hellenistic world, while remaining thoroughly Jewish, nourished by the Scriptures. Moreover, he constantly appeals to the Scriptures. Hence when addressing kings he assumes the character of Solomon. The Wisdom which he presents is not different from that of Prov. 8:1-9:6 and of Eccles. 24. The allusions to the origins of Israel, the exodus and especially the plagues of Egypt are very characteristic. But a detailed comparison shows at the same time the freedom and boldness with which the author used these texts of the Pentateuch which he venerated because of their divine origin. He supplements the traditional narratives, or rather, suppresses whatever would interfere with his own account; he embellishes to suit his arguments, or even for literary reasons; more, he rearranges the events, or gives them a new meaning; it is an "accomplished model of midrashic exegesis" (see E. Osty, "Le livre de la Sagesse" in *La Ste. Bible*, Paris, Ed. du Cerf, 1950, p. 19, 20-26).

4. In the Psalms.—(1.) Ps. 132—Opinions about the date and the historical setting of this psalm are very divergent. It seems clear however that the crux of the problem is to determine the genre of the psalm: should the

details of the description be taken literally? What situation, what psychology would evoke it? Let us see what the structure of the psalm reveals.

Verses 1-10. A prayer which praises the merits of David: he was trying to find a resting place for the Ark and with the consent of the people to rescue it from oblivion.

Verses 11-12. The first part implicitly uses 2 Sam. 7:1-17, which relates the interview with Nathan. The second part clearly refers to the divine response. The purpose of building on this response is to give reasons for hope that the prayer will be granted: the Davidic dynasty has the promise of an everlasting reign. The rejection of it was only temporary and was justified by its infidelities.

Verses 13-14. It follows from the same prophecy of Nathan that God has chosen Zion as his eternal dwelling place. Now given the circumstances in which Nathan's prophecy was uttered, the fate of the house of David will be the same as that of the house of Yahweh. The election is valid, then, forever.

Verses 15-18. It followed from this that the divine blessings would surely descend upon the priests and the faithful. Verses 17-18 suggest in veiled terms the prospects of a personal messiah.

In short, this psalm appears to be a midrashic reflection on the prophecy of Nathan, and the occasion of its composition may have been the reconstruction of the Temple and the disappearance of Zerubabel. The author reasoned rightly about the link between the Temple and the dynasty, which is presupposed by Haggai and Zach. 1-8. He responded to a question which was being raised: the Temple was rebuilt; why then did the Davidic line seem to be extinct forever? The psalmist recalls the divine promises, which he does not doubt, and in this psalm his affirmation of faith changes into supplication. While using the ancient narratives the psalm gives them new life; it "actualizes" them. The whole Jewish soul is there, with its trust in the Scriptures and its hopes, and it is badly misunderstood when this wonderful composition is reduced to a banal review of a historical fact in the time of David or given a false *Sitz im Leben* by relating it to a liturgical rite which cannot be defined.

(2.) Ps. 78. The midrashic genre is also evident in this historical psalm, which regards the entire history of Israel from the standpoint of the election of Judah and the rejection of Ephraim. Other features, too, are characteristic of the genre of this psalm and its dependence on the priestly tradition; as for example the waters raised *like a wall* (during the crossing of the Red Sea) in verse 13 (a characteristic of P, in contrast with J and E).

Psalms 73, 105, etc., the so-called historical psalms may also be seen as similar to many so-called royal psalms (2, 45, 72, 110). Other genres also provide us with a number of examples in addition to those noted above: for example Baruch, Jonah (which extends the doctrine of Jeremiah to combat the particularism of its time), etc. The problem of the priestly Code too would most likely benefit from a study in the light of the midrashic genre. It no longer seems overstated to consider Deuteronomy a work done in midrashic style. In its historical sections it follows the Yahwistic and Elohistic narratives word for word while developing them, commenting on them and grafting exhortations to faithfulness onto them.

5. Minor examples.—Next to these fundamental tendencies, which often bear on the extensive biblical works, there is room for a study of certain lesser literary methods which are characteristic of midrashic development; for example the marked interest in the etymology of proper names, alliteration and other types of verbal assonance and paronomasia (cf. F. M. Th. de Liagre Bohl, "Wortspiele im A.T.", in *Journal of the Palestine Oriental Society*, 1926, p. 196-216; and in *Opera minora*, Groningue, Wolters, 1953, p. 11-25; and I. L. Seeligmann, "Voraussetzungen der Midraschexegese," in *Supplements to Vetus Testamentum, Congress Volume, Copenhagen*, 1953, Leiden, Brill, 1953, p. 150-81). These methods undergo considerable development in rabbinic midrash (see the problems raised on this subject by J. D. Wynkoop, "A peculiar kind of Paronomasia in the Talmud and Midrash" in *JQR*, new series, 2 (1911), p. 1-23).

The *midrašim* which enlarge upon the biblical narratives are not always simply the interpretations or speculations of an individual. They also bear traditions which were not recorded in the Scriptures. Some of these extra-biblical traditions are alluded to in the Bible itself. Thus a gloss (the importance of glosses is too often minimized; a study of them would reveal, among other things, interesting midrashic tendencies) appears in Is. 29:22, which describes God as the *Savior of Abraham*, assuming a tradition which was not preserved by the biblical text and which the LXX ignored. The LXX has an entire theological elaboration in this verse, and inserts the idea of election in place of the midrashic theme of the deliverance of Abraham: "That is why, thus says the Lord to the house of Jacob, which he has *set apart* since Abraham. . . ." But this tradition is well attested in rabbinic literature: because he destroyed the idol of Nimrod, king of Ur, Abraham was thrown by the king into a fiery furnace, from which God rescued him safe and sound (see Renée Bloch, "Écriture et tradition dans le judaïsme", in *Cahiers sioniens*, 1954, n. 1, p. 29, note 62).

V. MIDRASH IN THE BIBLICAL MILIEU

1. The apocryphal literature: midrash and apocalyptic.—The preceding observations give a view of the midrashic method which is broader and yet more accurate than the notions commonly held . At the same time they show that this method was in common use in the Persian period. If rabbinic midrash appeared at the time of the Gospel as a genre whose characteristics were already shaped and even fixed, it is because the genre had developed slowly

during the course of the preceding centuries. In fact the apocryphal literature, which flourished alongside the canonical literature already in the second century B.C., arose essentially out of the midrashic genre. It includes, for example: Jubilees, a midrashic development of Genesis, called Little Genesis in Greek; the Testament of the Twelve Patriarchs, which contains moral and religious exhortations, using the biblical accounts about the twelve sons of Jacob as a point of departure, etc. This literature continued to develop until the end of the first century A.D., and was very important as well as extensive. The documents discovered in the Judean desert provide additional evidence. The Damascus Document contains a meditation on history from the fall of the "Watchers" to the time of the author, as well as halakhic expositions.

But there is a particularly close relationship between apocalyptic and midrash. In both cases, in fact, the authors intended to instruct and to edify by referring to Scripture or to revered traditions. Both have the fulfillment of the ancient promises in mind: they search the texts, discovering in them a deep and mysterious meaning, particularly showing how history is guided by Providence. They searched the past in order to identify the hand of God in current events and to announce the end of time, which was thought to be very near. The authors of the apocalypses saw the fulfillment of the prophetic utterances in the events of their time: they contemporized the ancient prophecies.

The prophecies are placed on the lips of the great figures of the past: Enoch, Moses, Job, Daniel, Ezra, etc., who had foreseen and resolved all the problems of the present. In the book of Jubilees, an excellent example of aggadic midrash, we encounter already the principle which recurs constantly in rabbinic midrashim: the response to all religious questions had been given to Moses by God (G. Vermès, "La figure de Moïse au tournant des deux Testaments", in *Moïse, l'homme de l'Alliance*, special number of *Cahiers Sioniens*, 1954; and Paris, *Desclée*. 1955, p. 77-78, 83-84, 91). But this constant reference to the past was well suited to bold transpositions: the wise Job of the Bible becomes, in the Testament of Job (K. Kohler, "The Testament of Job, An Essene Midrash on the Book of Job," in *Semitic Studies in memory of Alexander Kohut*, Berlin, 1897, p. 264-338), a mystic who saw the celestial chariot described by Ezekiel, and was raised from sheik to king, like his friends (chapter 7, ed. cit., p. 326f.—this tradition is also found in the LXX Job, 42:17d, e). The restrained narratives of the Bible are amplified by many details, and in places are transposed to represent current circumstances. Thus the Sabeans (Job 1:15) became the Persians (Test. of Job, 4:13); Job, who is not a Jew, though the author of the Testament wished to relate him to Israel by making him pass for a son of Esau and husband of Dinah, gives as last counsel to his sons the advice not to marry foreign women.

The Habakkuk Commentary, which is a contemporizing paraphrase of the first two chapters of Habakkuk, uses every known midrashic method. The preoccupation with actualizing prophetic pronouncements is in the foreground: the Chaldeans become the Kittim, conquering people of the end time; the "Righteous" designates the "Teacher of Righteousness"; the "Wicked" the wicked priest. The author argues from homophonic words; from *mašal* (proverb) he moves to *mašal* (ruler). His explanations sometimes attest textual variants as well as Masoretic readings (G. Vermès, "Le 'Commentaire d'Habacuc' et le N.T.," in *Cahiers sioniens*, 1951, p. 342-43).

The main difference between the two genres is that midrash is presented as a work of tradition and of reflection, while apocalypse (precisely as its name, which means "revelation," implies) intends to convey truths which elude the human intellect and were communicated from above. Moreover, midrash appears to be different from apocalypse because it is turned toward the past while apocalypse is turned toward the eschatological future. This is only an appearance however; such orientations are for the most part literary fiction. When midrash consults the past, it is thinking of the present, and even, in a veiled manner, of the future (cf. the implications of the priestly Code and the messianism of Chronicles). Conversely, in the apocalyptic genre the author recounts the past, by convention, in the form of prophecy, but with all the particulars of a history: this is in order to validate his eschatological predictions (cf. Daniel).

Finally, the two genres share a profound sense of the supernatural, which makes them neglect secondary causes and absorb the human into the divine. Hence the predominance of miracles and the often hyperbolic style. The midrashic and apocalyptic genres experienced an extraordinarily extensive development in the Jewish literature of the last centuries before the birth of Christianity and in the early Christian period. Apocalypse is only a type of midrash, and it established, as it were, some of the midrashic characteristics. Since it has been acknowledged that midrash exists in the Bible as a tendency and even as a developed genre, it would be most illogical to disregard the presence of the midrashic genre itself in the Bible. (On prophetic eschatology, which draws its substance from the history of Israel and intends to explain the unfolding of that history by relating the messianic future to the present and to the past, see A. Feuillet, "Le messianisme du livre d'Isaïe," in RecSR, 1949, p. 183-84).

2. The Versions.—Analogous observations can be made by studying the ancient versions, especially the LXX. On almost every page one finds modifications inspired by the theological ideas of the translator and his milieu, motifs taken from oral tradition, and identifications which relate the sacred text to the age of the interpreter. The midrashic tendency of the versions is even more understandable because the purpose of the ancient translators was not to produce a version which followed the letter but rather the spirit of the Scriptures so that they would be understood and explained in the liturgical assemblies. Precisely this adaptation to life is, as we have already pointed out, an essential characteristic of midrash. The correlative tendency

to actualize the content of the sacred text by transposing it in a way which would relate it directly to the present situation is also found in the versions.

The translation of Isaiah in the LXX, for example, reveals the influence of contemporary events. A typical case is Is. 9:11, in which the Greek translator replaces the Arameans and the Philistines of Isaiah's time with the Syrians and the Greeks of his own time. Even more interesting is the history of the name *Kittim* (Gen. 10:4). Originally given to the inhabitants of Cyprus (Is. 22:1, 12; Jer. 2:10; Ezek. 27:6) it came to designate successively the Macedonians (1 Macc. 1:1; 8:5), the Syrians (Jubilees 37:10), and the Romans (Dan. 11:30, in the LXX, Vulgate, Peshitta, Targum of Jerusalem, Habakkuk Commentary), because of the mysterious prophecy in Num. 24:24. The mysterious conqueror in Numbers was identified each time with the contemporary invader (G. Vermes, "Le cadre historique des manuscrits de la mer Morte," in *RecSR*, 1953, p. 210-13; *Les manuscrits du desert de Juda*, Paris, *Desclée*, 1953, p. 84-85).

Until now the versions have been studied almost exclusively from the standpoint of the history of the biblical text, and studies on them have been preoccupied with textual criticism. But the versions are also privileged witnesses to the development of religious ideas and they are equally important for the study of ancient Jewish exegesis. The versions actually laid the groundwork for the later midrashim, particularly the homiletic midrashim.

In this slow progression toward the characteristic literary forms of rabbinic literature one should not forget the exegetical and midrashic work which the establishment of the *consonantal text* of the Hebrew Bible presupposed. The choice of *qere* (the text which is read) as opposed to the *ketib* (the written text) is already an interpretation. The *tiqqune soferim* (corrections of the scribes) often intended to eliminate anthropomorphisms or other expressions which were considered shocking by the people of that time. This vast and obscure work is on the one hand basic to later rabbinic exegesis and on the other hand basic to the exegesis which was incorporated into the NT and which constituted the starting-point of Christian exegesis.

3. The Palestinian Targum.—This cannot be considered a version, which can be seen simply by reading it. While the Targum of Onkelos, edited in Babylonia in an artificial language, is less a true version than an adaptation of the Pentateuch to the discussions in the great Babylonian rabbinic schools (a sort of *pešat*, interpretation of the Torah according to the Talmudic halakhah), the Palestinian Targum comes much closer to *deraš*. It is much closer to midrash than to the versions. It is even quite likely that it was originally a sort of homiletic midrash, or simply the framework for a sequence of homilies on Scripture, made in the synagogue after the public reading of the Torah. It includes already the entire structure and all the motifs of midrash. It contains very ancient traditions (a study of the manuscripts from the Cairo Genizah demonstrates this; cf. P. Kahle, *The Cairo Genizah*, London, 1947, p.

121-30) and constitutes a type of midrash. Used as an immediate extension of the Scripture reading it constituted a sort of juncture or bridge between the biblical text and its interpretation.

4. The New Testament.—The tendencies which we have summarily described occur quite naturally in the NT. Study of midrashic processes in the NT—a field which has not yet been thoroughly explored—would be of very great interest, but it cannot be done within the scope of this article. At most we can mention some salient points.

The Gospel of Matthew uses almost all the midrashic methods, some in their most characteristic form. We might mention, for example, the exposition on Num. 24:17 in Matt. 2:1-12; on Hosea 11:1 in 2:13-15 (a typical transposition); on Jer. 31:15 in 2:16-18; on the resemblance between Nazarene and Nazareth in 2:23; on Zach. 11:12-13, and Jer. 32:6-15 in 27:3-10. Particularly significant is the development of Zach. 9:9 in 21:2-7.

In Luke, especially in the infancy gospel, and most notably in the Magnificat and the Benedictus, we have excellent examples of the anthological style, and in the first part of Acts, especially in the speeches of Peter, Stephen and Paul. The symbolism of the Fourth Gospel, its interest in the meaning of names, its penchant for wordplays, etc., are also related to certain midrashic tendencies. With Paul, especially in the major epistles, we find the most characteristic and authentic form of midrash, what might be called the great midrash: confronted with the immense problem of a change in economy—salvation by faith in Christ, the call of the Gentiles, the rejection by official Judaism—the Apostle, guided by the Spirit, searched ceaselessly in the ancient Scriptures to find divine answers to the questions posed by the new situation. We see this in Gal. 3-4 and Rom. 4, and 9-11, etc. Besides these examples (midrash on the justification of Abraham, in Gal. 3 and Rom. 4; on Sarah and Hagar, in Gal. 4) one could mention the midrash on the veil of Moses in 2 Cor. 3:7-18, etc.

The midrashic genre pervades the Epistle to the Hebrews, but it differs from the preceding examples in that the author wished to draw apologetic arguments from the biblical text rather than answers to actual questions. The great midrash on Melchizedek in chapter 7 is particularly characteristic in this regard.

It is evident that the Apocalypse of St. John draws its motifs and images from the OT. It is literally filled with biblical allusions. Its literary methods easily compare with those of Jewish apocalyptic.

Hence all the forms of midrash are found in the NT: the midrashic study of a character, an event or a collection of biblical texts; the midrashic exposition on a text (sometimes composite); the midrashic contemporization of ancient texts for the sake of applying them to the present (see the examples given for Matt., and among many others, Acts, 1:15-22; see also the contemporized application of many biblical texts in the Johannine Passion narrative; similarly Acts 7:42, where in a text quoted from Amos 5:27, Damascus is replaced by Babylon, following the requirements of the context); the homiletic midrash (some characteristic examples: Matt. 24:37-42: the lesson of the flood; 1 Cor. 10:1-13: the lesson of the exodus; Heb. 11: the example of the ancient heroes of the faith); and even halakhic midrash (see in Matt. 5:32; and 19:9 apropos divorce, a halakhic precise application peculiar to this Gospel; cf. 1 Cor. 9:8-10 on Deut. 25:4). Finally, there are certain non-biblical midrashic traditions in the NT (e.g., the Moses traditions in Acts 7:22-32; the tradition of the rock which accompanied the Israelites in the desert in 1 Cor. 10:4; the role of the angels in the promulgation of the Law in Gal. 3:19; the magicians opposed to Moses in 2 Tim. 3:8; the dispute of the archangel Michael with the devil on the subject of Moses' body in Jude 9), and certain classical biblical "occasions" of apostolic preaching which are equally amenable to the midrashic genre (thus Is. 6:9-10, on the hardening of the people: cf. Matt. 13:14-15; Mark 4:12; John 12:40; Acts 28:25-27; and Ps. 118:22, the stone which the builders rejected: cf. Matt. 21:42; Mark 12:10; Luke 20:17; Acts 4:11; 1 Pet. 2:4).

VI. CONCLUSION

Study of the midrashic genre and midrashic methods seems to be particularly fruitful for the exegesis of the OT as well as of the NT. Certainly since the development of biblical criticism Scripture is no longer thought of as a static unit. Archeology and history have enabled us to locate the biblical world in the setting of the ancient Near East and have laid the foundations for an extra-biblical comparison which, pruned of its excesses of imagination and method, could throw light on many points regarding the genesis of the biblical writings. Literary criticism has taught us to distinguish and to classify actual literary units according to their age, their provenance and their affinities. *Formgeschichte* has inaugurated, albeit in a form which is still usually too extrinsic and too conjectural, an attempt to return the texts to their *Sitz im Leben*. But we still need, among other things, to return the formation of the sacred books, and these books themselves, to their own historical, literary and doctrinal milieu; that is, the biblical milieu, their proper place, to the framework of a living tradition which is constantly in progress, deepening and reflecting on itself and the revelation which it transmits. We have yet to discover by careful literary analysis their links, their sources and their insertion into this tradition which originated with Moses and the prophets. Now it appears to follow from observations made in the course of this article that the midrashic genre, which comprises an explanation and a deepening of the Bible by the Bible, is the ideal area for this research, for it provides the key, especially for the post-exilic literature. Hence the importance of an accurate idea and sufficient knowledge of the midrashic genre for the study and understanding of the sacred Books (see, e.g., A. Robert, "L'exégèse des

Psaumes selon les méthodes de la 'Formgeschichteschule,'" an account and critique, in *Miscellanea biblica B. Ubach*, Montserrat, 1954, p. 211-25). Hence also the usefulness of the study of post-biblical midrashic literature, which can be of great help in giving this idea its accurate shape and acquiring sufficient knowledge of the literary genre itself which is the most characteristic and yet the least understood of the Bible.

III

Methodological Note for the Study
of Rabbinic Literature

RENÉE BLOCH

Translated by
WILLIAM SCOTT GREEN
UNIVERSITY OF ROCHESTER

with

WILLIAM J. SULLIVAN
ST. JOHN FISHER COLLEGE

I. THE SCOPE OF THE PROBLEM

The importance of the study of rabbinic literature[1] for the understanding of Judaism itself, its historical evolution and its invariant traits is too evident to require justification. The literature of medieval Judaism, despite its somewhat novel concerns and literary genres, remains above all a literature of elaboration and codification based for the most part on the heritage of the rabbinic tradition. It took up the basic elements of this heritage in order to reorganize, sometimes to develop, often to condense them, but did so without perceptibly deflecting the evolution of the traditions contained therein. It is obvious to anyone even slightly familiar with later Jewish literature that it is more profoundly shaped by the substratum *(le fond)* transmitted almost unchanged from the rabbinic tradition than it is by the traits peculiar to medieval Jewish thought. The study of the former thus is essential in every respect, and all the difficulties, all the uncertainties confronted by whoever comes to Jewish Studies are due to the scarcity of basic works dealing with this critical period.

It seems that until now much less attention has been paid to the benefit that the study of biblical literature—particularly of the later writings of the Old Testament—could derive simply from *the* understanding (we cannot speak of a *better* understanding) of the ancient strata of rabbinic literature, especially the exegetical and homiletical literature. Of course, this is said on condition that the literary character of these ancient rabbinic writings, which are nearly contemporary with the latest biblical books and which represent an

51

obvious continuity with them, be clearly distinguished and their historical situation determined. Let one think, for example, of everything a close study of the rabbinic commentaries and of their evolution in a period contiguous to the formation, or at least the definitive redaction, of the later biblical books could bring to the exegesis of those books, to the clear understanding of their literary genres and of their themes, as well as to the reconstruction of the history of the text and of the ancient versions. We recently have had occasion[2] briefly to point out the utility of the study of ancient rabbinic midrash for the clear understanding of the midrashic genre, numerous examples of which appear in the later biblical books.

For the past few decades, it has been admitted in theory and emulously rehearsed by very nearly everyone that the understanding of the contemporary Jewish milieu, its literature, its traditions, its flow of ideas, etc., is indispensible to any serious study of the New Testament and Christian origins. Indeed, for a good half-century this exigency of New Testament studies has stimulated a certain number of non-Jewish scholars to take an interest in rabbinic literature, which, on first inspection, is so barely accessible. Perhaps the true dimension of the problem generally is underestimated. When one attempts seriously to penetrate ancient rabbinic literature, one discovers that it is not only a matter of discerning a "semitic substratum" of a philological order, or simply of drawing comparisons of verbal order, but that the literary genres, the structures of thought, and the fundamental themes of the New Testament writings cannot fully be clarified—or clarified at all—without a sufficient knowledge of the Jewish tradition in which they are immersed and from which they spring. It is clear, however, that this work presupposes a serious, critical, historical and literary study of that tradition and of the writings which convey it; it is essential to determine their strata and evolutions, their themes, their structure, their language, their ideas and the role of these writings in life. But the few works at the disposal of exegetes hardly respond to these needs. They are manuals composed at second or thirdhand[3]—which is serious in an area where the reliable, firsthand works cover only a few prescribed questions—or encyclo-pedic catalogues *(répertoires)* undoubtedly representing considerable and worthwhile effort, but which, given the actual state of the works, address a basically impossible task and consequently are of exceedingly limited use-fulness.[4]

It also is appropriate, in passing, to point out a group of questions which remain particularly untreated and which cannot be otherwise until rabbinic literature itself is explored first: the problem of the Jewish sources of certain parts of ancient and medieval Christian literature. A sufficient knowledge of rabbinic literature, in fact, would make it possible to recognize an obvious Jewish substratum, sometimes of considerable importance, in many of the writings or passages which presently baffle researchers, especially in patristic literature, from Origen to Isidore of Seville (who draws extensively on Jewish chronicles) and well into the twelfth century, to the Victorines and Pierre Comestor, etc. From this perspective, a study of Christian Syriac literature, which constitutes a sort of bridge between the semitic world impregnated by Jewish tradition and the Christian world, would be of special interest.

One final example, chosen from among many, will serve to demonstrate the importance of the study of rabbinic literature. The entire scholarly world of orientalists, semiticists, and biblical exegetes was set atremble by the recent discovery of manuscripts in the Judean Desert. The number of works devoted to these manuscripts in the past few years is truly impressive. It has hardly mattered that this discovery deals only with a small and peculiar "side" branch of Judaism dating from around the birth of Christianity—a branch whose precise situation must be determined in relation to the major currents and official institutions of the Judaism of the time, and which cannot fully be understood without sufficient knowledge of these factors. Rabbinic literature also contains vast manuscript material, in part fairly ancient and in large measure utterly unexamined, especially in the case of the manuscripts and fragments from the Geniza at Old Cairo.[5] The quantity of work devoted to the immense corpus of rabbinic literature, however, is ridiculously small in comparison to the amount of research devoted to the recent finds from the Dead Sea.

II. THE DIFFICULTIES

Whence come the considerable difficulties encountered by those who try to undertake the study of rabbinic literature?

In the first place, it is well to remark that this literature often is approached incorrectly. One begins with the Mishnah, a choice which is easily explained. Here is a book which has played and continues to play a fundamental role in Judaism. It is dated fairly accurately; its text has been established; numerous and accessible editions and even translations of it exist. Thus one begins here, and, if he does not want to limit himself to the Mishnah, he then proceeds to the Talmud, the Babylonian Talmud of course, which is more accessible and less difficult, even though more voluminous. But in all this there is an inevitable tendency for the researcher to limit himself to the *halakhic* or legal aspect of Jewish tradition. Seen from the outside by someone who fails to replace it within the living framework of a religious life, and from whom a great part of the real significance of this tradition therefore is in danger of escaping, this literature quickly becomes forbidding. It is almost as if one were to begin the study of Christianity with the study of canon law without an awareness of the living context which gives this juridical system its meaning. In order to complete the analogy, one must imagine the state of canon law prior to its recent codification and the edition of the sources of the Code.

Misunderstanding is made almost inevitable by the fact that the

Mishnah, with its authorative commentary, the *gemara*, in the Talmud, actually is the code which regulates Jewish life, even in detail, according to the Torah. For this reason, it always has been the part of rabbinic tradition most studied and commented upon. Just as it did in the domain of traditional studies, the *halakhah*, especially the Mishnah and the Talmud, quite naturally has come to occupy the fundamental role in the more scientific studies undertaken in modern Judaism during the last century. So it is that in recent years the several interesting, though still fairly timid attempts at truly critical study, attempts which tend to distinguish and to situate in history different redactional strata in rabbinic literature, deal especially with the Mishnah.[6]

It even is an understatement to say that this primarily legal, or *talmudic* part (so named because it finds its most complete expression in the Talmud) of what is strictly *rabbinic* literature has been the most studied. In a certain sense, for quite a while it was the only one studied. This is not to say that the Jews ever have disregarded the incomparable richness of the *aggadah* contained in the ancient midrashim. But because the essence of these aggadic traditions rapidly had been integrated into the *gemara* and the liturgy, then into medieval commentators such as Rashi, and finally into anthologies destined to nourish private piety, the ancient midrashim themselves finally no longer were read or studied in the schools. There, specifically, the *gemara*, Rashi and other commentators formed the basis of rabbinic studies. When the emancipation of the Jews in the nineteenth century gave birth to a modern science of Judaism, the scientific study of the *aggadah* certainly knew a brilliant beginning with the works of Wilhelm Bacher, still indispensable, although at many points outdated. But this promising beginning has remained without a sequel.

Outside of Judaism, especially in Christian circles, it seems that hardly anyone has grasped the importance of the aggadic part of Jewish tradition, of midrashic literature. Indeed, it is obvious that *aggadah* is the aspect of rabbinic literature which is the most interesting for the study of the Old and New Testaments, Christian origins and ancient Christian literature, and which is the most important for the understanding of the living religious content of Judaism. Furthermore, the *aggadah*, essentially homiletic in nature, represents an intrinsically religious meditation on immutable sacred texts; it is much less subject to fluctuation, to adaptation to ever-changing circumstances, than is the *halakah*, whose nature is essentially *practical*. Thus the *aggadah* has a much more stable nature, one more apt to conserve extremely ancient traditions. To a far greater extent than halakhic literature, the *aggadah* allows one to distinguish the constant elements and the evolutions in ancient Jewish tradition and to situate both of these in the larger framework of the history of religions, particularly in relation to Christianity, and, for certain questions, also to Islam.

The principal difficulty, however, is historical in character. One confronts a vast literature which, from the viewpoint of the history of religions, contains extremely rich, varied and important materials. But where do these writings come from? How can they be returned to the milieux which witnessed their birth? What date should be assigned to them? How is one to classify them according to their dependents and filiations? To believe certain opinions which have been repeated incessantly for a century (and generally not supported with any serious proof), the redaction of many of the most important of these writings would date from the sixth, eighth, eleventh centuries, etc. If there is any basis to these opinions, we obviously cannot use these writings *in their present form* to illuminate questions about the New Testament or ancient Christianity. It is possible, however, that certain of these documents may be of late redaction and nevertheless contain traditions which date back to a very ancient period. In any case, so long as these questions are not resolved, this entire literature remains misleading and unusable.[7]

At present, the study of rabbinic literature is in a condition similar to that known in biblical studies a century ago, before the major works of critical ground-clearing had been done. Whatever uncertainties may continue to exist in this latter area, a certain number of givens concerning the history and formation of biblical writings, the respective antiquity of the traditions they contain, the determination of their principal redactional strata, etc., seem definitively established. As a result, it has become possible to undertake the study of the history and evolution of biblical traditions. In the domain of rabbinic literature, this work still remains to be done. Several preliminary works have convinced us that this necessary work is altogether possible. It even seems much easier than it was for the Bible, not only because it concerns later and better-known periods, but also because we deal with a much more tightly knit literary network which contains numerous witnesses for the same traditions at different phases of their evolution, and because there exist a number of well-dated witnesses both internal and external to this literature.

An additional difficulty, however, hinders the development of this work. We already have pointed out in passing that from a certain point in time, sufficiently remote in the case of certain documents, the midrashic writings were less read and studied. Consequently, they also were less recopied and reedited. The only presently accessible editions derive either from the great publishing work of the Renaissance and the first centuries of printing or from the renewal of a relative interest in these writings experienced in the nineteenth century. But in many cases the given texts do not meet the demands of scientific work. This is so especially for the more recent and most accessible editions, whose primary purpose often is practical. Lacking above all for any truly scientific work on this literature are critical editions, or at least usable editions. Therefore, one of the first tasks—a task, moreover, inseparable from the work of literary criticism—would be to resume the study of these documents from the manuscripts and to edit them in an attempt to establish some sort of *corpus* of midrashic literature. This would be an indispensible tool for all the historical, literary and comparative studies, etc., the possibility and utility of which we are just beginning to recognize.

III. A COMPARATIVE METHOD

The problem, then, is to determine, by a careful work of historical and above all of literary criticism, as well as by comparative study, the development and the respective antiquity of traditions,[8] the formation, the historical situation, and the interdependence of rabbinic writings. We already have noted that a systematic work of this sort never has been undertaken, that it is imperative at present if we are to advance on solid ground, and, finally, that there exist sufficient materials with which to undertake it.

Essentially, the goal of this article is to propose a *method* for this work by illustrating it with an example of requisite brevity, chosen particularly for Palestinian literature, from the traditions relating to the birth of Moses.[9] An analogous study, of course, can—and must—be made of any aggadic tradition. It is desirable that such a study be carried out not only on selected traditions (it would be unrealizable for the totality of traditions), but methodically, on the principal traditions contained in a given document. Given the present state of the question, this is the only possible method of study;[10] any synthesis, or even any sketch of an overall view, would be premature.

In order successfully to classify and date traditions and documents, in addition to employing the historical indicators of external criticism and the criteria of paleography and philology, we propose to resort to a *comparative study* comprising two stages: an external comparison and an internal comparison.

1. *The External Comparison.* This consists of a comparison between the Palestinian rabbinic, especially midrashic, writings which, along with the traditions they transmit, are not dated, and the texts external to Palestinian rabbinic Judaism which have at least an approximate date and in which the same traditions are found. Thanks to these dated witnesses, one can determine the *terminus ad quem* of certain Palestinian aggadic traditions and, at the same time, establish some guidelines for the history of the literature.

To give an idea of the material which ought to serve as the foundation of this comparative study, it will be useful rapidly to list the groups of writings which can be taken into account.

a. *The Writings of Hellenistic Judaism*

There sometimes is too great a tendency to identify Hellenistic Judaism with Philo. This Alexandrian philosopher doubtless represents the end result of certain tendencies of Hellenistic-Jewish thought, but his also is a very personal philosophy which, moreover, does not lack a deep affinity with Palestinian tradition. On the whole, a penetrating, exhaustive study of Hellenistic Judaism and of its exact relationship to Palestinian Judaism is still lacking. Certainly, Hellenistic-Jewish literature shares the characteristics of the surrounding Greek literature, both with respect to its literary forms (philosophical, poetic, historical—as distinguished from the "biblical," midrashic and rabbinic forms of Palestinian Judaism) and to certain of its inclinations, for example, its universalism. Some also think that this literature in particular has an apologetic preoccupation and a missionary goal: to spread the faith of Israel and, in order to do this, to adapt it to the surrounding world. But like Palestinian literature, it generally addresses itself primarily to Jewish readers in order to reaffirm them in their faith, to explain and revitalize their great past, and, with the hope of days to come, to support them in their struggles. In this essential aim it closely resembles Palestinian literature and very often uses the same tradition while adapting its expression when necessary to different surroundings and circumstances. We think that the studies like those recommended here will show that Hellenistic Judaism was much more oriented towards Palestine than is generally thought. In this manner, moreover, one can establish a distinct tendency in the Greek versions of the Bible progressively to approach the Hebrew text, which fundamentally remained the norm or basic authority, even for Hellenistic Judaism.

For the proposed study, Hellenistic Judaism offers us a good number of *witnesses* which either are dated with sufficient precision or have at least a well-determined *terminus ad quem*. This is the case especially for those ancient Hellenistic Jewish authors who were saved from oblivion by Alexander Polyhistor (between 80 and 40 B.C.). In his Περὶ Ἰουδαίων he provided a certain number of extracts from their writings; these were then copied and preserved by Eusebius of Caesarea,[11] and also by Clement of Alexandria.[12] These sources include: *biblical versions*, the Septuagint, Aquila, Theodotion, etc.; *Greek books* and *supplements (complements) to the Bible; philosophical writings*, especially those of Philo; *"historical" writings*, Demetrios, Eupolemus, Artapanus, Aristeas, Jason of Cyrene, etc., and *poetical writings*, Theodotus, Ezekiel.

b. *The Apocrypha*

Most of these writings can be assigned to a fairly well-determined period. This is especially true for several of the most ancient Palestinian apocrypha, which date back to the pre-Christian era or to the period of Christian origins. This literature could furnish important information, but here again, the essential work remains to be done. These writings were preserved only by Christians; to be able to use them with complete assurance, it is essential to distinguish their Jewish basis from the Christian revisions.

c. *Pseudo-Philo*

This sort of biblical history (analogous, for example, to Chronicles), which goes from Adam until the death of Saul, must have played a very important role.[13] Pseudo-Philo dates from the first century of the Christian era, probably from the year following the destruction of Jerusalem in 70 A.D.

It is a kind of aggadic commentary on the historical books of the Old Testament which unquestionably bears the mark of the ancient aggadic midrash. One certainly can discern the close points of resemblance between Pseudo-Philo, on the one hand, and the biblical Apocrypha, especially the Book of Enoch, the Book of Jubilees, the Syrian Apocalypse of Baruch and IV Esdras,[14] on the other. But it is more evident that Pseudo-Philo's version of the history of Israel to a great extent is derivative of the aggadic traditions[15] known to us through midrashic literature. At the least, this testifies that these traditions precede Pseudo-Philo.

d. *Josephus*

Dated with certainty and precision, Josephus naturally is an invaluable witness. Moreover, his work, *Jewish Antiquities*, reveals an extensive knowledge of the rabbinic aggadah. The problem is the same for Josephus as it is for Pseudo-Philo: since the present forms of the rabbinic writings through which we know the aggadic traditions are of later redaction, from where could these ancient authors have drawn the aggadic traditions they used in their work? (For no one would imagine that these traditions might depend on Josephus or Pseudo-Philo.) It is historically impossible to resort to the hypothesis of a purely oral tradition. It remains, therefore, to postulate one or several common, written aggadic sources anterior to both Josephus and Pseudo-Philo.[16]

e. *Glosses of the Biblical Text and Versions*
(Septuagint, Peshitto, etc.)

While contributing to the determination or precision of the sense or usage of an already established text into which they were inserted at a later period, the glosses sometimes simultaneously reveal *midrashic* traditions of this milieu. We have pointed out in a recent article a typical example of a gloss, taken from the biblical text and the Septuagint, which reveals aggadic traditions.[17] To our knowledge, however, no study as yet has been devoted to the problem of glosses of the biblical text.[18]

f. *The Damascus Document and the Qumran Manuscripts*

Since none of the extant ancient midrashic texts were edited *(rédiger)* prior to the second or third century A.D., and since the majority of these in their present form date from no earlier than the fifth, sixth or seventh century, in the Damascus Document[19] and in the manuscripts of the Qumran sect, we have for the first time writings which date from the initial period of rabbinic literature, very probably from the first half of the first century B.C. These texts also provide us with valuable evidence, particularly about the importance attached to the study of Scripture, about the *technique* of interpreting it during that period,[20] (already very similar to what will soon become the fully developed midrashic genre) and, finally, about certain specific aggadic traditions.[21]

g. *The New Testament Writings*

The authors of the New Testament are Jews raised in the Jewish tradition who to a great extent speak to and write for Jews who know this tradition as they do. The fact that the New Testament assumes this entire Jewish tradition cannot be stressed enough. Thus, in Chapter 7 of the Acts of the Apostles, when the deacon Stephen wishes to proclaim Jesus, he quite naturally speaks of Moses. This is not by chance: all of Jewish tradition considers Moses, first Savior of Israel, as the prototype of the coming Messiah. This idea was familiar to the authors of the New Testament and often is evident in their writings.[22] This is only one example among many. We deal here not with simple verbal comparisons, but with an utterly fundamental way of thinking confirmed by the New Testament writings.

Apart from this general climate, the well-dated writings of the New Testament also reveal a certain number of interesting traits of a purely aggadic character. An important example can be found in the account of the *"spiritual" rock, which*—according to I Cor. 10:4—*followed the Israelites in the desert:* this passage from St. Paul confirms the antiquity of this theme, which has parallels in midrashic literature. Like the best aggadists, Paul here resorts to the *midrash aggadah* for an illustration, in order to derive from it a doctrinal meaning: "this rock was Christ."[23]

h. *Some Ancient Christian Writers*

We already have mentioned Clement of Alexandria and Eusebius of Caesarea, both of whom directly preserved written evidences of certain traditions of Hellenistic Judaism. In their writings, but even more so in those of Origen, one also could find other traces of Jewish sources which they knew directly or indirectly. As we already have noted, the writings of the first Syrian Fathers, especially Aphrahat and Ephrem, offer abundant material, still accessible only with difficulty, for comparative study. As with Origen, it is their biblical commentaries which are most important in this regard.[24] But in Syriac literature the similarities to rabbinic tradition are particularly widespread. Despite the relatively late fourth century date of the major witnesses of Syriac tradition, there is no doubt that this is an important avenue to explore.

i. *Ancient Liturgical Sources*

Jewish liturgy undoubtedly preserves many very ancient texts; but given the present state of research, it is rare to find one which can be dated with sufficient probability to be used as an object of comparison. This *is* the case, however, for the *Qerobot* of Yannai, [25] which are based on the liturgical pericopae read in the synagogue every Sabbath, which follow the order of the triennial cycle, and which constitute, in poetic form, a sort of complete midrash on the Pentateuch.[26]

2. *The Internal Comparison.* This work essentially traces a single tradition through the various stages represented by the different documents. It tries to distinguish the most primitive elements and the variants, the developments, the additions and the revisions; it takes account of the diversity of literary genres and historical situations. It does all this in order provisionally to classify the writings according to the evolution of the observed tradition.

This comparative study, which even could be done with the aid of synoptic tables, begins with the biblical text and follows the selected tradition or traditions through the versions of the Bible (LXX, TO, Pesh., etc., making use of the *Hexapla* of Origen), the Jerusalem Targum, the different midrashim, the *Midrash Rabbah*, the Talmud, various rabbinic writings (*Sefer ha-Yašar, Sefer ha-Zikronot, Chronicle of Moses, Yalqut Šimᶜoni,* etc.) and concludes with Rashi. In certain cases, of course, this work opportunely can be combined with that of the *external* comparison.

Everything indicates that the point of departure can only be the biblical text. According to the counsel of the Psalmist, it is on this sacred text that one reflects, prays and meditates night and day. And in the synagogue, the *homily*,[27] which played an extremely important role in the establishment of the midrashic tradition, was constructed uniquely on these venerable texts.

In reality, none of this literature was created in an "ivory tower"; it is neither a collection of personal works nor even, in the first instance, the product of scholars and schools. It is a popular product. It springs from the preaching done in the synagogue every Sabbath and festival day, after the reading of the Torah, on that section of Scripture which had just been read. The preaching centered on Scripture, as did all the religious life of Judaism.

Within *rabbinic* literature, it is the *Palestinian Targum*[28] which we propose as a starting point. This text cannot really be considered a version (one need only to read it to realize this!), but belongs to a very different genre;[29] it is much closer to the midrash, properly speaking, than to a version. It even is probable that it originally was a homiletic midrash, or simply a series of homilies on Scripture, read in the synagogue after the public reading of the Torah.

Due to the limited scope of this article, we can consider neither the problem of the Targums, nor that of the Jerusalem Targum in particular, that extraordinary imbroglio of hypotheses, often of the most fantastic sort.[30] We merely wish to indicate here the reason for our choice. During a study of the Jerusalem Targum, it became obvious to us that this Targum lies at the base of later aggadic tradition, that by serving as an immediate extension of the scriptural given, it acts as a sort of hinge, a bridge between the Bible and later rabbinic literature, and that it represents the starting point, not of the midrashic genre as such (which is already present in biblical literature), but of *midrash*, properly so-called, all of whose structure and themes it already contains. This observation seemed to us important. It is no matter of indifference to have access to a firmly established starting point for the internal comparison.

IV. AN EXAMPLE: TRADITIONS CONCERNING THE PROCLAMATION OF MOSES' BIRTH: PHARAOH'S DREAM

Rabbinic tradition recognizes two versions of the proclamation of Moses' birth: (1) Pharaoh's dream and the magicians' prediction and (2) Miriam's prophecy. The example we provide here to illustrate the proposed method is based only on the first, Pharaoh's dream and the magicians' prediction.

It is not our intention to provide an exhaustive list of the different parallel versions of this account, but only to show that through the work of literary criticism and by the application of the internal comparative method, it is possible to analyze the evolution of a given tradition, and that, thanks to the dated witnesses for the tradition in question, it is possible successfully to fix, if not its origin, at least its *terminus ad quem*, a very important datum for the application of the results of such a study.

1. *An Attempt at Literary Criticism of Several Parallel Accounts.* The tradition concerning Pharaoh's dream seems to be the most natural and the most ancient. Reflecting on the biblical account, one is led to wonder what might have motivated the cruel decision of Pharaoh—who already was embittering the life of the Hebrews by forcing hard labor on them—to drown the male infants of the Hebrews.

The *Jerusalem Targum* (TgJ) itself appears to recount one of the ancient traditions which were to serve as the basis of later accounts, when, beginning at Exodus 1:15 (*The king of Egypt spoke to the Hebrew midwives. . . .*), it proposes this explanation:

> While sleeping, Pharaoh saw [in] a dream: Behold the whole country of Egypt was placed on one scale of a balance, and a lamb, [31] the offspring of a ewe, on the other side; and the scale holding the lamb sank down. At once he sent to call all the magicians of Egypt, and he repeated his dream to them.
> Immediately, Jannes and Jambres, the chief magicians, began to speak, and said to Pharaoh:
> "A son will be born in the community of Israel, who will destroy all of Egypt."[*]
> That is why Pharaoh, King of Egypt, gave the following order to the Jewish midwives . . .[31a]

---

[*]Lit.: By whose hand all of Egypt will be destroyed.

All rabbinic literature knows this tradition. But it suffices to compare the TgJ account with those of the midrashim and the chronicles to realize that it is the simplest and most primitive of them all, that it must constitute the basic text, and that all the other accounts must be classified in relation to it.

Thus, the *Chronicle of Moses*[32] follows the targumic account rather closely:

> It happened in the one hundred thirtieth year after the descent of the children of Israel into Egypt and sixty years after the death of Joseph, that Pharaoh had a dream: an old man stood before him and there was a balance in his hand; he made all the people of Egypt, men, women and children, climb into one scale of the balance, and in the second he placed a lamb, and the lamb outweighed all the Egyptians. The king was astonished and pondered in his heart over this prodigy, this great prodigy, this great vision. Then Pharaoh awoke, and behold, it was a dream. He assembled all the wise men and magicians of Egypt and told them his dream. All the people were seized by a great fear because of the dream, until there came before the king one of the princes who said to him, "This dream signifies a great misfortune and a calamity for Egypt." The king asked him, "What is it, then?" He replied, "A child will be born unto the children of Israel who will destroy all of Egypt. But now, my Lord King, I would like to give you good counsel: Give the order to kill every boy who will be born to the children of Israel. Perhaps then the dream will not come to pass?" These words found favor in the eyes of Pharaoh and in the eyes of his court and the king of Egypt spoke to the Hebrew midwives . . .

In comparison with the primitive account, however, we note signs of a certain elaboration. Instead of beginning *ex abrupto*, the account opens with the exact chronological setting: "It happened in the one hundred thirtieth year after the descent of the children of Israel into Egypt . . ." The holder of the scales is specified: "An *old man* stood before him, and there was a balance in his hand . . ." Details are supplied: "the whole country of Egypt" becomes "all the people of Egypt, men, women and children." Some psychological notations appear: "The king was astonished and pondered in his heart this prodigy . . ."; "All the people were seized by a great fear because of the dream . . ." We note variations: In place of Jannes and Jambres, it is "one of the princes" who interprets the dream. Finally, the conclusion of the TgJ text was a simple statement: the dream *explains why* Pharaoh gave the order to kill all the male infants; but in the conclusion of our account, the same person both interprets the dream and advises Pharaoh how to prevent its realization.

The *Sefer ha-Yašar*[33] contains an account which is very similar to the one found in the *Chronicle of Moses:*

> And it happened in the 130th year of the descent of the children of Israel into Egypt that Pharaoh dreamed that he was seated on his royal throne. He raised up his eyes and looked: behold an old man stood before him, and in his hand was a balance (like) the balance of merchants. And the old man took the balance and hung it in front of Pharaoh. And the old man took all the elders of Egypt, and all the princes and all the great ones and bound them together, and placed them on one of the scales of the balance. And he took a suckling lamb and put it on the other scale of the balance, and

the lamb outweighed all the others. Pharaoh was troubled by this terrible vision: why would a lamb outweigh all the others? And Pharaoh told them his dream, and the men were seized by a great fear. And the king said to his wise men: Now, explain to me the dream that I had so that I may know what is in it. And *Balaam*, the son of Beor, answered the king and said to him: It can only mean that a great evil will befall Egypt at the end of days. For behold, a son will be born to Israel who will devastate all of Egypt, exterminate her people and lead the children of Israel out of Egypt by a powerful hand.[34]

Certain modifications of this text, the supplementary details, and the explanations which the author believed it necessary to insert, show that we deal with a more advanced elaboration.

Thus, the diverse circumstances of the dream are specified: Pharaoh "was seated on his royal throne. He raised up his eyes and looked . . ."; similarly, the type of balance: "like the balance of merchants." The explanation of the dream is much more developed, and to the destruction of Egypt is added the prediction that this *son* "will lead the children of Israel out of Egypt by a powerful hand." Moreover, it is Balaam, instead of Jannes and Jambres (TgJ) or one of the princes *(Chronicle of Moses)* who explains Pharaoh's dream. It might be possible to establish a relationship between the prophetic meaning of Balaam's prediction in Numbers and his prediction here of the birth of a son who will lead the children of Israel out of Egypt "by a powerful hand." In biblical terminology this expression signifies the Power of God, his mighty intervention, and this son could be a *messenger* of God. This could well give the text a messianic, or even an eschatological resonance, a notion further reinforced by the variant here which specifies that the event will occur "at the end of days."

Concerning Exodus 1:15, the *Yalquṭ Šimᶜoni*[35] incorporated an account very similar to that of *Sefer ha-Yašar*. Furthermore, this collection is very useful precisely because it has preserved numerous aggadic traditions, certain of which have come down to us only in this work.

Here is the text from the *Yalquṭ*:

In the 130th year of the descent of Israel into Egypt, Pharaoh had a dream: he was sitting on his royal throne. He raised up his eyes and saw an old man standing before him, and in his hand was a balance like the balance of merchants. And the old man took the balance and hung it before Pharaoh. And he took all the elders of Egypt, the princes and great ones and bound them together on one of the scales of the balance. And after this he took a suckling lamb and put it on the second scale of the balance, and the lamb outweighed all the others. Pharaoh was troubled because of this terrible vision. Why would a lamb weigh more than all the others? And Pharaoh awoke, and behold, it was a dream. And he arose that morning and called for all his servants and told them the dream, and the men were seized by a great fear. One of the eunuchs of the king replied, saying: It can only mean that a great evil will befall Egypt at the end of time. A child will be born in Israel who will destroy all of Egypt. . . .[36]

The text follows the *Sefer ha-Yašar* almost word for word. The two differences in detail which can be detected, however, furnish interesting clues and allow us to conclude that the compiler of the *Yalqut* probably knew the *Chronicle of Moses* and had the text in front of him.

The first difference concerns Pharaoh's counsellor, who here is designated as a eunuch. It may be conjectured that this is not a variant, but a mere slip of the pen: instead of *ᵓeḥad min haśarim* (with a *sin*), "one of the princes," which he read in one of his models, the scribe would have written: *ᵓeḥad misarise (hammelek)* (with a *samek*), "a eunuch of the king."[37]

As in the *Chronicle of Moses*, the content of the prediction consists of only the destruction of Egypt, omitting the second part, the deliverance of Israel.

We also can note that the term used to designate the one to be born is no longer *ben*, "son," as in the preceding writings, but *yeled*, "child," a less precise term.

If we have deemed it necessary to quote not only its few interesting modifications, but the entire passage from the *Yalqut*, it is because we again encounter it almost in full in another compilation, as yet unedited, whose only known manuscript is in the Bodleian Library,[38] and which we will call *Sefer ha-Zikronot*.[39]

Here is this text:

> In the 130th year of the descent of Israel into Egypt, Pharaoh dreamed that he was sitting on his royal throne. He raised up his eyes and looked: *behold*[40] an old man stood *before him*,[41] holding in his hand a balance like that of merchants. And the old man took the balance and hung it before Pharaoh. And he took all[42] the elders of Egypt and all the princes and all the great ones[43] and bound them together on one of the scales of the balance. And after that he took a suckling lamb and put it on the other scale of the balance, and the lamb outweighed all the others. Pharaoh was troubled because of this terrible vision: Why would a lamb weigh more than all the others? And Pharaoh awoke, and behold it was a dream. And Pharaoh[44] arose that morning and called for all his servants and told them the dream, and the men were seized by a great fear. One of the eunuchs of the king replied *saying*:[45] It can only be a great evil which will envelope Egypt at the end of days. *The king then responded to the eunuch saying: "What is it?" The eunuch said to the king*:[46] "A *child* shall be born in Israel who will destory all of Egypt."[47]

With the exception of the short dialogue inserted in lines 11 and 12 of the manuscript, this account is similar, word for word, to that of the *Yalqut Šimᶜoni*, with a few variations which always correspond to the *Sefer ha-Yašar*.

The literary analysis of these parallel accounts thus demonstrates that it is possible to establish certain filiations among them and that the account in the Jerusalem Targum appears to be the least developed, while that of the *Sefer ha-Zikronot* must have used the *Yalqut Šimᶜoni* and the *Sefer ha-Yašar*, and therefore is of a later date.

It is understood that, before advocating a precise chronological order, an analagous exercise of literary criticism must be carried out for a certain number of important traditions contained in these books. In the present article we simply suggest a method and illustrate it with an example.

2. *A Dated Witness: Josephus.* Josephus knows this Palestinian aggadic tradition and reproduces it integrally:

> One of the scribes in sacred matters[48]—for these men were extremely skilled in speaking the truth about things to come—announces to the king that at about that time someone will be born to the Israelites who, when grown, will crush the power of the Egyptians, exalt that of the Hebrews, surpass all with his grandeur, and acquire a glory, the memory of which will never fade. Seized by fear, the king following his counsel, orders that every male infant born of the Hebrews be killed by being thrown into the river.[49]

We can establish that all the elements characteristic of this tradition are found again in the above text in a somewhat different form and with some stylistic traits peculiar to the author, to the language he used, and to his era. To stress the significance of such evidence would be superfluous.

3. *Some Indicators from a Related Tradition.* According to certain sources, astrologers predicted to Pharaoh the birth of a Savior of Israel, but they did not know whether he would be a *Hebrew or an Egyptian*; hence the command, given by Pharaoh, to throw *all* the male infants, Hebrews or Egyptians, into the river. Claiming that the Savior of Israel would only be a Hebrew, the Egyptians refused to obey the decree. Pharaoh then modified his decree and ordered that only the male infants of the Hebrews be thrown into the water.

It is the *Midrash Rabbah*[50] which gives the most developed account of this view:

> *Then Pharaoh gave this order to all his people* (Ex. 1:22): R. Jose b. R. Hanina explains that this decree also was directed against his own people. And why was this so? Because the astrologers had told him, "His mother already carries the Savior of Israel, but we do not know whether he is Israelite or Egyptian." Then Pharaoh assembled all the Egyptians and said, "During the next nine months give me your (newborn) sons so that I may throw them into the river." For this is what is written [Ex. 1:22]: *You will throw into the river every son who will be born.* It is not written, *every Israelite son,* but *every son,* Jewish or Egyptian. But they did not accept, saying, "An Egyptian could never deliver them; this must be a son born of Jewish women."— *You will throw [them] into the river* [Ex. 1:22]: Why this decree to throw into the river? Because the astrologers had seen that the Savior of Israel would be punished by water, and they thought that he would drown in the water.[51]

This tradition, in an abridged form, has left numerous traces. For example, the midrash *Tanḥuma* reads:[52]

> The astrologers said to them, "On this day is born the Savior of Israel, but we do not know if he is an Egyptian or not.[53]

Similarly, in the *Pirqe de R. Eliezer:*

The astrologers predicted to Pharaoh that a little boy was going to lead Israel out of Egypt.[54]

This tradition is assumed in the Talmud[55] and taken up again by Rashi:

The decree was also for them. For at the moment of Moses' birth, his [Pharaoh's] astrologer's said to him, "On this day their savior is born, but we do not know if he is an Egyptian or an Israelite; but we see that in the end he will suffer by the waters of Meriba.[56]

This tradition, most of whose witnesses seem relatively recent, may well not be foreign either to the Septuagint text of Exodus 1:22, which states explicitly (compared to the Masoretic text): ὃ ἐάν τεχθῇ τοῖς Ἑβραίοις, or to the Jerusalem and Onkelos Targums, which conclude the biblical verse with the same statement: "every son who will be born *to the Hebrews.*"

What can be the origin of this slightly different, but thematically similar tradition? It seems more developed, which would indicate a more recent origin. We have just seen, however, that it well could have been attested in a very ancient period, namely, that of the formation of the Septuagint. Perhaps it simply is based on a different verse than is the first tradition, on Ex. 1:22—since we habitually find it in reference to this verse—while the first tradition, as we have shown, had as its point of departure Ex. 1:15.

4. *The Evidence from the New Testament.* Since the antiquity of these traditions already has been sufficiently confirmed, especially by Josephus, it is no surprise also to find traces of them in the New Testament. For the traditions we have just presented, this evidence certainly remains implicit; it is clear nevertheless, and it merits additional interest because it deals with the totality of the theme in question.

The messianic resonances of this theme, several instances of which we have pointed to throughout this investigation, explain in an obvious way its application to the story of Jesus, the use made of it by the first Christians. Let us simply recall some of these instances, such as the appearance of Balaam, son of Beor, in the *Sefer ha-Yašar,*[57] and even the very use of the term "son" *(ben)*[58] to designate the one whose birth is predicted.[59] We cannot here offer expanded treatment of the evolution of the messianic character of this tradition, a character which several observations made during this brief inquiry seem to confirm. They are: to the simple prediction, made by Jannes and Jambres, of the birth of a son who will destroy Egypt, which we find in the Jerusalem Targum and the *Chronicle of Moses,* the *Sefer ha-Yašar* adds, in addition to the role it attributes to Balaam, that this great calamity will befall Egypt "in the end of days," and that the child to be born not only will devastate Egypt, but simultaneously "will lead the children of Israel out by a powerful hand." The *Midrash Rabbah* will go even farther by calling the one who will deliver Israel from the hand of the Egyptians a *goᵓel*, that is, a savior, a redeemer, and by noting that the savior of Israel will be punished by water, also a mark of the messianic character. It perhaps is interesting to note that these traits were eliminated from later compilations such as the *Yalqut Šimᶜoni* and the *Sefer ha-Zikronot*.

In order for us to grasp the full significance of these traits, they naturally must be returned to the larger context of the ancient Palestinian aggadah. In that context, as we already have noted, Moses is seen as the prototype of the messiah to come. He would be like a second Moses, a suffering figure like the first and the author of a final deliverance, the model for which is the deliverance from Egypt,[60] accomplished by Moses.

The first Christians, including the evangelists themselves, knew these traditions, placed their new faith within their perspectives, and often expressed their faith following these traditional themes. Thus it is that Matthew in particular, the most "rabbinic" of the evangelists, in the account concerning the birth of Jesus (contained in his Chapter II), obviously presupposed the aggadic tradition of Moses' birth. Jesus, acknowledged as Messiah, was considered a second Moses, and it was natural for the evangelist constantly to refer to the traditions concerning Moses' birth in order to formulate those relating to the birth of Jesus. We note the parallelism of the two figures and their role as saviors; parallelism of the predictions of their birth, attributed in each case to official scribes; parallelism of the two tyrants, Pharaoh and Herod; parallelism of the massacre ordered by each to kill the future savior and thereby to prevent the realization of the prediction. The obvious relationship between the two traditions can only help the New Testament exegete grasp the full significance of Matthew's account. At the same time, it constitutes an invaluable confirmation of the antiquity of a tradition attested with remarkable continuity by all of midrashic literature, from the Jerusalem Targum to the Jewish—and even Christian—chroniclers and commentators of the Middle Ages.

CONCLUSION

To more completely illustrate the proposed method, it undoubtedly would have been necessary to present several examples and to exposit them in detail, but the limits of the article prevented this. In conclusion, let us again recall that this method must be employed together with philological analysis, research which is properly historical, etc., and can provide sufficiently complete and certain results only in conjunction with these disciplines. And yet, due to the nature of the literature and the present state of studies in this area, we believe this method of work to be not only fundamental, but also capable of providing results from which proximate disciplines can greatly benefit. This is what we hope to have illustrated somewhat by our presentation.

Yalqut Šimᶜoni

בשנת מאה ושלשים לרדת ישראל
מצרים ופרעה חולם והנה יושב על
כסא מלכותו וישא עיניו וירא והנה זקן אחד
עומד כנגדו ובידו מאזנים ממאזני
הסוחרים ויקח האיש הזקן את
המאזנים ויתלם לפני פרעה ויקח כל
זקני מצרים שריה וגדוליה ויאסרם
ויתנם יחד בכף מאזנים האחת ואחר
כן לקח טלה חלב אחד ויתנהו בכף
מאזנים השנית ויכריע הטלה את
כולן ויתמה פרעה על החזון הנורא
ההוא מדוע יכריע הטלה את כולם
וייקץ פרעה והנה חלום וישכם בבקר
ויקרא לכל עבדיו ויספר להם את
החלום וייראו האנשים יראה גדולה
ויען סריס אחד מסריסי המלך אין זה
כי אם רעה גדולה אשד תצמח למצרים
באחרית הימים כי ילד יולד בישראל
ויחריב כל ארץ מצרים.

Jerusalem Targum

פרעה דמך הוה חמי בחילמיה והא
כל ארעא דמצרים קיימא בכף מודנא
חדא ושלייא בד אישוותא בכף מודנא
חדא והות כרעא כף מודנא מטליא
בגווה מן יד שדר וקרא לכל חרשי
מצרים ותני להון ית חולמיה מן יד
פתחון פומהון ינים ויימברם רישי
חרשיא ואמרין לפרעה ביר חד עתיד
למהוי מתיליד בכנישתהון דישראל
דעל ידוי עתידא למחרבא כל ארעא
דמצרים.

Chronicle of Moses

בשנת מאה ושלשים שנה לרדת בני
ישראל למצרים מקץ ששים שנה
לאחר שמת יוסף חלם פרעה חלום
אחד והנה בחלום זקן אחד עומד לנגדו
ובידו מאזנים והיה מעלה כל דרי
מצרים אנשים ונשים וטף בכף אחד
של המאזנים והיה משים בכף שנייה
טלה אחד והטלה מכריע לכל אנשי
מצרים והוא משתאה ומהרהר בלבו
הפלא ופלא גדול על המראה הגדולה
הזאת ויקץ פרעה והנה חלום ויקבוץ
לכל חכמי מצרים ואת כל חרטומיו
ויספר פרעה להם את חלומו ויראו כל
העם מאד מן החלום עד שבא א' מן
השרים לפני המלך ויאמר לפניו זה
החלום רעה גדולה הוא למצרים ובהלה
ויאמר לו המלך ומה היא ויאמר לו בן
יולד לבני ישראל שיחריב כל מצרים.

Sefer ha-Zikronot

בשנת מאה ושלשים לרדת ישר'
מצרימה ופרעה חלם והנה יושב על
כסא מלכותו וישא עיניו וירא והנה
זקן אחד עומד לנגדו ובידו מאזנים
ממאזני הסוחרים ויקח האיש הזקן
את המאזנים ויתלם לפני פרעה ויקח
את כל זקני מצרים ושריה וכל גדוליה
ויאסרם ויתנם יחד בכף מאזנים האחת
ואחרי כן לקח טלה חלב אחד ויתנהו
בכף מאזנים השנית ויכרע הטלה את
כולם ויתמה פרעה על החזון הנורא
ההוא מדוע יכריע הטלה את כולם
ויקץ פרעה והנה חלום וישכם פרעה
בבקר ויקרא לכל עבדיו ויספר להם
את החלום וייראו האנשים יראה
גדולה ויען סריס אחד מסריסי המלך
ויאמר אין זה כי אם רעה גדולה אשר
תצמח למצרים באחרית הימים ויען
המלך את הסרים ויאמר לו ומה יהיה
ויאמר הסרים למלך ילד יוולד בישראל
ויחריב כל ארץ מצרים.

Sefer ha-Yašar

ויהי בשנת מאה ושלשים שנה לרדת
ישראל מצרימה ופרעה חולם והוא
יושב על כסא מלכותו וישא עיניו וירא
והנה איש זקן עומד לנגדו וביד הזקן
מאזנים ממאזני הסוחרים ויקח האיש
הזקן את המאזנים ויתלם לפני פרעה
ויקח הזקן את כל זקני מצרים וכל
שריה וכל גדוליה ויאסרם יחד ויתנם
בכף המאזנים האחת ויקח טלה חלב
אחד ויתנהו בכף המאזנים השנית
ויכרע הטלה את כלם. ויתמה פרעה
על החזון הנורא ההוא מדוע יכרע
הטלה את כלם.
וייקץ פרעה והנה חלום וישכם פרעה
בבקר ויקרא לכל עבדיו ויספר פרעה
להם את החלום וייראו האנשים יראה
גדולה ויאמר המלך אל כל חכמיו
פתרו נא אלי החלום הזה אשר חלמתי
ואדענו ויען בלעם בן בעור את המלך
ויאמר אליו אין זה כי אם רעה גדולה
אשר תצמח על מצרים באחרית הימים
כי הנה בן יולד לישראל אשר יחריב
את כל מצרים והשחיח את כל יושביה
והוציא את ישראל ביד חזקה
ממצרים.

NOTES

[1] By the term *rabbinic literature* we understand—as one generally does—all Jewish literature extending from the end of biblical literature to the end of the elaboration of the Talmud in the sixth century.

[2] Renée Bloch, "Écriture et tradition dans le Judaïsme, Aperçus sur l'origine du Midrash," in *Cahiers Sioniens*, No. 1, 1954, pp. 9-34.

[3] Even such a work as *Le Judaïsme avant Jésus-Christ*, by Pére Lagrange (*Collection Etudes Bibliques*, Gabalda, Paris, Third Ed., 1931), which has received wide acceptance from an entire generation of Catholic exegetes due to the name of its author, is based not on any primary sources nor editions, nor even existing (often very faulty) translations, but entirely on Strack, Moore, Schürer and several other obsolete or questionable works. Works which, in turn, usually do no more than take as established facts the often dangerously uncertain "hypotheses" of the "ancestors": Zunz, Geiger, Weiss, etc.

[4] For example, G. F. Moore, *Judaism in the First Centuries of the Christian Era*, 3 vols., Harvard University Press, Cambridge, Mass., 1927; J. Bonsirven, *Le Judaïsme palestinien au temps de Jésus-Christ*, 2 vols., Beauchesne, Paris, 1935; and *Exégèse rabbinique et exégèse paulinienne*, *ibid.*, 1939; H. L. Strack & P. Billerback, *Kommentar zum Neuen Testament aus Talmud und Midrasch*, 5 vols., Beck, Munich, 1922-1928.

[5] For the documents found in the Cairo Geniza, see the excellent work of Professor Paul Kahle, *The Cairo Geniza*, Schweich Lectures 1941, the British Academy, London, 1947. A new, modified and augmented edition of this work, in German, is in preparation. In this book, Professor Paul Kahle, who is the undisputed expert on this important material and the problems which it poses, gives the only comprehensive view existing at the present time. More recently, Professor S. D. Goitein expressed the wish—taking up an idea which was dear to Solomon Schechter—for a corpus of all the fragments of the Geniza: see Shelomo Dov Goitein, "What would Jewish and General History benefit by a Systematic Publication of the Documentary Geniza Papers?" in *Proceedings of the American Academy for Jewish Research*, Vol. XXIII, 1954, pp. 29-39.

[6] See, for example, P. R. Weiss, *Mishnah Horayoth, its History and Exposition*, Manchester University Press, Manchester, 1952.

[7] We are not discussing here practical difficulties which have nothing to do with the state of the question; what we are noting is the absence of reference materials which could prove useful in giving a certain initiation to rabbinic literature. The only existing and widely used introduction, that of H. L. Strack, *Einleitung in Talmud und Midrasch*, Beck, Munich, 5th ed., 1920, and *Introduction to the Talmud and Midrash*, Jewish Publication Society of America, Philadelphia, 1945, is a "second hand" manual, very analytical, purely skeletal, which gives no idea of the content, particular structure, or the inner life of the rabbinic tradition. On the whole, it also is quite approximate, often erroneous, and inexact. Furthermore, since the first edition of 1887 has never been revised, it still contains, for example, ideas based on the first edition of *Die gottes-dienstlichen Vorträge der Juden* (1832) by Zunz, ideas which Zunz himself later abandoned, as is evident in the second edition of this classic work in 1892. Similarly, a large number of facts repeated by Strack have been rendered obsolete by the discoveries—essential to the understanding of Jewish tradition and history—of the Cairo Geniza. Moreover, no attention was paid to these new facts when the first edition was reissued and the English translation of the work appeared.

[8]Our primary concern is with *traditions*. It is more important to date these than it is to date the redactions which have preserved them for us. We possess certain writings which are probably late but which seem to preserve very ancient traditions. It is known that the midrash as a literary genre probably did not die out until very late, only in the twelfth or thirteenth century.

[9]Cf. our study, "Quelques aspects de la figure de Moïse dans la tradition rabbinique," in *Moïse, l'homme de l'Alliance*, special issue of *Cahiers Sioniens* and published by Desclée & Co., Paris, 1955, pp. 93-167.

[10]All the work, of course, is to be done first hand, since critical editions, and sometimes any editions at all, are lacking. Nor are there concordances, indices, or other similar reference works.

[11]*Preparatio evangelium*, IX, 17-39, ed., Karl Mras in *Die Griechischen Christlichen Schriftsteller der ersten Jahrhunderte*, Eusebius, Vol. VIII, Part One, Akademie-Verlag, Berlin, 1954, pp. 502-48.

[12]*Ier Stromate*, Otto Staehlin edition, *ibid.*, Clemens, Vol. I. 1905, XXI, 130, p. 80 (Alexander Polyhistor and his Περὶ Ἰουδαίων); XXI, 141, pp. 87-88 (Demetrios, Philo, Eupolemus); XXIII, 153, pp. 95–96 (Philo and Eupolemus); XXIII, 154, p. 96 (Artapan); XXIII, 155–57, pp. 96–98 (Ezekiel the Tragedian, from whom Eusebius copies a long passage).

[13]This has come down to us only in a Latin translation, made from a Greek text, itself translated from a Hebrew original which is still well recognizable through these two translations. It is not known by what chance it has been placed under the name of the great Alexandrian Jewish philosopher of the first century. A critical study of those chronicles which have obvious relationships to Pseudo-Philo, certain of which probably have used, or perhaps even incorporated large parts of the work—*Josippon, Sefer ha-Yašar, Yalqut Šim^c oni* and *Sefer ha-Zikronot* (cf. [below] p. 000, Note 38)—would probably allow us to shed some light on the Hebrew original of this work, which enjoyed such a great vogue during the first centuries of the Christian era, and whose influence is still apparent in the Christian chroniclers of the Middle Ages. We will not quote from the text of the recent edition of Guido Kisch, *Pseudo-Philo's Liber Antiquitatum Biblicarum*, Notre Dame, Indiana, 1949, which reproduces the text of the Admont (MS. no. 359) and Melk manuscripts. This text is inferior to that of the *editio princeps* of Basel (1527), which is based in part on the Fulda and in part on the Lorsch manuscript. Therefore we will use the *editio princeps*, Basel, 1527.

[14]See the numerous parallels indicated in M. R. James, *The Biblical Antiquities of Philo*, S.P.C.K., London, 1917, pp. 43-58.

[15]In the very suggestive article of L. Cohn, "An Apocryphal Work ascribed to Philo of Alexandria," in JQR, Vol. X, 1898, pp. 277-332, a number of interesting indications are to be found, especially pp. 315-22.

[16]S. Rappaport, *Agada und Exegese bei Flavius Josephus*, Kauffmann, Frankfurt-on-Main, 1930, correctly emphasized the relationship between Josephus and the rabbinic aggadah and formulated the hypothesis (p. xx of his introduction) of an Aramaic translation of the Bible as the source of his aggadic information. We intend to return to the question of this common aggadic source.

[17]Renée Bloch, "Écriture et tradition dans le Judaïsme," pp. 28-30.

[18]A paper having as its subject, "Gloses sur le texte hébreu de l'Ancien Testament," was read

by Mr. G. R. Driver at the *VIe Journées bibliques de Louvain*, 7-9 September 1954, but we are unaware of its content, since the text has not yet been published at the time of this writing.

[19]Coming from the Cairo Geniza and belonging to the same sect as the manuscripts recently discovered in the Judean desert.

[20]Cf. W. H. Brownlee, "Biblical Interpretation among the Sectaries of the Dead Sea Scrolls," in *The Biblical Archaeologist*, XIV, No. 3, 1951, pp. 54-76.

[21]Thus, for example, the tradition attested by St. Paul (see below, p. 000) in I Cor. 10:4. The rock, identified by Philo as Wisdom or the Word of God, in the Damascus Document, VI, 3, is identified with the Torah, as it later will be in certain rabbinic midrashim.

[22]Cf. our already cited article, "Quelques aspects de la figure de Moïse dans la tradition rabbinique," the section entitled, "Témoignage du Nouveau Testament," pp. 161-66.

[23]If the last aggadic account itself belongs to the core of Palestinian tradition, the identification of the rock with Christ also finds strict parallels in Alexandrian Jewish thought. *Leg. alleg.*, II, 21; *Quod deterius*, 31 (commentary on *Deut.*, XXXII, 13); *De somn.*, II, 41; *De ebr.*, 29. For the reference to Jannes and Jambres in II Tim. 3:8, see "Quelques aspects de la figure de Moïse dans la tradition rabbinique," note 21.

[24]See for example the soon to be published edition by the R. P. R. M. Tonneau of Saint Ephrem's *Targum on Exodus*, in *Corpus Scriptorum Christianorum Orientatum*.

[25]A collection of *piyyutim* (liturgical poems) intended for the *Amidah* (prayer).

[26]Cf. Menachem Zulay, *Piyyutè Yannaï*, Schocken, Berlin, 1938, pp. ix-xiii.

[27]On the importance of preaching in ancient Judaism, see Zunz, *Die gottesdienstlichen Vorträge der Juden*, 2nd ed., Kauffmann, Frankfurt-on-Main, 1892, pp. 342-73.

[28]We prefer to discard the inaccurate designation, "Targum Jonathan" or "Targum Pseudo-Jonathan" (for the Pentateuch), which is not even ancient and which risks clouding the issue; we prefer to restore to this targum its true name of "Jerusalem Targum," and to designate the so-called "Fragmentary Targum" as the "Second Collation of the Jerusalem Targum." We will therefore use the following abbreviations: TO = Targum Onkelos; TgJ = Jerusalem Targum; 2TgJ = Second Collation of the Jerusalem Targum (Fragmentary Targum). Since at present no critical edition of the Targum exists, we will quote from the current editions of Rabbinic Bibles, and neither from the Berliner (for TO) nor Ginsburger (for TgJ and 2TgJ) editions, which are based on insufficient manuscript materials.

[29]Contrary to accepted opinion, we are more and more convinced that the TgJ and even the TO do not fit into the category of translations. Even though it resembles a translation more than the TgJ, the TO, edited in Babylonia in an artificial language, is more an adaptation of the Pentateuch based on the debates of the great Babylonian rabbinic schools than a true version. While the TgJ comes much closer to *deraš*, the TO is a sort of *pešat*, an interpretation of the Torah according to the talmudic halakah.

[30]In preparation for an edition of the Palestinian Targum, we intend to publish several studies on the problem of this Targum, on its existing editions, the currently accessible manuscript materials, dating criteria (study of the manuscripts and of the vocalization of manuscripts coming from the Cairo Geniza, various traces of this Targum in dated documents, etc.), the structure and the language of the TgJ as compared with those of Onkelos.

[31]The Aramaic *talya* can also mean "little child" and "servant." In the *Midrash ha-Gadol* on Exodus (David Z. Hoffman edition, Itzkowski, Berlin, 1913-1921, p. 12), we find *seh* (lamb) instead of *talya*.

[31a]The original Hebrew texts which we are comparing are to be found at the end of this article.

[32]*Dibre ha-Yamin šel Mošeh.* This is an aggadic account of the life of Moses written in pure Hebrew. Nathan ben Yehiel, the author of the Talmudic Dictionary *ᶜArukh*, who lived in Rome in the eleventh century, cites this midrash under the title which it bears today, and Rashi, his contemporary, certainly used it in his commentary on Exodus and the Song of Songs. The numerous manuscripts which we possess of this brief aggadic midrash bear witness to the great popularity which it must have enjoyed. It contains traditions which are undoubtedly very ancient, but until now no serious attempt has been made to date it. Written anonymously, the text contains no mention of any talmudic authority or scholar. We are quoting from the *editio princeps* of Constantinople, 1516, 5 non-paginated folios, reworked by A. Jellenek, *Bet ha-Midrasch*, II, Leipzig, 1853, pp. 1-11.

[33]The *Sefer ha-Yašar* is an aggadic account of Biblical history covering the period from the creation of Adam until the time of the Judges. Neither a study nor critical edition of this important book exists. Such a study would be rich in discoveries, due to the close link which must exist between, on the one hand, the *Sefer ha-Yašar* and the *Jewish Antiquities* and, on the other hand, *Josippon* and the *Jewish War*. Furthermore, this text presents interesting parallels to Pseudo-Philo. Considerable portions of the *Sefer ha-Yašar* are also to be found in the *Yalqut Šimᶜoni* and in other compilations of this type. The hypotheses set forth by Zunz, Strack, and others, concerning the origin of the book, do not appear to be founded on any convincing reason. The *editio princeps* of this work is the Venice edition of 1625. We are quoting from the edition of Lazarus Goldschmidt, Harz, Berlin, 1923.

[34]*Op. cit.,* p. 238.

[35]This is a sort of midrashic *Thesaurus* which follows the biblical narrative (but in the talmudic, not masoretic, order), inserting for each account juxtaposed, unrelated commentaries, be they aggadic or halakhic. It includes commentaries ranging from the most ancient up to those of the gaonic period and perhaps certain aggadic writings which are even more recent. *Editio princeps*, Salonika, 1526-27 for the Torah, 1521 for the Prophets and the Writings (Hagiographa). We are quoting from the Levin-Epstein edition, two volumes, Jerusalem, 1952.

[36]*Op. cit.,* Vol. I, Section 174, p. 106.

[37]The confusion between the *sin* and the *samek*, on the one hand, and the *sin* and *mem*, on the other, can occur very easily.

[38]Oxford MS Heb. d.11 (= Catalogue No. 2797). This manuscript of 388 parchment folios contains a collection of diverse writings assembled by Eleazar ben Asher ha-Levi. Two hands are clearly distinguishable in the manuscript. The older one (in a very different script, on a much older parchment, annotated in the margins by the redactor) covers folios 22a-25b, 30a-34b, 38a-46b (we here present the beginning of this section), 47a-50b, 62a-63b, 65a-66b. The other, the "redactor's" hand covers all the rest of the manuscript with his German rabbinic script; this handwriting certainly is much more recent. In addition to long passages from *Josippon*, the *Sefer ha-Yašar* and the *Yalqut Šimᶜoni*, the compilation contains numerous midrashim and other interesting accounts, notably some long pericopae which are literal Hebrew translations from the *Liber Antiquitatum Biblicarum* of Pseudo-Philo (cf. "Quelques aspects de la figure de Moïse dans la traditions rabbinique," where we provide examples). M. Gaster, in *The Chronicles of Jerahmeel,*

Oriental Translation Fund, IV, London, 1899, offered an English translation of part of the manuscript without either editing the text himself or even giving the description and number of the manuscript. The translation is rather capricious, and the introduction (112 pages!) is even more so. This manuscript provides evidence and constitutes an especially interesting link in the study of the megilah

[39]Following the name given in the preface, folio 7a (and also in folio 376b): *zehu sefer ha-zikronot*, "Here is the Book of Remembrances."

[40]Line 2 (of the manuscript) *wehineh*, as in the *Sefer ha-Yašar*. (In these notes, we will indicate changes only.)

[41]Line 2, *lenegdo*, as in the *Sefer ha-Yašar*, while the Yalqut has *kenegdo*.

[42]Line 4. The text gives the preposition *ʾel* before *kol zikne*, as in *Sefer ha-Yašar*.

[43]Line 4, as in *Sefer ha-Yašar*, preposition *we* before *śareha*, and adverb *kol* before *gedoleha*.

[44]Line 8, Pharaoh, as in *Sefer ha-Yašar*.

[45]Line 10, *wayomer*, *ibid*.

[46]Lines 11 and 12: short dialogue peculiar to this account, but having some affinity with the *Chronicle of Moses*.

[47]Quoted manuscript, folio 38a, lines 1-13.

[48]Concerning this, we may point out the Numerius, in Eusebius *Preparatio evangelium*, IX, 8, 1 (*op. cit.*, note 11), employs for Jannes and Jambres, the very term (ἱερογραμματεῖς) used by Josephus to designate, without naming him, one of those who predicted Moses' birth to Pharaoh (τῶν ἱερογραμματέων τις).

[49]Τῶν ἱερογραμματέων τις, καὶ γάρ εἰσι δεινοὶ περί τῶν μελλόντων τὴν ἀλήθειαν εἰπεῖν, ἀγγέλλει τῷ βασιλεῖ τεχθήσεσθαί τινα κατ' ἐκεῖνον τὸν καιρὸν τοῖς Ἰσραηλίταις ὃς ταπεινώσει μὲν τὴν Αἰγυπτίων ἡγεμονίαν αὐξήσει δὲ τοὺς Ἰσραηλίτας τραφεὶς ἀρετῇ τε πάντας ὑπερβαλεῖ καὶ δόξαν ἀείμνηστον κτήσεται. Δείσας δὲ ὁ βασιλεὺς κατὰ γνώμην τὴν ἐκείνου κελεύει πᾶν τὸ γεννηθὲν ἄρσεν ὑπὸ τῶν Ἰσραηλιτῶν εἰς τὸν ποταμὸν ῥιπτοῦντας διαφθείρειν. . . . (Antiquities, II, 9, 2).

[50]We quote from the Vilna edition under the abbreviation for the biblical work commented upon, followed by R. *(Rabbah)*, with the chapter and verse notation.

[51]Exodus R., I, 18.

[52]Ed., Buber, Vilna, 1885. We quote from the photostated New York edition, 1946, with biblical book and page notation.

[53]*Tanḥuma*, Exodus, 122.

[54]Sabionetta editon, 1567, chapter 48.

[55]Babylonian Talmud, Vilna edition, quoted by tractate and folio. Sanh. 101a, Soṭah 12b.

[56]Commentary on Exodus 1:22 (we quote from current rabbinic bibles). It is necessary to remember that the substratum of Rashi's commentaries is taken over integrally from the traditional, and generally ancient, aggadah. Thus, in relation to TgJ, it constitutes a point of arrival; between these two points we can follow the evolution of a given tradition which, while being enriched and sometimes diversified, always retains its original essence.

[57]We also can note in Balaam's oracle, Num. 24, that the predicted destruction is linked to the appearance of one who will "arise" from Israel, as in our text the destruction of Egypt is linked to the child who will be born and who will liberate Israel from Egypt.

[58]See, for example, Is. 9:5, Ps. 2:7, etc.; on the other hand, see Matt 2:15, 3:17.

[59]Except in the *Yalqut Šim^c oni* and the *Sefer ha-Zikronot*, which depends on the former, where the term *yeled* (child) is used instead of *ben* (son).

[60]A more detailed discussion of this entire subject (which only can be outlined here), including the necessary references and supporting arguments, may be found in our previously mentioned article, "Quelques aspects de la figure de Moïse dans la tradition rabbinique," pp. 149-61.

IV

What's in a Name?—The Problematic of Rabbinic "Biography"

WILLIAM SCOTT GREEN

UNIVERSITY OF ROCHESTER

Arnaldo Momigliano's remark that in his youth "scholars wrote history and gentlemen wrote biography"[1] is an apt portrayal of the uncertain and inconsistent career of biography both as a source and a tool of history. Despite Dilthey's insistence that "the course of an individual life in the environment by which it is affected and which it affects" is the "germinal cell of history," the most fundamental context for understanding the past,[2] the Hellenistic distinction between biography and history has obtained, in varying degrees, into modern times.[3] Because biography, "the account of the life of a man from birth to death,"[4] easily lends itself to a variety of literary forms and styles and rapidly succumbs to varied motives and purposes, it often is suspect in historical circles either as a source of accurate information about its subject, as a technique for investigating the past, or as both.

The purpose of this essay is to examine and reassess the propriety of biographical studies to the critical investigation of rabbinic Judaism and thereby hopefully to contribute to the discussion of the problems just mentioned. The remarks which follow pertain principally to examinations of the traditions of the masters of Yavneh, those Tannaim who allegedly lived and were active in Palestine between the destruction of the Temple in 70 and the Bar Kokhba rebellion in 135. Specifically, this essay is constructed around the following questions: Is it likely that studies which focus exclusively on the traditions ascribed to a single master will result in an authentic biography of that figure, in the story of his life? If we cannot produce rabbinical "lives," what kinds of things can be known, for instance, about the historical Eliezer b. Hyrcanus or Joshua b. Hananiah? If such studies will not produce biographies, what problems, if any, can they solve, and what is the place of their problematic within the larger, critical investigation of rabbinic Judaism?

Since the results of any historical investigation ultimately are governed by the quality and nature of the available evidence, it will be useful, before turning directly to our questions, to describe the sorts of material out of which any rabbinical "life" must be constructed and to say a few words about the distinctive character of the groups who produced them.

So long as the Temple in Jerusalem stood, it was the central religious institution of Palestinian Judaism, and the primary religious leaders were the priests. The Temple was the point at which the threads joining heaven to earth were knotted, and God's power, although "produced in heaven" was "distributed from the Temple."[5] The rituals of the Temple cult, when properly performed, certified the availability of that power for Israel's needs. By preserving and protecting God's presence in the Temple, the cultic rites exhibit what Mary Douglas calls "instrumental efficacy."[6] But she suggests that religious rituals possess another sort of efficacy which "is achieved in the action itself, in the assertions it makes and the experience which bears its imprinting."[7] Following this analysis, the Temple rites assume an added dimension: they reflect, shape, and indeed constitute that which is truly real, or holy. From the priestly perspective, reality was reflected in and holiness only could be achieved through the ritual complex of the Temple cult. The Temple was a saving institution.

Early rabbinic Judaism, which emerged in the aftermath of the Temple's destruction in 70, certainly shared that fundamental levitical perception. More than half of the materials of Mishnah, the authoritative collection of rabbinic law allegedly produced *ca.* 200 by the Palestinian Patriarch, Judah, and its corollary collection, Tosefta, directly pertain to matters of the cult. But early rabbinism altered the priestly world-view in one fundamental respect. It claimed that the holy life, once centered in the cult, applied everywhere to all Israel. This idea came from the Pharisees, the pre-70 sect of whom the rabbis were heirs, and its concrete realization engaged the Tannaitic masters in substantial, if not compulsive, theorizing about the detailed nature of the rituals themselves and about their actual or hypothetical application to life outside the cult. This largely accounts for the centrality of *halakhah* (law, the "way" of doing things) in rabbinic Judaism and helps explain why legal dicta predominate in the traditions ascribed to early rabbinic masters. If the performance of rituals within the Temple exposes the lines of God's revealed reality, then thinking and debating about those rituals outside the Temple, even without the possibility of performing all of them, has the same result. "The Mishnaic rabbis express their primary cognitive statements, their judgments upon large matters, through ritual law, not through myth or theology, neither of which is articulated at all."[8] Early rabbinism took ritual beyond the realm of practice and transformed it into the object of speculation and the substance of thought. Study, learning and exposition, became not only the basic rabbinic activity, but a principal expression of piety as well. Early rabbinic masters were men for whom "comprehension was both a means and an end,"[9] men, as we shall see, who possessed an "interior need to penetrate beyond the screen of immediate concrete experience."[10] In other words, they were intellectuals.[10a]

I think it fair to say that in the approximately 130 years following the demise of the cult the Tannaitic rabbis created a culture, "a framework of beliefs, expressive symbols and values in terms of which individuals [could] express their feelings and make their judgments . . . a fabric of meaning in terms of which human beings [could] interpret their experience and guide their action."[11] A principal goal of rabbinic culture was to overcome the vertigo initially brought on by the Temple's destruction and severely intensified by the disaster and failed messianism of the Bar Kokhba rebellion. The avoidance of ambiguity and confusion was accomplished largely through the techniques of making distinctions among and between actions, times, places and persons, through the extension of levitical categories, of paradigms of holiness, to the world outside the cult. If everything in the outside world can be defined, classified, catalogued and thereby understood, it is difficult to be lost.[12] The world-view of rabbinic culture, its "picture of the way things in sheer actuality are, [its] concept of nature, of self, of society, [its] most comprehensive ideas of order"[13] is expressed, as we have seen, primarily in rabbinic legal materials. Its ethos, "the tone, character, and quality of life, its moral and aesthetic style and mood,"[14] emerges most vividly in the non-legal materials, whether these be fanciful interpretations of biblical narrative or tales of the activities of the sages. It is important to point out that the cultural products of rabbinic Judaism are literary documents which, to adapt a term used by Basil Bernstein, constitute a restricted code.[15] That is, the contents of these documents are meaningful particularly, if not exclusively, to members of the rabbinical group; the general principles behind them are implicit and rarely spelled out. Indeed, rabbinic literature, as it extends from Tannaitic through post-Talmudic times, offers a virtually unparalleled and astonishingly rich record of the *inner* life of an intellectual elite. Whatever we say about individual rabbinic figures must be conditioned by, and in fact depends upon, our ability to elaborate and comprehend the restricted code of rabbinic culture, and the intellectual character of that culture determines the sort of evidence we have. Let us now turn to a consideration of the nature of the rabbinic evidence itself to see how it affects the theoretical possibility of knowing anything about the lives of early rabbinic masters.

The literature of rabbinic Judaism offers no systematic or coherent biographies of its important sages. Indeed, unlike other religious systems of late antiquity, rabbinic Judaism seems to have produced no hagiographies, no lives of "holy men," and no literary form uniquely suited to that enterprise.[16] Rabbinic literature does contain, however, legal dicta and exegetical sayings which allege to report the words or opinions of given masters and some narrative material which purports to depict details of their activities or to describe important events in their careers. The diverse sorts of material relating to the life of a single master are nowhere gathered under his name, but are scattered throughout rabbinic literature in documents of equally diverse character which date from Tannaitic through post-Talmudic times.

These documents appear to be not accidental, inchoate collections, but carefully and deliberately constructed compilations. Each document has its own ideological or theological agendum, and it is axiomatic that the agendum of any document, though shaped to a degree by inherited materials, ultimately is the creation of the authorities, most of whom are anonymous, who produced the document itself. They have determined the focus, selected the materials, and provided the framework that unites the discrete pericopae and gives the document its internal consistency and coherence.[17] The features of these documents suggest that their agenda surpass the teaching of any single master. First, rabbinic documents contain a substantial amount of unattributed material. This gives them an almost transcendent quality and creates the sense that the document, or the tradition, is speaking for itself, independent of any individual mind. Second, rabbinic documents are not constructed around the sayings of any individual, but follow either a thematic, formal, topical or scriptural arrangement in which the teachings or opinions of various masters are gathered to address a single issue or to interpret a particular verse of scripture. Indeed, early rabbinic figures rarely appear alone. Within the documents, moreover, the comments of the masters and their disagreements with each other almost always focus on matters of detail, so that they appear as glossators, never as innovators. The larger conceptions which inform the documents themselves are never called into question. This sort of arrangement points to a process of selection in which the teachings of individuals have been made subservient to the goals of the documents. Third, although every teaching in rabbinic literature originated in the mind of an individual, the continued vitality of those teachings depended on the rabbinic circles and communities who preserved and transmitted them. The chain of tradents, only occasionally mentioned by name, the redactors and the editors who stand behind the present form of both discrete pericopae and entire documents substantively revised, embellished and refined received materials, and sometimes invented new ones, to suit their various agenda. Rabbinic documents are "bright with names that men remember, loud with names that men forget."[18] All of this means that we know about early rabbinic figures what the various authorities behind the documents want us to know, and we know it in the way they want us to know it. Consequently, the historical context, the primary locus of interpretation for any saying attributed to a given master or story about him is the document in which the passage appears, *not* the period in which he is alleged to have lived. It follows that the earliest rabbinic documents, Mishnah-Tosefta, ought in the first instance to provide better information about Yavnean masters than should the *gemarot* or later exegetical collections.

But when we turn to those theoretically more useful materials, we still find ourselves well removed from rabbinic masters as historical figures. All rabbinic materials, certainly those in Mishnah-Tosefta and the (later) Tannaitic *midrashim*, have been made to conform to a literary agendum as well as a theological one. In the processes of transmission and redaction the discrete sayings and rulings have been cast into rhetorical patterns, many of them stereotyped, which now characterize the documents, or sections of them, in which those materials appear. W. Sibley Towner has given us a superb illustration of the use of forms in Tannaitic exegetical literature,[19] and Jacob Neusner's extensive investigations of the tractates of the Mishnah Order *Tohoroth*[20] demonstrate the astonishing pervasiveness of formalism in that document. Indeed, he shows that constructions in the Order of Purities are rarely capricious and that six or seven rhetorical patterns can account for almost all of its materials.[21] Let us first assess the effects of formalism on the representation of rabbinic figures.

Forms by nature remove us from a historical figure because they "package" or epitomize his thought, obscure idiosyncracy and unique modes of expression, and thereby conceal distinctive elements of personality, character and intellect. The very presence of forms means at the outset that we cannot claim to have the exact words spoken by any Yavnean master. But if we cannot claim access to a master's language, perhaps we nevertheless can claim to possess formalized but accurate representations of *ideas* and *positions* held by him. To evaluate this last allegation, let us examine one form important in the traditions of Yavnean masters, the dispute-form.[22] The structure of that form is as follows:

A. Statement of a legal problem or issue
B. Rabbi X says . . .
C. Rabbi Y says . . .
[D. Rabbi Z says . . .]

The opinions of the authorities often are balanced either with respect to meter, word choice, or both, and the order in which their views are presented remains constant. The language of B and C sometimes simply provides the masters with fixed positions, as in the following example:

No. 1 A. [Concerning] one who scratches his flesh [on the Sabbath]—
B. R. Eliezer obligates [him] for a Sin-offering.
C. And R. Joshua exempts [him].

Mishnah Shabbat 12:4

Often, however, B and C appear as complete sentences, as in the following case:

No. 2 A. [Concerning] one who dedicates his goods [to the Temple] and intends to divorce his wife—
B. R. Eliezer says, "He should make her vow [not to give him any] benefit, and she [may] collect her *ketuvah* from the sanctuary, and if he wanted to remarry her, he [may] remarry her."

C. R. Joshua says, "If he wanted to remarry her, he [may] not remarry her."

Tosefta ᶜArakin 4:5

The legal issues of these two passages need not detain us. The two examples have been included here because they concretely demonstrate that in the dispute-form it is the referent and the context provided by the superscription, A of each case, that makes the positions of the masters, B and C of each case, understandable. The positions ascribed to Eliezer and Joshua in example no. 1 could be, and in fact are applied in their names to any number of cases within and outside the laws of the Sabbath. By themselves, they tell us little; their significance is wholly a function of the situations to which they are attached. In example no. 2 the statements of Eliezer and Joshua, although complete sentences, are incomprehensible without the case described in A. It is easy to see that if the conditions of A were changed, so would be the importance, indeed the meaning, of B and C. The centrality of the superscription is further shown by the fact that Ushan revisions of Yavnean disputes consistently alter only the superscriptions, leaving intact the discrete lemmas or opinions. This means that in the dispute-form the language attributed to the master himself is secondary for an interpretation of the passage. The precision and subtlety of an individual's opinions are more likely to be determined by the superscription. But the superscriptions themselves are synthetic by definition and therefore must admit of a measure of artifice. It is clear that the purpose of the dispute-form is to transmit in a single context the (usually conflicting) views of more than one master. As the examples above demonstrate, in authentic disputes the superscription must be consensual; that is, it must be substantively appropriate to at least two opinions.[23] Since it is unlikely that two individuals perceive issues, define problems and express themselves in identical ways, the dispute-form by nature requires the alteration and modification of the language and also perhaps of the precise meaning of the originally independent, individual statements and rulings that almost certainly stand behind it. This means that we cannot be certain of the extent to which a master's views on a given matter have been revised in the tradental and redactional processes, and we therefore cannot automatically suppose that the superscriptions in disputes involving him accurately depict his perceptions and definitions of the issues and problems they represent.

Forms can misrepresent a given master in yet another way. By definition forms are used irrespective of the ideas they express, and the model of the dispute-form, with its terse language and fixed order of names, is applied to a wide variety of cases. The continued reduction of a master's thoughts on a variety of issues to stereotypic language and rigid formal structures can create an illusion of consistency and thereby transform a distinctive, individual intellect into the personification of a single posture or position.

These observations apply, *mutatis mutandis*, to other forms and rhetorical patterns in which the statements of masters have been truncated and incorporated into a larger structure.[24]

To all this must now be added the results of Jacob Neusner's commentaries to Purities. They show that particular forms do not characterize the traditions either of specific masters or of generations of teachers. To the contrary, they demonstrate that forms are basic to the construction and organization of the chapter divisions in Mishnah-Tosefta.[25] That is, a particular form commonly does not appear in isolation, but is joined with other pericopae which share the same form. These clusters of formally consistent materials routinely cut across generational lines and give whole chapters of Mishnah-Tosefta, or large segments of them, their distinctive character. It is argued that these

> . . . formal and formulary patterns were imposed only at the point at which the materials were grouped together in the first place. That means that the aggregation of two or three or more units of thought assigned to authorities at diverse periods was accompanied by the imposition, upon those several distinct units of thought, of uniform formal or formulary traits.[26]

The imposition of formal traits is apt to be the work of the penultimate redactors of Mishnah and Tosefta.

> . . . the preferences exhibited in a given chapter for a form or set of forms are going to reflect the character of the penultimate redactional circle responsible for the chapter, not the formulary preferences of the authorities cited in it, the materials relevant to it, or the earlier, already redacted pericopae assembled in it.[27]

For our purposes this observation means that we have to take account at the outset of the likelihood that the extant traditions of any Yavnean master have been shaped by several redactional circles removed from him in time by possibly two generations and the Bar Kokhba war. We therefore cannot suppose that the present forms of the materials attributed to a single master derive from a common origin.

But if we can neither assign the words of a given pericope to a given master nor show that he or his immediate disciples stand behind the formal structures in which those words appear, how shall we understand the attributive formulae which associate his name with a given opinion? Indeed, Towner has argued that the attributions cannot be taken seriously.

> The apparently unique tie to specific cultural and historical settings provided by the names of rabbinical authorities associated with particular traditions proves on closer inspection to be of little help in reconstructing the "setting in life" of those traditions. The attributions are simply not historically reliable data.[28]

The assumption of the unreliability of attributions also is implicit in Neusner's research on the Mishnaic law of Purities. He argues that attributions can help in reconstructing the history of the law, but he regards them as "reliable" only when they are verified by other criteria. If, for example, a legal rule assigned to a Yavnean master is elaborated upon or assumed in a saying attributed to an Ushan master, it is argued that the law attributed to the Yavnean reliably may be placed in the Yavnean stratum. The other mode of verification is the attestation. If an Ushan master substantively revises or comments upon a Yavnean rule, the rule is to be located in the Yavnean stratum. Attributions not corroborated by one of these techniques are defined as "probable" but not "reliable." It must be stressed that in Neusner's research attributions serve principally to locate traditions within a generational time period. It is not argued that even corroborated attributed traditions report the words of the individuals to whom they·are assigned.[29]

It should not be supposed that a reluctance to adopt the tacit claims of attributions is the result of excessive skepticism or groundless nihilism. To the contrary, aspects of the literature itself encourage such a posture. First, the record of attribution is not always consistent. Manuscript readings not uncommonly conflict and attribute the same saying to different masters. But even when the manuscript record is firm, traditions assigned to one master in one document sometimes appear either anonymously or in the name of a different master in another. Also, later tradents sometimes supply a lemma with a double attribution, or announce that attributions are confused, or reversed.[30] Although these phenomena are not comparable and differently affect our evaluation of the material, they nevertheless justify caution in the way attributions are used.[31] On a different level, attributions also are suspect because of the collective character of rabbinic literature itself and the apparent importance of disciple-circles in the transmission of rabbinic materials. It is not unusual for the disciples of a teacher to perceive in or derive from his teachings, and then to attribute to him, positions he did not hold but which are consonant with their own, contemporary concerns. It therefore cannot automatically be supposed that all the views assigned to a given master actually originate with him. Specific opinions may be interpretations or inventions of the followers of a particular sage. The names attached to specific sayings consequently may not represent an individual at all, but rather a group or circle which identified itself with a particular master or others who adhered to his teachings.[32] Pseudepigraphy is always a possibility, and there is evidence, for instance, that some teachings of the Houses of Hillel and Shammai are the inventions of later tradents.[33]

The arguments and evidence adduced thus far suggest how thoroughly the legal and exegetical traditions of early rabbinic masters have been conditioned by the formal and ideological biases of their tradents and redactors, how deeply they are imbedded in their various documentary contexts, and, hopefully, how that situation limits their usefulness as sources for biography.

The considerations raised above apply no less to the non-legal materials, specifically the so-called rabbinic *aggadot*, narratives about the activities and careers of the sages. These materials occupy only a small part of the dossiers of Yavnean masters, and most are suspect because they appear initially in post-Tannaitic documents. Like the legal and exegetical materials, the *aggadot* show signs of development and manipulation, and it therefore would be a mistake to underestimate either their formal character or the care with which they have been constructed.[34] Even if the impetus to create such stories derived from an actual event in the life of a particular master, in their present form their purpose evidently is other than the depiction of his individual, "private" personality.[35] That is, the identity of the master himself generally is not decisive for an understanding of the story. For example, stories which describe how a sage suffered poverty and deprivation for the sake of Torah only to be rewarded later make the same point whether they are told, with different and distinctive details to be sure, about Hillel, Eliezer, or Aqiba.[36] Even after form-analysis strips away some of the embellishment, the provenance and date of such stories remain exceedingly difficult to determine. The presence of one or more plausible details or the absence of miracles or other improbabilities hardly constitute adequate criteria for authenticity. Moreover, because such materials serve a cultural purpose different from that of legal rulings and generally treat issues or solve problems inappropriate to a legal context, it should not be expected that they will find corroboration in the legal materials.[37]

The use of rabbinic *aggadot* for the purposes of biography is rendered more difficult by the utter disharmony and lack of consensus in contemporary scholarship on these materials. At the outset of his treatment of the Talmudic accounts of conversations between rabbis and Roman officials, for example, Moshe D. Herr argues that "the important question is not whether the event actually occurred, but whether it could actually occur."[38] But in his very next paragraph, verisimilitude becomes fact: "To suggest . . . that such incidents never occurred in reality and were pure figments of the imagination is certainly out of the question."[39] In Herr's view, the meeting between Yohanan B. Zakkai and Vespasian is accurately reported in the various Talmudic accounts, and the "only question which remains to be settled is the date of the conversation—when could it have taken place?"[40] In the materials Herr produces, no rabbi ever loses an argument to an Emperor or Roman official or is outwitted or seduced by the ubiquitous Roman matron (who apparently found all rabbis irresistible!), but his analyses never raise the possibility of self-serving invention. Ephraim E. Urbach's lengthy studies of the character and class-status of the Talmudic and Palestinian sages likewise presuppose the general historical reliability of rabbinic *aggadot*.[41] Samuel Safrai's conviction that despite their "aggadic-didactic embellishment," the "common feature of all . . . *aggadot* is their genuine historical core"[42] seems somewhat more critical, but essentially offers the identical view.

Adopting a different approach, Henry A. Fischel[43] and A. A. Halevy[44] supply catenae of "parallels" between rabbinic narratives and Greco-Roman literary materials. Fischel argues that many biographical pericopae in rabbinic literature illustrate a "general context in late antiquity the representative and ideal of which was the *sophos-sapiens-hakham* . . . [a] special brand of scholar-believer-bureaucrat   ."[45] To support this claim he draws heavily on rhetorical passages characteristic of various Greco-Roman philosophical schools and attempts to show that they substantively and formally were adopted and adapted by early rabbinic culture. Fischel's arguments frequently are ingenious and intriguing, but his demonstrations have not enjoyed a consistent success.[46] While Halevy resorts to a larger sample of comparative materials, his demonstrations are less rigorous and consequently less suggestive than Fischel's. If deduced with care and precision,[47] the results of such comparativist exercises certainly can help to locate aspects of rabbinism within a broad cultural milieu, but their importance should not be overstated.[48] Indeed, since one goal of this approach is to specify the paths of cultural interaction and to highlight intercultural similarity, it can bypass or obscure issues which are fundamental to research into rabbinic narratives. Even if it can be shown, for example, that various rabbinic narratives mirror Greco-Roman rhetorical forms, we still need to ask why such stories were told and preserved in rabbinic circles, what sorts of problems they try to solve, and how they exemplify what is "rabbinic" about rabbinic Judaism.

Finally, Dov Noy[49] and Dan Ben-Amos[50] have made important contributions to our understanding of the internal structure of some rabbinic narratives. Their approach, however, presupposes that these narratives constitute folklore and thereby reflect a long oral tradition and a popular imagination. Given the intellectual, paradigmatic and self-enclosed character of most of rabbinic literature, it would be preferable to inquire first how such stories functioned within a rabbinic environment. The critical study of rabbinic *aggadot*, then, must begin with primary attention to the ways these narratives behave within their present documentary setting.

Hopefully, the above materials demonstrate that the critical study of rabbinic Judaism in every instance depends on and must begin with the examination and assessment of rabbinic documents themselves. Until we understand the motives and techniques of the men responsible for the present state of rabbinic literature, it will be difficult to apprehend the full meaning of the discrete materials it contains. This has an important bearing on the studies of individual figures, as we shall see. Let us now turn to the issues raised at the outset of this essay.

Is it likely that studies which focus exclusively on the traditions ascribed to a single master will result in an authentic biography of that figure, in the story of his life? We have observed that rabbinic literature does not offer biographies of its important sages, and the goal of most modern rabbinic biographers was to supply the "lives" that the sources omitted. Most scholars interested in individual figures supposed that the words ascribed to a rabbinic master were really said by him and that the narrative accounts accurately reflect events which actually occurred. This much is evident from the sorts of biographies they wrote. To fashion a biography of Joshua b. Hananiah, for example, Joshua Podro[51] simply collected materials about him from a variety of sources, used the narrative materials to determine a chronology, and inserted legal dicta and exegetical sayings when he imagined they "happened." He then glossed this new arrangement of materials with tidbits of historical information and his own subjective estimations of Joshua's thoughts, attitude, or states of mind. This same, uncritical approach characterizes Louis Finkelstein's celebrated biography[52] and J. Goldin's psychological "profile" of Aqiba,[53] and it is evident in virtually every article on an early rabbinic figure in the recent *Encyclopedia Judaica*. Like the others, Podro's biography depends heavily on his own contributions because the plot line for Joshua's life provided by all the available narrative material about him has all the complexity and interest of a Dick and Jane story. Indeed, had he been utterly faithful to his sources, Podro's chapter headings should have read as follows: "R. Joshua Takes a Boat Trip to Rome with his Friends" or "R. Joshua Talks Back to the Emperor." This is not to ridicule rabbinic literature or the activities of the sages, but to point out that, even ignoring the critical considerations raised above, any attempt to recover the life of an early Tanna is doomed from the start because of insufficient information. In the strict sense of the term, rabbinic biography is an impossibility.

But if it is not possible to recover the life of an early rabbinic master, perhaps it is possible to say other things about him. Since, as we have seen, the bulk of materials about early rabbinic masters consists of legal dicta and exegetical sayings, perhaps it is possible to describe their minds, that is, to gather together all of the lemmas and rulings of a single master and identify the comprehensive principles of thought which inform and underlie them. Such an exercise, though tempting, is fraught with difficulties. First, to achieve results of any real importance, we should require a rather large number of sayings and rulings. Thirty or fifty opinions on specific matters of detail are not apt to reveal the character of a distinctive intellect. This automatically rules out most of the names which appear in Mishnah-Tosefta. Second, the distinctiveness of any opinion or ruling will first emerge in a documentary setting. Before we can abstract it from that context, we first need to see it as the redactor saw it and then as the tradent manipulated it. But our understanding of the construction and ideologies of rabbinic documents is still primitive. The systematic, critical investigation of Mishnah is just now under way. Let me describe the problem differently. Given the nature of the sources, reconstructing a master's mind is analogous to an attempt to see an atom. Just as scientists have never observed an atom or any of its parts, but have conjured its shape on the basis of reflected images, so, too, we do not have direct access either to the words or thoughts of early rabbinic masters, but must reconstruct their intellects on the basis of their reflection in the minds of others. Scientists understand what makes their reflecting machines work. As yet, we do not possess an equivalent understanding of our own reflectors. Indeed, it is not even clear who they are. Third, even if we successfully could abstract the rulings from their various contexts, on what criterion should we determine that a single mind stands behind them? "Coherence" and "consistency" are the most obvious choices, but it hardly needs to be said that these categories do not necessarily point to a single intellect. Indeed, as I suggested earlier, they may indicate just the opposite. S. C. Humphrey's observation is apposite here: "Our understanding of patterns of combination or contrast on the level of ideas has yet barely progressed beyond pure intuition even for individual cultures, let alone comparative studies."[54]

I think it is now fair to say that studies of the traditions ascribed to a single rabbinic master which stress the recovery either of his life or his mind are apt to yield very little. Conventional biography, the story of the life of an early rabbinic figure, is impossible to produce. Intellectual biography, the description of a mind, even if possible, at this stage is premature.

If biographical studies will not result in biographies, can they contribute at all to an improved understanding of rabbinic Judaism? What is their problematic, if any? The answer to this question depends on the recognition that the focus of biographical studies is not the lives of men, but a particular trait of rabbinic culture, the preservation of names. We earlier observed that the inclusion in rabbinic documents of much unattributed material and their organization according to topic or scriptural verse lends them a transcendent quality and suggests that their development is the result of a collective enterprise. The preservation of named traditions in rabbinic literature, then, cannot be regarded as inevitable. It consequently is a fact to be assessed. The problematic of rabbinic "biography" will emerge from our understanding of how names function in rabbinic culture. It is clear that in legal and exegetical materials names function merely as a label. That is, the logical or substantive relationship of one law to another or one exegetical comment to another could be discerned even if the names were not attached. It therefore is unlikely that biographical studies will make important contributions to our understanding of the law or its development. The names facilitate the discrimination of one tradition from another, but no more.

However, if we adopt a broader perspective of rabbinism, it becomes evident that it is the preservation of the names of individual masters that gives rabbinic Judaism its *diachronie*, its "pastness," its traditionality. It is primarily because of the names that rabbinic Judaism appears to unfold and we are able to chart change and movement in it through time. That factors other than chronology guided the construction of rabbinic documents need not mean that the past or its representation were irrelevant in rabbinic culture, especially in its early manifestations. The contrary is suggested by the fact that within early rabbinic documents masters of different generations usually are not brought into dialogue with one another. Yavneans dispute with other Yavneans, not with Ushans, and when that order is violated, the pericope in question immediately is suspect. The presence of the names of rabbinic masters, then, provides a tangible connective between the present and the past, and the demarcation of the past in terms of generations not only avoids one sort of temporal vertigo, it also palpably establishes the inter-generational chain of communication fundamental to a traditional culture.[55] These are not inconsequential functions. As Edward Shils points out, the ability to identify a practice or idea as having occurred in the past is essential to the stability and continuity of a tradition.

> . . . even though one—perhaps the chief—constitutive feature of a traditional belief is that it has been believed previously, of a traditional action that it has been performed previously—its present acceptance or performance—its continuation in the present—depends upon its being perceived by those who recommend acceptance or perform it as having been existent previously.[56]

This discussion suggests that the basic problematic or rabbinic "biography" ought to be conceived in terms of understanding the dynamics of tradition rather than the recovery of an individual life or a particular period in the history of Judaism. Because of the materials they necessarily include, the "biographical" studies offer us, as it were, a cross-section of rabbinic culture. It is the biographical studies which take us across the boundaries of documents and through time and make it possible to observe the internal processes of rabbinic tradition. Thus, in the study of the legal traditions of individual masters, we shall want to know not only the cluster of ideas associated with a given master, but also if later figures attribute to him positions not justified by the views he already is known to hold in early documents. Is rabbinic traditionality capricious or conservative? The same sorts of issues can be raised in the study of rabbinic *aggadot*. We shall want to know not only the kinds of portraits which emerge from aggadic materials, but also if the figures of the past continually are remade and reimaged by later tradents. Is their individuality discarded over time or is some sort of distinctive identity preserved?[57] To what degree is the past authoritative in the present? It is through attention to these matters that the biographical studies can help us understand the mechanisms of change in a tradition which is both communal and intellectual.

To summarize: By limiting the range of issues open to question, by organizing discrete sayings of individuals to address a single point of law or to interpret a verse of scripture, and by shaping narrative accounts of rabbinical activities to serve public goals, the authorities behind rabbinic documents created a literature dominated by consensus, by collective opinion. It is a literature in which individual figures appear to gloss and refine tradition, but never to invent it, a literature in which the sense of separate existences is minimal. The structure of rabbinic documents severely limits the expression of individuality. Idiosyncracy or personal charisma rarely appear. No biographies are preserved; the inner, private, psychic, imaginative and intellectual lives, as well as the public careers of early rabbinic masters, are almost totally obscured. No individual emerges as a "whole person" in whom all wisdom and piety are centered and who might threaten or serve as a focus of resistance against the rabbinic collective itself. We know that the names of these figures are attached to certain rulings and opinions, but we have few grounds to assert that they actually thought them, much less why they thought them, or how passionately they felt about them. Although questions about rabbis as historical figures ought not be ignored, the character of the evidence suggests that the basic problematic of rabbinic "biography" is not the recovery of the life or mind of a given master, but the study of how and if his traditions change and develop across documents and through time.[58]

NOTES

[1]A. Momigliano, *The Development of Greek Biography*, Cambridge, 1971, p. 1.

[2]Wilhelm Dilthey, *Pattern and Meaning in History*, Edited and Introduced by H. P. Rickman, New York, 1961, p. 89.

[3]Momigliano, *op. cit.*, pp. 1-22.

[4]*Ibid.*, p. 11.

[5]Baruch A. Levine, "On the Presence of God in Biblical Religion," in J. Neusner, ed., *Religions in Antiquity: Essays in Memory of Erwin Ramsdell Goodenough*, Leiden, 1968, p. 82.

[6]Mary Douglas, *Purity and Danger*, Pelican, 1966, p. 84.

[7]*Ibid.*

[8]Jacob Neusner, *A History of the Mishnaic Law of Purities*, Part 10, *Parah: Literary and Historical Problems*, Leiden, 1976, p. 230.

[9]The phrase is Durkheim's, "L'individualisme et les intellectuels," *Revue Bleu*, 1898, pp. 7-13. It is cited in S. C. Humphreys, "'Transcendence' and Intellectual Roles," *Daedalus*, 104:2, 1975, p. 93.

[10]Edward A. Shils, *The Intellectuals and the Powers and Other Essays*, Chicago, 1972. p. 3.

[10a]These two paragraphs are abbreviated from my "Palestinian Holy Men: Charismatic Leadership and Rabbinic Tradition," in the forthcoming volume on religion of *Aufstieg und Niedergang der römischen Welt*, Berlin-New York, 1977.

[11] Clifford Geertz, *The Interpretation of Cultures*, New York, 1973, pp. 144-45.

[12] For a description of the international, "scribal" character of rabbinic intellectuality, see Jonathan Z. Smith, "Wisdom and Apocalyptic," in Birger A. Pearson, ed., *Religious Syncretism in Antiquity: Essays in Conversation with Geo Widengren*, Missoula, 1975, pp. 131-56. See especially, pp. 135-36, 144-45.

[13] Geertz, *op. cit.,* pp. 126-27.

[14] *Ibid.*

[15] See Mary Douglas, *Natural Symbols*, New York, 1973, pp. 44-46, 52, 54-57, 77-79, 96, 91-98, 200-1.

[16] For descriptions and analyses of biographical forms in other ancient religious traditions and the problems associated with their study, see Moses Hadas and Morton Smith, *Heroes and Gods*, New York, 1965; Morton Smith, "Prologomena to a Discussion of Aretalogies, Divine Men, the Gospels, and Jesus," *Journal of Biblical Literature*, XC, 1971, pp. 174-99; C. W. Votaw, *The Gospels and Contemporary Biographies in the Greco-Roman World*, Philadelphia, 1970; David L. Tiede, *The Charismatic Figure as Miracle Worker*, Missoula, 1975; Jonathan Z. Smith, "Good News is No News: Aretalogy and Gospel," in J. Neusner, ed., *Christianity, Judaism and other Greco-Roman Cults: Studies for Morton Smith at Sixty*, Leiden, 1975, Part I, pp. 21-38.

[17] For a critical discussion of various perspectives on this point, see Jacob Neusner, ed., *The Formation of the Babylonian Talmud*, Leiden, 1970, and *The Modern Study of the Mishnah*, Leiden, 1973. For midrash, see Joseph Heinemann, "Profile of a Midrash: The Art of Composition in Leviticus Rabbah," *Journal of the American Academy of Religion*, XXXIX, 1971, pp. 141-50.

[18] A. C. Swinburne, *Eaton: An Ode.*

[19] Wayne Sibley Towner, *The Rabbinic "Enumeration of Scriptural Examples,"* Leiden, 1973.

[20] Jacob Neusner, *A History of the Mishnaic Law of Purities*: Part One, *Kelim: Chapters One through Eleven*, Leiden, 1974; Part Two, *Kelim: Chapters Twelve through Thirty*, Leiden, 1974; Part Three, *Kelim: Literary and Historical Problems*, Leiden, 1974; Part Four, *Ohalot: Commentary*, Leiden, 1974; Part Five, *Ohalot: Literary and Historical Problems*, Leiden, 1975; Part Six, *Negaim: Mishnah-Tosefta*, Leiden, 1975; Part Seven, *Negaim: Sifra*, Leiden, 1975; Part Eight, *Negaim: Literary and Historical Problems*, Leiden, 1975; Part Nine, *Parah: Commentary*, Leiden, 1976; Part Ten, *Parah: Literary and Historical Problems*, Leiden, 1976; Part Eleven, *Tohorot: Commentary*, Leiden, 1976 (hereafter, *Purities*).

[21] *Ibid.,* Part Three, pp. 192-236. Part Five, pp. 131-48, Part Eight, pp. 108-21, Part Ten, pp. 93-109

[22] For analysis and discussion of this and other typical Yavnean forms see Jacob Neusner, *Eliezer ben Hyrcanus: The Tradition and the Man*, Parts One and Two, Leiden, 1973, especially Part Two, pp. 18-62 (hereafter, *Eliezer* I or II).

[23] For a critical discussion, see Gary G. Porton, "The Artificial Dispute: Ishmael and ᶜAqiva," in J. Neusner, ed., *Christianity, Judaism and Other Greco-Roman Cults: Studies for Morton Smith at Sixty,* Leiden, 1975, Part IV, pp. 18-29.

[24]Most of the legal materials of Mishnah-Tosefta in which individual masters appear exhibit these characteristics. See the listing in *Eliezer* II, pp. 18-31, and the material cited above, note 21.

[25]See the material cited above, note 21.

[26]*Purities*, Part Sixteen, *Niddah: Literary and Historical Problems*, Chapter Fourteen, Conclusion. I thank Professor Neusner for making the typescript available to me in advance of publication.

[27]*Purities*, Part Three, p. 209. To be sure, particular forms may be proportionally significant in a given corpus of early traditions about an individual master (disputes, for instance, in the traditions of Eliezer and Joshua, narratives in the early legal traditions of Gamaliel), but at present none of these forms appears to be unique to a particular master or atypical of early rabbinic literature in general, and no single corpus is composed of only one form. Questions about the dominating formal traits of a master's tradition therefore should begin as questions about redaction, selection and stylistic preference and not as questions about the man himself. In this area, Neusner's results and their implications impose important and useful perspectives. The forthcoming works of Gary G. Porton on Ishmael, Jack Lightstone on Yose the Galilean, and Shamai Kanter on Gamaliel II promise to significantly inform the discussion on this matter.

[28]Towner, *op. cit.,* p. 34.

[29]*Purities*, Part Eight, pp. 206-220.

[30]See b. Meg. 31b-32a. Professor Gary G. Porton brought this passage to my attention. Also see Sifré Deuteronomy, ed., Finkelstein, p. 227.

[31]See the discussion in Robert Goldenberg, *The Sabbath-Law of Rabbi Meir*, University Microfilms, Ann Arbor, 1974, pp. 239-70.

[32]See the materials cited above, note 26. Other factors as well can cause a master's name to be associated with a view he did not hold. With respect to Meir, for instance, Goldenberg, *op. cit.,* p. 225, remarks, "There was apparently a strong tendency for later transmitters to add the words, 'R. Meir's opinion' whenever the named authority in the second clause was Meir's contemporary."

[33]See the argument in Neusner's forthcoming *Purities*, Part Seventeen, *Makhshirin*, Chapter Ten, Section iv.

[34]The arguments of J. Fraenkel, "Bible Verses Quoted in the Tales of the Sages," and Z. Kagan, "Divergent Tendencies and their Literary Moulding in the Aggadah," both in *Scripta Hierosolymitana*, XXII, pp. 80-99 and 151-70 respectively supply evidence for this assertion. Also see Robert Goldenberg, "The Deposition of Rabban Gamaliel II: An Examination of the Sources," *Journal of Jewish Studies*, XXIII, Autumn, 1972, pp. 167-90, also in W. S. Green, ed., *Persons and Institutions in Early Rabbinic Judaism*, Missoula, 1977. For a Mishnaic illustration, see my "Palestinian Holy Men: Charismatic Leadership and Rabbinic Tradition."

[35]Dan Ben-Amos, *Narrative Forms in the Haggadah: Structural Analysis*, University Microfilms, Ann Arbor, 1967, pp. 160-79, points out that the purpose of many rabbinic biographical narratives is the illustration of a particular cultural or ethical value. He identifies such narratives as exempla, and he argues (p. 163) that "the haggadic exemplum is a narrative form at the core of which lies an ethical value." For another illustration of a biographical narrative which makes a non-biographical point, see Jacob Neusner, *The Academic Study of Judaism*, New York, 1975, pp. 75-76 and the articles of Goldenberg and Kagan above, note 34.

[36]Ben-Amos, *op. cit.*, p. 166, observes that in such narratives the general reputation or image of the protagonist is essential to an understanding of the passage. But he notes that "personalities of equal status can replace each other in parallel versions." This is not to suggest that no *aggadot* focus on the activities of particular masters. For instance, the accounts of Eliezer's death (see *Eliezer* I, pp. 409ff.) obviously presuppose knowledge of reports of his excommunication. The problem is knowing what to do with such information. See note 37.

[37]Aggadic materials, for instance, report that Eliezer was excommunicated and that hostility between Joshua and Gamaliel led to the latter's deposition. Eliezer's alleged excommunication seems to have had little effect on legal traditions. None of them exhibit any hostility towards Eliezer (*Eliezer* II, p. 133). Likewise, Shamai Kanter (*Legal Traditions of Rabban Gamaliel II*, Leiden, 1977) observes little hostility towards Gamaliel in legal materials, and my own research reveals the same for Joshua. In other words, the materials are sufficiently diverse so that the aggadic stories could not be deduced from the legal materials.

[38]Moshe D. Herr, "The Historical Significance of the Dialogues between Jewish Sages and Roman Dignitaries," *Scripta Hierosolymitana*, XXII, 1971, pp. 123-50, p. 125.

[39]*Ibid.*

[40]*Ibid.*, p. 128.

[41]E. E. Urbach, "The Talmudic Sage—Character and Authority," *Cahiers d'Histoire Mondiale*, XI, 1968, pp. 116-47, and his "Class-Status and Leadership in the World of the Palestinian Sages," *Proceedings of the Israel Academy of Sciences and Humanities*, Vol. II, Jerusalem, 1968, pp. 38-74. Also see his *The Sages*, trans. Israel Abrahams, Jerusalem, 1975, Vol. I., pp. 525-648.

[42]Samuel Safrai, "Tales of the Sages in the Palestinian Tradition and the Babylonian Talmud," *Scripta Hierosolymitana*, XXII, 1971, pp. 209-32, p. 210.

[43]Henry A. Fischel, "Story and History: Observations on Greco-Roman Rhetoric and Pharisaism," in *American Oriental Society, Middle West Branch, Semi-Centenniel Volume*, Denis Sinor, ed., Bloomington, 1969, pp. 59-88; "Studies in Cynicism and the Ancient Near East: The Transformation of a *Chria*," in J. Neusner, ed., *Religions in Antiquity: Essays in Memory of Erwin Ramsdell Goodenough*, Leiden, 1968, pp. 372-411; "The Uses of Sorites (*Climax, Gradatio*) in the Tannaitic Period," *Hebrew Union College Annual*, XLIV, 1973, pp. 119-52; *Rabbinic Literature and Greco-Roman Philosophy*, Leiden, 1973.

[44]A. A. Halevy, *The Historical-Biographical Aggadah* (Hebrew), Tel-Aviv, 1975. Professor Baruch M. Bokser called my attention to this work and generously made it available to me.

[45]*Rabbinic Literature and Greco-Roman Philosophy*, p. xii.

[46]See the reviews of *Rabbinic Literature and Greco-Roman Philosophy* by A. Wasserstein, Journal of Jewish Studies, XXV, 1974, pp. 456-60; Anthony Saldarini, S.J., *Catholic Biblical Quarterly*, XXXVII, 1975, pp. 252-54; Seymour Feldman, *Association for Jewish Studies Newsletter*, June, 1976, pp. 20-22.

[47]The essential theoretical work in this regard remains Morton Smith's *Tannaitic Parallels to the Gospels*, Philadelphia, 1951.

[48]In *Rabbinic Literature and Greco-Roman Philosophy*, p. 34, for instance, Fischel claims to show that "certain beliefs, maxims, habits and legends belonging to the academic lore of the Epicureans were common knowledge in the ancient world, that they spread abroad by popular media and personal encounters—whether employing Greek or Aramaic—and that they played a significant role in the academic tradition of scholar-bureaucracies which resembled each other to a certain degree and were in contact with each other in the classical, Christian and Jewish worlds in the first two to three centuries of Roman Imperial times." But in the book itself, Fischel analyses only a handful of non-legal, aggadic pericopae which concern four early rabbinic figures, only one of whom (Aqiba) occupies a position of importance in rabbinic documents. So even if all of Fischel's demonstrations were uniformly persuasive, and they are not, the phenomenon he identifies hardly could qualify as major. The "significance" of Epicurean beliefs, maxims, habits and legends in early rabbinism remains difficult to specify.

[49]Dov Noy, "The Jewish Versions of the 'Animal Languages' Folktale (AT 670)," *Scripta Hierosolymitana*, XXII, 1971, pp. 171-208. His two-volume doctoral dissertation, *Motif-Index of Talmudic Midrashic Literature*, University Microfilms, Ann Arbor, 1954, is an essential research tool.

[50]Ben-Amos, *op. cit.*

[51]Joshua Podro, *The Last Pharisee: The Life and Times of Rabbi Joshua ben Hananyah, A First Century Idealist*, London, 1959.

[52]Louis Finkelstein, *Akiba: Scholar, Saint and Martyr*, New York, 1970. The original version appeared in 1936.

[53]Judah Goldin, "Toward a Profile of the Tanna, Aqiba ben Joseph," *Journal of the American Oriental Society*, 96.1, 1976, pp. 38-56. The abstract (p. 38) summarizes Goldin's argument as follows: "For the tanna Aqiba ben Joseph of the first third of the second century A.D., the verb plus the object suffix of Exodus 15:2, w^{ɔ}nwhw, understood by him as "I will declare His glory to the world," is Israel's proclamation to the Nations: I am His and He is mine. This exclusive relation between Israel and God is based on love. And Aqiba's theological insistence on love is illuminated by his teachings about ideal relationships between husbands and wives."

Goldin selects several pericopae from a variety of documents and tries to weave them into a consistent doctrine of love. Specifically, he asserts (p. 52) that ". . . a recognition of the emphasis by Aqiba on the seriousness of love—on what I would like to call the literalness of love—between husband and wife, helps restore for us the force and freshness of his well-known sayings about transcendent love. The word is still ^{ɔ}hb, ^{ɔ}hbh, but it has risen to a plane where it is completely transfigured, spiritualized, where only heart and soul are embraced; where the direction is from desire to zeal, from receiving to surrendering to the other's needs, the other's demands." To achieve a credible "profile" of Aqiba as the teacher of love, Goldin must demonstrate the correlation between Aqiba's teachings about the husband-wife relationship and the relationship of God to Israel. If his correlation does not stand, neither does his description. The entire exercise, therefore, depends on the quality of Goldin's exegeses.

The pericopae which in Goldin's view reveal Aqiba's emphasis on the "literalness of love between husband and wife" are as follows:
1. Avot de Rabbi Natan A, ed., Schechter, p. 83. Aqiba holds that a man who marries a woman unsuited for him transgresses five negative commandments: *Thou shalt not take vengeance* (Lev. 19:19); *Nor bear any grudge* (*ibid.*); *Thou shalt not hate thy brother in thy heart* (Lev. 19:17); *But thou shalt love thy neighbor as thyself* (Lev. 19:18); *That thy brother may live with thee* (Lev. 25:36). If he hates her, he desires her death, and thus neglects the commandment to be fruitful and multiply.
Whatever this passage may mean, it hardly supports Goldin's case because its attribution is

inconsistent. Tosefta Soṭah 5:13 (ed. Lieberman, p. 108, ls. 77-84) assigns the lemma to Meir. Goldin notes this fact (p. 45, note 52), but utterly ignores its implications.

2. Mishnah Giṭṭin 9:10. Aqiba holds, apparently extending a Hillelite rule, that a man may divorce his wife if he finds another woman more attractive than she.

Goldin argues (p. 49) that Aqiba's lemma suggests divorce and "ignores the strategem of marrying an additional wife . . . because he insists . . . that in a marriage, first, the relationship must be based on love, and, second, that love is an exclusive relationship. . . ." But the pericope itself neither requires nor encourages divorce; it simply states the grounds on which it is permissible. Moreover, it is utterly silent on the question of polygamy. It therefore is difficult to see how the language of the pericope itself calls forth Goldin's rather elaborate interpretation. Without the supposition that Aqiba's lemma here is an explicit rejection of polygamy, however, Goldin's exegesis about love appears extraneous, if not irrelevant, to the plain sense of the ruling.

3. b. Pesaḥim 112a. Aqiba says that the pot in which your fellow did his cooking is not for you to cook in. The anonymous *gemara* takes this to mean that one should not marry a divorcee whose former husband still lives, because then there will be "four in bed." It extends the saying to marriage to a widow. Goldin writes (p. 50), "When Aqiba talks about love in passages like this, there is nothing ambiguous about his emphasis. . . ." But the pericope itself does not mention love, and its culinary metaphor does not necessarily connote it. More important, the lemma attributed to Aqiba and the *gemara*'s interpretation of it are not necessarily the same thing. Goldin nonetheless ascribes both to Aqiba himself.

4. Sifra, ed., Weiss, 97c/b. Shabbat 64b. Aqiba holds that during her period of impurity a woman may adorn herself as usual, lest she appear unattractive to her husband and he divorce her.

5. Mishnah Nazir 4:5. Aqiba holds that if a wife's Nazirite vow must be repeated in cleanness, her husband may annul it, claiming that he "cannot stand a squalid wife."

Of these two pericopae Goldin writes (p. 52), "All this from the man who ruled that if the husband found another woman who pleased him more, he might divorce his wife! But there is no paradox or inconsistency here, for Aqiba sensed that once a man ceased to *love* his wife, to desire her, it was no longer a marriage of true minds. Hence, his strong objections to what is corrosive of love." Goldin's understanding of these last two passages clearly derives from his reading of 2; but here, as there, nothing in the language of the pericopae themselves suggests his exegesis.

Of the five passages Goldin lists, two are irrelevant (1, 3) to his argument. The other three treat the problem of a wife who is physically unattractive to her husband. The rules they contain neither suggest Goldin's notion of the "literalness of love between husband and wife," nor do they require it to be understood. It therefore appears that Goldin's "profile" of Aqiba is not derived from the texts, but is imposed upon them, necessitated by his assumption that passages attributed to Aqiba, no matter where they appear, can be removed from their documentary contexts and made to offer reliable testimony about a single mind.

[54]S. C. Humphreys, *art. cit.,* p. 91.

[55]Edward Shils, *Center and Periphery: Essays in Macrosociology,* Chicago 1975, p. 186.

[56]*Ibid.*

[57]Cf. the phenomenon described by Hippolyte Delehaye, *The Legends of the Saints,* Donald Attwater, trans., New York, 1962, p. 19ff.

[58]Thanks are due to my teacher Jacob Neusner, Brown University, for encouraging the undertaking of this project, for his help as the work progressed, and for his willingness to read and comment on the typescript. Professor Gary G. Porton, University of Illinois, discussed many of these matters with me in detail and thereby prevented errors of both fact and reasoning. His help is acknowledged with gratitude. Colleagues at the University of Rochester kindly took time to

discuss problems only peripherally related to their own fields, and they considerably broadened my perspective. Gratitude is owed to Professors Barbara I. Sobieszek, Dean A. Miller, Harmon R. Holcomb, Thomas Spence Smith, Donald R. Kelley and Fitz John Porter Poole. An earlier, somewhat abbreviated version of this paper was read at the Second Annual Max Richter Conversation, Brown University, July 26, 1976. Its present form is enriched by the comments of other participants in the conversation, particularly Professors Morton Smith, Columbia University, Geza Vermes, University of Oxford, Jonathan Z. Smith, University of Chicago, Jakob J. Petuchowski, Hebrew Union College-Jewish Institute of Religion, David Weiss-Halivni, Jewish Theological Seminary, Baruch M. Bokser, University of California (Berkeley), and Richard S. Sarason, Brown University. Responsibility for the paper's deficiencies is mine.

V

On the Use of Method in the Modern Study of Jewish Liturgy

RICHARD S. SARASON

BROWN UNIVERSITY

The task of modern critical scholarship often has been likened to solving a jigsaw puzzle. The scholar must assemble and examine the manifold individual data which are deemed relevant to a particular field of inquiry and then attempt to "put all of the pieces together" into a coherent and intelligible whole. Although the final construction usually is put forth with a claim to objective validity, there are critical points in the process where subjective elements inevitably are present. Data frequently are subject to a variety of interpretations. But more crucial to the scholarly enterprise is the fact that the "intelligibility principle," the *logos*, or general schema which is employed to draw all of the data together, always is the mental construct of a particular person, the scholar, who lives and thinks in a particular social and intellectual milieu. Our claims to objective, scientific knowledge always are historically and subjectively conditioned—especially in the social sciences and the humanities, where the human mind itself is both the subject and the object of inquiry.

In the fields of history and literary history the problem is further complicated by considerable gaps in the data as the scholar proceeds further and further into the past. The element of subjectivity thereby is increased, since these gaps usually will be filled in with hypothetical constructions which extrapolate on the basis of the surviving data. It is clear, then, that the question of *methodology* is of absolute, fundamental importance to scholarly endeavor. By method we mean the configuration of basic axioms, presuppositions, criteria for deduction and inference, etc., according to which the scholar combines, juxtaposes, and otherwise manipulates the data and by which he or she seeks to arrive at a coherent picture of the whole. In the area of historical studies we also mean the model of development according to which the data are related sequentially. While it undoubtedly is true that "a method is to be judged by its results,"[1] we nevertheless must not lose sight of the converse, that the results of any scholarly inquiry are only so good as the basic assumptions and types of inference with and upon which they are constructed. A method, then, also must be judged by the plausibility of its assumptions and by their applicability to the data under examination. We must ask whether the method flows from the data themselves and is sufficiently responsive to adjustment and correction or whether it is imposed onto the data and forces them into a pre-conceived mold. The final court of appeal for any method is the nature of the data in question.

An excellent case in point is the modern study of Jewish liturgy, not yet 150 years old, to which the methods of classical philology were transferred at the outset without prior determination of the extent of their applicability. For a century, the so-called "historical-philological approach" was applied with increasing rigor, while basic methodological questions were left unasked.[2] There are historical reasons for this fact, the most prominent being the pioneering nature of the *Wissenschaft des Judenthums*, which took time to establish itself and to mature to the point at which meta-historical and methodological issues became matters of primary concern. But Christian biblical scholarship also did not begin to construct new methods for dealing with similar materials (such as that of literary form-criticism) until the turn of the century.[3]

Only in 1939 was the applicability of the historical-philological method to Jewish liturgical materials seriously questioned by Arthur Spanier,[4] who concluded that the basic assumption of an *"Archetypus,"* an *Urtext* for each of the statutory prayers, was not valid, and that consequently the philological approach of "peeling off the layers" in order to arrive at the "original kernel" could tell us nothing about the earliest forms of the prayers. Spanier previously had made a few preliminary attempts at applying a modified type of form-criticism to the materials,[5] and now summed up:

> Was aber die historisch-philologische Erforschung des Gebetes für die Zeit vor 200 zu
> leisten vermag, kann grundsätzlich nur der Formen- und Motivgeschichte gelten.[6]

Spanier was unable to expand on his important methodological insights; he perished in Bergen-Belsen in 1944. In the meantime, philological research in Jewish liturgy proceeded on apace, best exemplified as late as 1960 by Daniel Goldschmidt's research on the Passover *Haggadah*.[7] Only in 1960 was Spanier's line of criticism taken up again, this time to be developed more forcefully, by Joseph Heinemann in a review of Goldschmidt's *Haggadah*.[8] Later, in his doctoral dissertation, Heinemann for the first time attempted systematically to apply the method of form-criticism to the entire range of Jewish liturgy. The dissertation, *Hatefillah bitequfat hatanna꜄im weha-꜄amora꜄im: Tibah udefuseha (Prayer in the Tannaitic and Amoraic Periods: Its Nature and Form-Patterns)*, was first published in 1964 and appeared in English in 1977. In it, Heinemann convincingly argues against the assumption of an *Urtext* on the grounds that we are not dealing here with "literary" texts in the full sense of the word, but rather with an oral, folk literature, and he criticizes several other standard operating procedures of classical philology: that the simplest version always is the earliest, that the development always proceeds in a simple, "evolutionary" fashion from simplicity to complexity, etc.[9]

In the following pages we shall present a general overview of the history of Jewish liturgical studies from Zunz to Heinemann, paying particular attention to the methodological bases upon which the various scholarly superstructures have been erected and according to which they frequently can be called into question. Moreover, since the critical study of post-Biblical Jewish literature always has drawn its basic methodological approaches and historical models from the surrounding world of classical scholarship, particularly from the fields of Old and New Testament studies, we also examine the origins of the form-critical approach and its broader significance for the study of folk-literatures, which initially were not "literary" creations in the full sense of the term. We therefore shall look at several pioneering efforts in form-criticism which had a direct bearing on the application of the method to the field of Jewish liturgy. Finally, we shall suggest a number of problems in the study of Jewish liturgy which remain unresolved. The studies which follow are not intended to be exhaustive; they merely aim to point to certain general methodological traits and problems which characterize the work of each of the scholars in question.

I. HISTORICAL-PHILOLOGICAL STUDIES

Zunz

Leopold Zunz (1794–1886), the father of the *Wissenschaft des Judenthums*, also was the founder of the modern study of Jewish liturgy.[10] Zunz published his monumental work, *Die gottesdienstlichen Vorträge der Juden*, in 1832. In the twenty-first chapter, entitled, "The Later Development of the Haggadah," in the context of a broader discussion on the use of aggadic materials in liturgical poetry *(piyyuṭim)*, Zunz also deals with the major rubrics of the statutory prayers *(Stammgebete)*—the *šema^c* and the *tefillah*.

Zunz was the first scholar to stress the gradual, evolutionary development of the *siddur* and of all of the individual prayers contained therein. But his interest in demonstrating historical development in the liturgy, as well as in the Jewish sermon, was not purely scholarly. In 1832, Zunz was still partial to the cause of liturgical reform. By demonstrating both the antiquity of the *šema^c* and the *tefillah* as well as the relative newness of the *piyyuṭ*[11] and by showing that even these oldest elements of the liturgy developed gradually over time, Zunz sought to justify both the elimination of *piyyuṭim* from the worship service and the addition to it of new, modern prayers.[12] He also advocated the "restoration of the *pristine* and the *legitimate* in place of the existing and decaying elements"[13] (italics mine) of the service. The results of Zunz's research eventually were used by others as a justification for abbreviating the statutory prayers.[14] The congruence between scientific liturgical studies and a penchant for practical liturgical reform also is evident in the works of Elbogen and Kohler, as we shall see.

Since Zunz's analysis of the statutory prayers became paradigmatic for all subsequent studies down to the time of Heinemann, it is well to consider his methodological axioms and procedures in some detail. We first should realize that what Zunz intended in the concept of *Wissenschaft des Judentums* was precisely the application of the methods of classical philology, as he had learned them at the University of Berlin from his teachers Friedrich August Wolf and August Boeckh, to the areas of classical and later rabbinic literature.[15] "In 1795 Wolf's *Prologomena to Homer*, in which he proved that Homer's work was a composite of several authors, had launched the critical scholarship of the nineteenth century."[16] This clearly became Zunz's model in the field of Rabbinica.

Since the philological method was the embodiment of German literary scholarship of the time, Zunz naturally assumed that it could be applied with equal validity to Jewish liturgical texts. Other factors also gave this assumption some credence. Zunz had access to a large number of manuscripts containing the prayer texts for the various rites. Comparing the different manuscripts, he noticed wide divergences in custom with regard to the recitation of various *piyyuṭim*. On the other hand, he noted the basic similarity in the wording of the statutory prayers in all of the European rites. Those differences which did exist seemingly could be explained as variations on, and additions to, a single *Urtext* which lay at the base of all of the rites. Thus, those elements and actual phrases common to all the rites necessarily must be of higher antiquity than those which vary among the rites, and the latter consequently have to be viewed as later additions to the "basic" text. This being the case, it follows that by an exact comparison of the variations in wording among all of the rites, one could reconstruct the "original," or *Urtext*, in its pristine form.

This is in fact what Zunz does in the case of the three benedictions surrounding the *šema^c* in the morning. He assumes, on the basis of a simple evolutionary model of liturgical development, that the original texts must have been much simpler than those which are presently recited,[17] and accordingly cuts them down to size. Other criteria[18] which Zunz uses to "peel away the layers" basically are stylistic: the use of rhyme or alphabetical acrostic (which he views as later artifices), the presence of messianic petitions (which later were opposed by the *ge^{ɔ}onim*), the presence of whole phrases which recur in other prayers as well (thus the passage in the third benediction which begins, *^{c}ezrat ^{ɔ}abotenu*, and contains phrases which recur in *nišmat*, cannot have been original).[19] The *qeduššah deyoṣer* is also to be viewed as an addition to the text, albeit an early one. Other deletions are made which seem arbitrary and only could be based on the desire to reduce the text to a minimal number of words in accordance with the assumption of simplicity. Thus, Zunz arrives, for example, at a *yoṣer* benediction which contains only 45 words![20] Such a brief form of this benediction is in fact found in Saᶜadya's *Siddur*, where it is designated for private recitation (when the *qeduššah* was not be be recited),[21] although the existence of the *Siddur* in manuscript was not known to Zunz. Subsequent scholars have pointed to this version as validation of Zunz's hypothesis.[22] In reconstructing the "original text" of the *šemaᶜ* benedictions, Zunz set a pattern from which only Heinemann tried to break away.

Zunz's analysis of the *tefillah* also is the prototype of later investigations. He notes that the Eighteen Benedictions recited on weekdays do not form a monolithic entity and did not all come into being at the same time. While he gives some credence to the Talmudic dictum which ascribes the institution of the daily prayers to the Men of the Great Assembly (b. Ber. 33a), Zunz nonetheless sees the *tefillah* as having been created over a span of five or six separate periods.[23] We shall designate the particular historical model which Zunz employs as a sequential, monolinear one, a temporal continuum in which the various developments follow each other in time in a cumulative fashion, rather than occurring simultaneously. Such a model presupposes that changes and additions are instituted from above in an orderly fashion at a certain point in time and that textual variations can best be explained sequentially. This is the opposite of Heinemann's model which might be labeled, "simultaneous, multilinear," in which numerous variations can exist simultaneously while many strands ultimately may converge together. Zunz's model is one of organic development; it is his conviction that literary analysis can separate the earlier from the later elements. Thus, the Eighteen Benedictions can be separated into four *typological* strata, each of which must correspond, according to Zunz's schema, with a different *chronological* stratum.

The first stratum consists of the three opening and three concluding benedictions—the "framework" into which the petitionary prayers are placed. Zunz dates this stratum as early, on the linguistic ground that it contains late biblical idioms. But a closer look at the language of Jewish liturgy in general reveals an *overall* tendency to make use of biblical idioms and citations. Consequently, Zunz's criterion disappears. Zunz next tries to establish the possible historical settings in which such benedictions first could have been recited. This came to be a very common procedure among scholars, but it must be applied with great caution. Zunz suggests, for example, that the prayer for the messianic "Redeemer" in the first benediction is appropriate to the Seleucid period—although a prayer for redemption certainly could be characteristic of *any* period in Jewish history, and such prayer-insertions were the subject of great controversy as late as the Geonic period.[24] There is no firm basis on which this petition can be assigned to such an early period. Similarly,

Zunz concludes that the language of these benedictions is appropriate to the time of Simon the Just.[25] But since we have no written records from the time of Simon the Just and are not even certain in our knowledge of who this Simon was and when he lived, Zunz's determination must be viewed as completely arbitrary. As for Zunz's general characterization of this stratum, it might be objected (as Elbogen[26] later was to object) that the weekday *tefillah* would not then have functioned from the outset as a petitionary prayer.

The second stratum is that of the personal petitions, which fits nicely into Zunz's "organic" scheme, since it would be "natural" for the worshippers to insert private petitions. These apparently were added "gradually," not at one time. Zunz was the first to point out that the seventh benediction, *go'el yiśra'el*, a plea for national redemption, is thematically inappropriate to its context, and he concludes that it probably was added "during some period of national emergency, perhaps at the time of Antiochus Epiphanes or of Pompey [!]," when there were as yet only *twelve* benedictions in the *tefillah*.[27]

Zunz suggests that the next stratum, the national petitions, was added either immediately preceding or immediately following the destruction of the Second Temple. Again we note the attempt, according to the sequential, monolinear model, to pinpoint the events which "caused" the insertion of each benediction or series of benedictions. It was at this time as well that the "additional phrase" which asks for the restoration of the sacrificial cult was "added" to the seventeenth, or *'abodah*, benediction.[28] The total number of benedictions now reached eighteen.

The final step was the addition of the nineteenth benediction, *birkat ha-minnim*, at Yavneh. Zunz here follows the explanation of b. Ber. 28b. This account seemed plausible at the time since Zunz did not have at his disposal any of the Palestinian-Egyptian texts of the Cairo Genizah in which *birkat ha-minnim* is included among the eighteen, while the separate prayer for the restoration of the Davidic dynasty is lacking.

There are a number of problems with this approach. On the one hand, it fails to account for the special pre-eminence of the number "eighteen," which is referred to by the Mishnah in a fixed fashion (M. Ber. 4:3, *et passim*). Using a sequential monolinear model, there really is no reason that nineteen should not be preferred to eighteen, or that twelve should not have been mentioned as well. Furthermore, although Zunz's analysis is typologically accurate, the identification of typology with chronology seems somewhat arbitrary. Zunz's only claim for the antiquity of the first stratum which has some validity, because it relates to an actual observation, is that the six "framework" benedictions are recited on *all* liturgical occasions while the intermediate unit varies, depending on the occasion. The basic assumption here is that "primitive elements" would tend to maintain their position and function with greater tenacity. This does not *prove*, however, that the *tefillah* originally consisted of these six benedictions exclusively.[29]

On the other hand, there is no reason to affirm the antiquity of the private petitions over the national petitions. The order in which they are recited today is not conclusive. Only on the assumption that personal petitions are psychologically more primary could this assertion be made, but it seems more valid for the individualistic ethos of the nineteenth and twentieth centuries than for Palestinian Jewry of the first century and earlier. This is not to espouse the opposite view that the "collective" necessarily precedes the "individual"[30] but merely to caution that we have no firm basis in the data for making such an assertion and to propose that both types of petitions may be of equal antiquity.

It is significant that Zunz does not attempt to reconstruct the *Urtext* of the *tefillah*. In fact, he notes that "for a long time there were doubts and divergent customs with regard to the wording of the benedictions."[31] Unlike his treatment of the *šema*^{c}, then, Zunz is ambiguous with regard to the question of whether or not there ever had been an "original" text of the *tefillah*. We shall note that this ambiguity is perpetuated in the work of Zunz's successors, especially Elbogen.[32]

In addition to his analysis of the *šema*^{c} and the Eighteen Benedictions, Zunz provides a relative chronology for many other prayers and liturgical elements based on citations in the Talmudic and Geonic literature. The latter provide attestations to the existence of particular prayers in certain periods and are relatively reliable indexes (occasionally a prayer will be older than its first citation in the literature, but the burden of proof will always be on the scholar to provide corroborating evidence).[33] Zunz draws no distinction, however, between the citation of a prayer and its exact *wording*.[34]

Zunz's subsequent works in the liturgical field were devoted to a detailed comparative examination of the later rites and particularly of the *piyyuṭim* which they contain. By the mid-1840's, Zunz had broken with the Reformers, and "he now set himself, in a series of weighty works, to demonstrate to the Reformers, the importance of Hebrew liturgy and *piyyuṭ*."[35] But more fundamentally, his decision to examine the *piyyuṭim* and the medieval European rites grew out of his historical model, according to which *diversity* in the liturgy is relatively *late* and was brought about primarily by the geographical dispersion of the Jews.[36] It is difficult to speculate as to how Zunz would have altered his model had he had at his disposal the vast amount of material discovered by Solomon Schechter in the Genizah of the synagogue in old Cairo (Fostat) in 1896, among which are found liturgical fragments of a distinct Palestinian character whose wordings in many cases differ sufficiently from those of the European rites to seriously call into question the applicability of the classical philological method. But if we are to judge from the work of his successors, the Palestinian fragments probably would not have called forth a radical change of method.

If we have devoted an inordinate number of words to Zunz, this is only because he stands at the very beginning of the modern study of Jewish liturgy and because it was he who fixed the parameters of research in this field, as in

so many others, establishing as well the basic methodological approach to the
material. In all that follows we shall detect the influence of Leopold Zunz.

Luzzatto

The importance of the liturgical work of Samuel David Luzzatto (1800-
1865), an Italian Jewish sage and a younger contemporary of Zunz, lies
primarily in the Introduction he wrote to accompany the 1856 Leghorn
edition of the Italian *Maḥzor*.[37] Luzzatto, like Zunz, saw the distinction
between the various rites to consist in their use of *piyyuṭim*,[38] and he therefore
devoted the bulk of his composition to a description of the *piyyuṭim* in the
Italian rite. His method, of course, was philological, and he had at his disposal
a number of manuscripts and early printed editions of the *Maḥzor*. But even
Heinemann does not deny the validity of the philological method in its
application to *piyyuṭim*, which *are* literary, artistic creations in the full sense
of the word and were all composed by *individuals*, the great majority of whom
are known to us by name.

What interests us here is the beginning of Luzzatto's Introduction, in
which he gives a brief historical account of the development of the statutory
prayers, leading up to the origin of *piyyuṭim* as a genre. Like Zunz, Luzzatto
holds to an authoritarian model of the origin of the prayers themselves: they
all were instituted from above by the rabbis.[39] Nonetheless, according to
Luzzatto, the rabbis did not fix the *wording* of the prayers, only their content,
order, and number.[40] The precise wording was left up to each individual and
Prayer Leader to improvise for himself. Luzzatto thus challenges the
assumption of an *Urtext*. He supports his claim not only by noting, as did
Zunz, the various Tannaitic formulations which differ from those of the later
European rites (". . . and had it been the ruling of our ancient Sages of
blessed memory that we were to recite the Eighteen Benedictions in a standard
wording without any variations, how could it be that the wording of the
prayers which has been common among the Jews for many generations differs
from the wording of the Tannaitic authors of the *Sifre debe Rab*?"),[41] but also
by pointing to the various formulations which are singled out in Talmudic
literature as being improper (". . . but had the wording actually been fixed,
how could it have occurred to [the Sages] that someone would use these
expressions in his prayer, which are not to be found in the wording which has
come down to us?").[42] Both of these arguments are taken up again by
Heinemann[43] and are developed to the extent that they must be viewed as
decisive.

Luzzatto points to the Saboraic period (approximately 500-700) as the
crucial turning point in the fixing of the wording of the prayers. The
Saboraim, who committed the Talmud to writing, also wrote down the
prayers and fixed their wording: "From this point on, the wording of the
prayers remained fixed, and the Prayer Leaders could no longer elaborate as

they saw fit," although the ruling did not completely succeed "as is evident from the variations in wording which still persist in the different rites."[44] Luzzatto,then, still must account for the prevailing variations in wording.

But, although we have no written prayer texts until Geonic times, Luzzatto is compelled for another reason to date standardization from the Saboraic period. This reason is his theory that the *piyyuṭ* could only have come into being *after* the wording of the statutory prayers had been fixed.[45] This issue is still being debated by scholars of Hebrew liturgical poetry,[46] but we now know that the *piyyuṭ* originated at a much earlier date than either Zunz or Luzzatto had thought, and we incline more toward the view that this development did *not* require the previous fixing of the wording of the statutory prayers.

Since Luzzatto did not analyze the statutory prayers themselves, it is difficult to conceive how he would have dealt with them. If it is possible, however, to extrapolate from what he did write, we may surmise that he probably would have made use of the philological method (since it was the prevailing scholarly method at the time), but might have added the *caveat* that such analysis can only take us back to the Saboraic period at the earliest, when the wordings were "fixed."[47] At any rate, as regards the *Urtext* assumption, we find in Luzzatto an interesting precursor of Heinemann.

Elbogen

Research in the field of Jewish liturgy more often than not is associated with the name of Ismar Elbogen (1874–1943), who in 1913 published the most comprehensive study of "the Jewish worship service and its historical development" ever written, *Der jüdische Gottesdienst in seiner geschichtlichen Entwicklung,* a work which, some sixty years later, is still basic to the field.[48]

Elbogen, like Zunz in 1832, was committed to the idea of religious reform, and a number of his prejudices come out rather strongly in the historical section of his book.[49] His research also had practical consequences when, in 1929, he served as one of the three editors (along with Caesar Seligmann and Hermann Vogelstein) of the German Liberal *Einheitsgebetbuch.*[50] Thus, in his discussion of the *yoṣer* benediction, which parallels that of Zunz, Elbogen first argues that everything except the "core" is superfluous, artificial, and can be eliminated without any great loss.[51] He then indicates that the Reform version has indeed returned to the pure, "brief" wording as it is found in Saᶜadya's *siddur.*[52]

Much of the material on the statutory prayers in *Gottesdienst* actually derives from a number of earlier works by Elbogen, most notably his "Geschichte des Achtzehngebets" (published in MGWJ, XLVI [1902]), and "Studies in the Jewish Liturgy" (published in JQR [O.S.], XVIII-XIX [1906-7]), and it is to the latter that we first direct our attention.

In "Studies," Elbogen attempts to account for the origin and development of the *šema^c* and the *tefillah*. Although he already has a substantial amount of Genizah material at his disposal, he retains the philological approach of Zunz, and his conclusions consequently are merely a refinement of those set down by Zunz. Whereas the latter simply subjected the *šema^c* and its benedictions to a linguistic analysis, Elbogen attempts to show the gradual crystallization of the entire unit. He gives what might be called a "psychological" history of the *šema^c*, showing how a natural need was felt at each stage to add another unit. The historical model employed is that of evolution from simplicity to complexity.[53] There is a certain amount of support in the data themselves for particular assertions (that the last of the three biblical paragraphs, for example, might not originally have been part of the unit), but others are purely speculative and depend primarily on the presupposition of absolute original simplicity. Thus, as regards the first two biblical paragraphs of the *šema^c*: "As far back as our information reaches they are quoted together . . . [but] it is *improbable* that both sections found their way into the service at the same time" (Italics mine.);[54] here it is the *model* which determines the probability or improbability. So, too, with regard to the eventual motivation for adding the surrounding benedictions: "The bare recital of a profession of faith is too meagre to make up, for any length of time, the only element of a congregational service";[55] here we detect the assumption that at one time there had been an extremely simple congregational service consisting solely of the recitation of the three biblical paragraphs. Although the early synagogue services indisputably were simpler at the outset than they subsequently became, there is a methodological danger in reductionism, which itself is the outgrowth of the philological approach.

Another of Elbogen's assumptions, which is articulated in his "Studies" and later recurs in *Gottesdienst*, is that "the liturgy was, in its earliest period, quite general in its contents and adaptable to every religious occasion at will, and it was only later that it became more specified . . . the general elements are the older, to which the more specific were attached."[56] This assumption also derives from the philological method and the historical model which presupposes a development from simplicity (generality) to complexity (specification).

As was noted earlier,[57] Elbogen accepts Zunz's philological analysis of the *yoṣer* benediction and finds confirmation for this hypothesis in the short version found in Sa^{c}adya's *siddur*. Elbogen's complete acceptance of the presuppositions of the philological method is demonstrated in his treatment of this short version. At first glance it appears to be a "contraction" (rather than an independent alternate version), "but an analogous case of the contraction of an already existing long prayer is not known, and moreover, even if the Kedusha were not to be said, it was still not necessary to dispense with the whole of the richly worded section *ha-me^{ɔ}ir la^{ɔ}areṣ*."[58] Within this frame of reference, Elbogen can only conclude that this text is primary, particularly as it agrees more or less with a number of Palestinian texts in various Genizah fragments. The same conclusions are taken over into *Gottesdienst* almost without alteration. Yet, in the historical section, Elbogen asserts that as late as the Amoraic period none of the benedictions which surround the *šema*ᶜ had received a fixed wording![59] Thus a certain tension arises between the results attained by the philological examination of an actual prayer text and the historical conclusions which are arrived at by examining the Talmudic sources themselves. This tension becomes more evident when we turn to Elbogen's analysis of the *tefillah*.

In its broad outlines, this analysis is an expansion and refinement of the schema proposed by Zunz; Elbogen takes Zunz's major strata and further subdivides them. Thus, in the first stratum, or "framework" benedictions, the last three are singled out as having belonged originally to the Temple service. The second stratum, or "private petitions," can be divided into petitions for material and spiritual welfare. Since the former are more "instinctive," they are deemed to be primary, while the latter reflect the interests of "those circles which created the ᶜ*amidah*."[60] The first distinction is valid because it has a firm basis in the sources themselves, which Elbogen quotes. The second distinction may be questioned because it lacks such a basis. Elbogen argues, on functional grounds, that Zunz's first stratum never could have existed independently as the *tefillah*,[61] but the assumption of simplicity leads him to propose instead that the six "general" and "private" petitions, as well as the prayer for Jerusalem (which for some reason is not considered here to be a "national" petition!), originally belonged to the earliest stratum and were recited together in *one* intermediate petitionary prayer with a single eulogy at its conclusion. The *habinenu* prayer is cited as proof, but it is inconclusive. This earliest stratum is dated by Elbogen back to pre-Maccabean times, since the traditional ascription of the institution of the *tefillah* to the Men of the Great Assembly (b. Ber. 33a) seems to indicate its great antiquity.

Elbogen follows Zunz's chronological distinction between "personal" and "national" petitions, arguing for the primacy of the former since they are both more "instinctive" and more "general" in content.[62] His suggestion that the national petitions should be viewed as a unified messianic group (and particularly, on the basis of certain versions, that the prayer for the "Judges" was originally a prayer for the speedy coming of the Divine Judgment) is an intriguing hypothesis and has won general acceptance among scholars.[63] While Zunz assigned the introduction of this stratum to the period before or after the destruction of the Temple, Elbogen dates it back to the time of the Maccabean Revolt. Both of these datings are equally speculative. Elbogen connects the problematic *goʾel yiśraʾel* benediction with the ritual for fast-days, as have a number of scholars after him,[64] and thereby explains its introduction into the daily liturgy. In general, he regards the fast-day ritual and the *maᶜamad* service to have been the precursors of the *tefillah*.

Zunz had assumed the historicity of the Babylonian Amoraic account (in b. Ber. 28b) of the origin of the nineteenth benediction. Elbogen, who now had

Genizah fragments of a Palestinian-type ͨamidah at his disposal, correctly concluded that the Babylonian nineteenth benediction was not *birkat ha-minnim*, but rather the benediction for the restoration of the Davidic dynasty. Nonetheless, he still maintained the historicity of the Talmudic explanation and thereby came to assert that *birkat ha-minnim* was the *eighteenth* benediction to be "instituted," and that only *seventeen* benedictions were recited prior to the time of Rabban Gamaliel II.[65] He concluded as well that the "David" benediction was composed in Babylonia and found the "rationale" for this novel institution in the growing independence of Babylonian Jewry from Palestinian authority; the benediction contains a hidden "polemic" supporting the Exilarchate. In general we should be wary of such explanations—the more "hidden" and esoteric the agenda, the less is the likelihood that it actually inheres in the data and is not merely being imposed onto them. In this particular case, there is good evidence in Tos. Ber. 3:25 that the benediction in question (though not necessarily its formulation) was Palestinian in origin.[66] Elbogen himself cites this passage,[67] without fully exploring its implications. It seems that the culprit here is his authoritarian, sequential historical model, which structurally precludes certain options in interpretation.

We recall having encountered a certain tension in Zunz's analysis of the *tefillah* with regard to the question of an *Urtext*. This same tension is present and magnified in Elbogen. In his 1906 "Studies," Elbogen suggests that the framework benedictions were fixed at an early stage while the intermediate petitions originally "could make no claim in the popular estimate to immutability or inviolability, to any *fixed wording* or determined sequence."[68] (Italics mine.) In addition, "too much emphasis cannot be laid upon the saying of R. David Abudraham, that, namely, there cannot be the slightest question of a final and decisive redaction of the text of the Tefillah."[69] Thus Elbogen accounts for the numerous variations in the late European rites as well as for the original variety before the editing at Yavneh. He also has reservations about the "original" poetic version of the *tefillah* purportedly "discovered" through philological reconstruction by Joseph Dérenbourg and Gustav Dalman, warning against "too elaborate pedantry in the treatment of an old prayer, especially as it did not take its rise at any one particular time and was never definitely edited."[70]

> As for the archetype of the Tefilla, we are still very far from possessing it in this old text. . . . It is nevertheless quite impossible to reconstruct the original text for several passages. The great advantage gained by having so many varying texts, is the insight they afford us into the several intermediate stages of development through which the growth and elaboration of the Tefilla passed.[71]

In these last remarks, Elbogen affirms the validity of the application of philological analysis to the various versions of the *tefillah* and would also seem to assert that there *was* in fact an *Urtext* of the *tefillah*, although we may not in all cases be able to *recover* it.[72]

In his 1913 *Gottesdienst*, Elbogen has reversed this earlier opinion and now asserts categorically that no such *Urtext* ever existed and cannot possibly be reconstructed.[73] Nonetheless, he continues to perform philological operations on texts and frequently reduces them to their "simplest" or "original" form.[74] Moreover, none of the other philological assumptions are challenged. Thus a common formulation in all of the rites indicates antiquity,[75] while variation is a sign of late orgin;[76] the simpler form is the older form,[77] and variation *per se* demands an explanation.[78] The historical section of *Gottesdienst* begins by positing a conception of historical development in which the original "seed" of the liturgy gradually is encapsulated in layers of "rind."[79] This simile unquestionably derives from Elbogen's philological orientation, for if the original "seed" has been preserved intact, it certainly must be recoverable by "peeling off" the outer layers.

If, then, we note a certain degree of inner tension and contradiction between Elbogen's general assertion that no *Urtext* had ever existed (at least so far as the *tefillah* is concerned) and his specific statements about specific prayer texts, we must conclude once again that the origin of the inconsistencies lies in the method itself. The parameters of the philological method are such that all of its operations imply a basic primary text. We thus arrive at the paradoxical situation in which the scholar to some extent has been imprisoned by his own methodology.

Kohler

Occasionally we find that a scholar who otherwise proceeds according to the assumptions of the philological method will modify or even oppose those types of conclusions which we have come to regard as typical, on the basis of his adherence to an additional set of assumptions. Usually these latter are tied to a particular (and sometimes idiosyncratic) historical thesis. Such a scholar was Kaufman Kohler (1843-1926), whose fame rests primarily on his work as a theologian and as an eloquent spokesman for classical Reform Judaism. Kohler's theological writings are thoroughly tinged with apologetics. He stresses the relationship between Judaism and Christianity as that of "mother" to "daughter"[80] and calls for wider cooperation and understanding between the two religions in the optimistic spirit of the times:

> . . . For are they not branches of the same tree of life? Have they not, each in [its] own way, a common providential task to accomplish and a common historical goal in view? And since the great Jewish thinkers of the Middle Ages, such as Maimonides and Judah Halevi, had the vision and the courage to declare Christianity and Mohammedanism to have been selected by divine Providence as agencies to lead mankind ever nearer to the prophetic goal of one God and one humanity, all the more

does it behoove us today, with our larger historic view of the past and our wider outlook into the future, to bring the relationship and kinship of Synagogue and Church to greater recognition.[81]

Kohler attempts to ground this theological and apologetic position historically by laying heavy emphasis upon the common "origins of the Synagogue and the Church" in the ethos of the hassidim hariᵓšonim, "the pious ones of antiquity," whom he links up with the authors of the biblical Psalms[82] and, ultimately, with the Essenes,[83] from whose midst (according to Kohler) sprang up John the Baptist,[84] Jesus,[85] and most of the early Palestinian Judeo-Christians.[86] The identity of these hassidim and their relationship to the Pharisees is never quite made clear by Kohler.[87] The entire theory, as Enelow points out,[88] was soundly criticized by both Dérenbourg and Geiger "as an attempt to explain the unknown by something equally unknown and obscure."

When we turn to Kohler's analysis of the liturgy, particularly of the "origin and development" of the šemaᶜ and the tefillah, we note the pervasive influence of his "Essene" historical theory. This influence is manifest primarily in two areas—first, with relation to Kohler's account of the genesis of the various prayer structures and their components, and second, in his assertion that certain early Christian liturgical texts can shed light on the ancient Jewish liturgy, since both sprang from a common origin.

The šemaᶜ and its benedictions, for example, are held by Kohler to have been instituted by the hassidim as a protest against Persian dualism [!] and originally had been recited at sunrise "neither in the Temple nor in the Synagogue but under the free heaven and before the very eyes of the surrounding Mazdean priests."[89] The identification of this setting to no small extent is prompted by Josephus' description of Essene sunrise prayers. It is also for this reason that Kohler views the yoṣer benediction as primary.[90] The qeduššah in the yoṣer is characterized as an "enlargement," but it is attributed to the ancient hassidim rather than to the yorde merkabah. Kohler even holds that the response, "Praised be the glorious Name whose Kingdom is forever and ever," is an indication of the Hasidean origin of the prayer, since it "can only be explained by the assumption that the leader of the service pronounced the sacred Name as was done by the priests in the Temple and loud enough to make the assembly respond aloud forthwith, as was done on the Day of Atonement after the high priest's pronunciation of the Name."[91] Kohler rightly notes that this custom is intrinsically connected with the Temple usage,[92] and there certainly is no basis for associating it in addition with a hypothetical sunrise assembly of hassidim!

In his analysis of the tefillah, Kohler further subdivides those strata which previously had been isolated by Zunz and Elbogen, particularly the stratum of the personal petitions. Thus, the prayer for Understanding "was originally offered by the learned who began the weekday's work as Judges called upon to decide questions of the Law . . . [and] was only afterwards made a Congregational prayer when the original purpose was forgotten."[93] The prayers for Repentance, Forgiveness, and Redemption originally belonged to the fast-day liturgy, while the prayers for Healing and Prosperity were taken over from the *ma*ᶜ*amadot* service, etc. Again, the results are purely speculative and occasionally, as in the case of the prayer for Understanding, would seem to be examples of overspecification, i.e., beyond the limits of the extant data. Kohler's approach is not as rigidly cumulative in a chronological sense as that of Zunz and Elbogen. The *tefillah* rather consists of "various groups of prayer which were in the course of time combined, and *not always systematically*."[94] (Italics mine.) Thus, he rejects Elbogen's notion that *birkat ha-minnim* was the eighteenth benediction, added at Yavneh. He also recognizes (on the basis of parallels in Ben Sira and the Palestinian rescension of *habinenu*) the Palestinian origin of the "David" benediction. Yet Kohler has to ignore the evidence of the Genizah fragments in order to conclude that the nineteenth benediction must have been *go*ᵓ*el yiśra*ᵓ*el*, which is in any case problematic.[95] Kohler considers the Temple Psalm in *Ben Sira* 51:12ff., to have been the "original" prototype of the Eighteen Benedictions,[96] but he never reconciles this observation with his theory of the Hasidean origin of the prayers, *outside* of the Temple.

Kohler's theory occasionally brings him to contradict in practice certain assumptions of the philological method. Most notably is this the case with regard to the primacy of the *qeduššah* in the *tefillah*. The Hasidean mystics originally recited the full *qeduššah* while "a more sober form of the Benediction with the elimination of the specific mention of the different classes of angels was preferred for the Congregational prayer."[97] In addition, the Palestinian custom of reciting the *qeduššah* only on Sabbaths and Festivals represents, for Kohler, a curtailment of the original custom. This constitutes a "retrograde" development from complexity to simplicity. Kohler also disagrees with Elbogen's determination that the phrase, "who rememberest the pious deeds of the fathers," etc., must be a later addition, since it is not found in the Palestinian Genizah fragments—a typical philological operation. Rather, this phrase, which expresses the Hasidean doctrine of *zekut* ᵓ*abot*, "the merits of the fathers," must be seen as expressing the "main idea" of the benediction.[98] Once again in the case of the thirteenth benediction, for the *ḥassidim*, the *soferim, et al.*, Kohler concludes that the Palestinian version, which mentions only the *gerim* ("proselytes"), must for some reason have been "mutilated."[99]

The second practical outcome of Kohler's theory, as we noted above, is that early Christian prayers can be used to shed light on Jewish liturgical development. Kohler was the first scholar to insist on the Jewish character of a series of prayers in Chapters 33-38 of the Seventh Book of the *Apostolic Constitutions,* and there is no question that his assertion is basically correct, although we would hesitate to designate these prayers as the "Essene version" of the Seven Benedictions (recited on Sabbaths and Festivals). In structure, order, content, and occasionally phraseology, though not in style or length, these prayers are virtually identical to the Jewish benedictions, and they certainly have been modelled after the latter. Obviously these prayers are of great antiquity, but it is a methodological error to regard them, therefore, as somehow more "authentic" than the extant Hebrew versions and to use them as a standard for measuring the degree to which our texts subsequently have been "altered," as do both Kohler and Spanier.[100] For these ultimately remain Greek-language Judeo-Christian prayers, and we cannot assume that they themselves have not been "altered" beyond the simple Christological interpolations which Kohler points out.

From the fact, for example, that the style of the Christian parallel is hymnic and elaborate, Kohler concludes (as we noted previously) that the original character of the Jewish Eighteen Benedictions also was hymnic and relatively elaborate. The simple Palestinian and Yemenite versions, on the other hand, "bear on their face the artificial character and the signs of a very late construction or misconstruction. . . . On the contrary, everything speaks in favor of [a development] from the more elaborate to the simpler rhythmic form *which has its parallels also in the Christian liturgy.*"[101] (Italics mine.) Here, too, we note that it basically is because of his particular historical thesis that Kohler proceeds against the direction of the philological method. His conclusion also is questionable on the grounds that it may be based on a false analogy, and that in matters of style and wording it is hazardous to rely on a Christian parallel to the *tefillah*. On the other hand, the use which Kohler[102] and Heinemann[103] make of the *Apostolic Constitutions* to demonstrate the antiquity of the *qeduššah* in both the *yoṣer* and the *tefillah* (though not necessarily its *originality* in either) is methodologically sound, since it is based on content and not on formulation.

In the work of Kaufmann Kohler, then, we discern the importance of the historical model which is used in conjunction with a particular methodology and note how historical and philological assumptions can influence and modify each other.

Finkelstein

If the philological approach of Zunz was expanded and refined in the works of Elbogen and Kohler, then it inexorably was drawn to its logical conclusion in the liturgical studies of Louis Finkelstein (1895-   ). Although Finkelstein's erudition is considerable, his articles nonetheless raise grave questions of methodological propriety—questions which, in fact, cast doubt on the validity of many of his conclusions. Finkelstein's assumptions frequently are arbitrary, that is, they bear only an external, not an intrinsic, relationship to the data on which they are based. His inferences for the most part proceed from these same unproved assumptions, and when the assumptions are shown to be incorrect, the entire scholarly superstructure collapses. Other flaws of methodology characterize Finkelstein's work: overspecification and overinterpretation, i.e., beyond the limits which the sparsity of data permits; circular reasoning and *ex post facto* rationalizations; hazardously early datings of rabbinic materials. All of these exaggerations, as we shall see, result from a highly *rigid* approach to both the materials under investigation and the historical-philological method by which their "secrets" may be unlocked.

Such characteristic rigidity may be observed in a number of areas. For example, the *Urtext* assumption of classical philology is rigorously applied by Finkelstein to the Eighteen Benedictions[104] and the Grace after meals.[105] While Zunz had reconstructed the "original text" of the *šema*ᶜ benedictions, he never made any such attempt with regard to the *tefillah*. Elbogen, the preponderance of his philological operations notwithstanding, came to the conclusion that such an attempt was fundamentally wrong-headed, since no *Urtext* of the *tefillah* ever existed. Finkelstein, on the other hand, is convinced that if no *Urtext* had previously been reconstructed, then "this is largely due to the fact that scholars have not yet sufficiently availed themselves of the important texts of the Palestinian ritual that have come to light as a result of the discovery of the Genizah."[106] He then proceeds to reconstruct the "original text," basing himself on all of the available materials as well as on a number of his own stylistic presuppositions which, as we shall see, depend solely on his particular dating criteria.

His operational assumptions are set out in full:

> In attempting to establish on the basis of these later forms, the earliest text of the benedictions we must bear in mind that for many centuries the prayers were not written down but transmitted orally. Under these circumstances new material could be added, but changes or omissions were difficult. It is comparatively easy to issue an edict changing the wording of written prayers, and in an age of printing it is a slight matter to prepare a new edition of a prayer book. But when people recited their prayers from memory, they were willing to learn new verses or phrases, but found it difficult to unlearn what they already knew.
>
> It follows that in dealing with various formulae of prayer we must remember that *in general* these rules hold. 1. The old text is retained as a nucleus of the later formula. 2. Where various versions differ, the part that is common to all of them is the more likely to contain the original form. 3. The briefest form is very often the most akin to the original.[107]

Finkelstein here has articulated not only the basic operational assumptions of the philological method, but also their justification in a particular model of historical process which is authoritarian, sequential and monolinear. Original variety can only be accounted for in such a system by assuming broad geographical dispersion[108] or by positing linear development.[109]

It is only on the assumption that the texts of the prayers were originally fixed from above and were not subject to spontaneous "changes and omissions" by individual Prayer Leaders or by the people themselves (which implies a particular socio-psychological model as well) that one validly can attempt to reconstruct an "original text" of a piece which was not composed by a single author. It is precisely this configuration of models, and the assumptions upon which they are based, that is called into question by Heinemann. More than anything else, it is Finkelstein's rigorous application of the *Urtext* assumption which pushed Heinemann to search for a new approach to the materials and to put forth an alternative historical, socio-psychological model by which to justify that approach.[110]

But the *Urtext* assumption is only one of the several areas in which Finkelstein's methodology suffers from hyperrigidity. Following the path of Zunz, Elbogen, and Kohler, he also attempts to fix the precise date or period in which each of the various prayers or groups of prayers was taken into the Eighteen Benedictions. Whereas thematic content served as the primary criterion for such dating by his predecessors, Finkelstein's criteria, for the most part, are stylistic peculiarities which are external and unrelated to the ideational core of the prayers themselves. His first and most basic distinction, for example, is between prayers which make use of the divine address, *ʾadonay ʾelohenu* ("O Lord, our God!"), and those which do not. The former group, in the Palestinian rite, must be early since these epithets were not used in the generation of R. Gamaliel II, under whom the *tefillah* was redacted—so Finkelstein argues. But where the address occurs in the Babylonian rite with no Palestinian parallel, we must assume that the prayers in question were later additions to the Babylonian rite. As it happens, Arthur Marmorstein[111] has shown that this address was used during the time of R. Gamaliel, such that the entire superstructure which Finkelstein erected on these two words collapses.

But even without this proof, the hypothesis is subject to many criticisms on methodological grounds. Elbogen,[112] for one, did not feel that Finkelstein had adduced sufficient evidence to prove his case, and indeed only four examples are brought by the latter in which the epithets are not found. Elbogen also notes correctly that these examples are of quite a different character than those in which the epithets *are* found. In fact, Heinemann's typological analysis of the prayers allows us to go even further and to note that *all* of Finkelstein's examples, except for one, are drawn from the category of non-statutory and private prayers, from which he wishes to draw stylistic conclusions about the statutory public prayers.[113] More fundamental, however, is the question of the liturgical *function* of such epithets in the petitions of the *tefillah*. It is more reasonable to assume that they are merely interjections, a form of liturgical "padding" which makes use of stock phrases and addresses, and that their presence or absence in a particular prayer is more a matter of coincidence than of inherent significance.[114] Since these epithets are not intrinsically related to the content of any particular petition, Finkelstein's use of them as a primary criterion for dating purposes is in any case highly arbitrary.

Among the additional criteria which Finkelstein employs to date the various component prayers, two in particular must be singled out for their arbitrariness. The first is the "word count," or "seven-word formula."[115] Finkelstein notes that the body of four of the petitions (in the Palestinian versions) consists of seven words only, while a fifth is found in two forms— one containing seven, the other, eight words (and it is "obvious" which form is the "original"!). Special significance was attached to the mystic number seven during "the period of the rise of the pupils of Hillel"[116] (and not at any other time?), hence these prayers, varied as they are typologically, must have originated together during that period. But word counting is a form of artifice; as such it is external to the sense and primary function of the prayer itself.[117] Once again, we are confronted with an arbitrary, even capricious criterion for dating. The "use of scriptural expressions" also is an arbitrary criterion. Since the use of biblical idioms and diction, and occasionally the full citation of scriptural verses, is characteristic of the language of rabbinic prayer in general, it is inappropriate on methodological grounds to base any far-reaching conclusions on the presence of such citations in particular petitions of the *tefillah*. It is impossible to pinpoint the characteristic use of biblical phraseology to one particular period or another because the phenomenon is much too widespread. Finkelstein's determination that "the use of scriptural expressions in these benedictions is doubtless to be associated with the new interest in the canonical works that developed during the generation preceding the Rebellion of 66-70"[118] is not only arbitrary, it is methodologically impossible.

As regards the "emphasis on the Kingship of God," the lengthy scholarly debate which has been raging on this very question[119] indicates that the concept of God's Kingship was emphasized in some periods over others, but the interjectory occurrence of the term, *malkenu* ("our King"), as a parallel to *ᵓabinu* ("our Father"), in two petitionary prayers of the *tefillah* ("Babylonian version") which both employ the distich pattern, does not seem significant. Finkelstein in principle should be treading on safer ground when he bases himself on "evidence from Talmudic sources," were it not for the fact that we cannot always accept the testimony of these sources at face value. Thus, the Babylonian Amoraic statement about the institution of *birkat ha-minnim* by R. Gamaliel II and his colleagues at Yavneh does not prove *ipso facto* that this benediction was "added" to the *tefillah* at this time. In fact, on the basis of Tos. Ber. 3:25, the contrary seems likely, as we previously have noted. Finkelstein's additional inferences from the Talmudic sources are too heavily conditioned by his other dating criteria to be able to stand on their own merit. The prayer for peace, for example, both as a response to the priestly benediction and as a petition whose content is extremely general and equally appropriate to *any* period, simply cannot be pinpointed to "about the year 60, when the country was in a state of anarchy, and the people were torn in factions that bitterly hated each other."[120] This type of overdetermination is totally speculative and should be eschewed on the grounds that it goes far beyond the limits of legitimate inference, viz., that which is securely based in the sources themselves. On the other hand, Finkelstein's identification of an anti-Sadducean polemic in the *geburot* benediction, with its emphasis on the Pharisaic doctrine of resurrection (as has been noted by other scholars as well),[121] has a greater claim to legitimacy, since it has some support in the sources.

While Zunz thought that the *tefillah* originally consisted of the six "framework" benedictions, Finkelstein's historical and philological assumptions lead him to suggest an extremely brief formula consisting of one benediction as the original, to which *all* of the specific petitions were added on later occasions.[122] Here we have an example of philological reductionism carried to its logical extreme.[123] But Finkelstein, like Kohler, occasionally modifies such philological reductionism when it conflicts with his particular thesis. He holds, for example, that the verse *šemaᶜ yiśraᵓel* was always a part of the *qeduššah* in the *tefillah*, and on this assumption constructs an elaborate theory according to which the *qeduššah* is primary in the *yoṣer* benediction and was taken over from that context *together* with the *šemaᶜ* verse into the *tefillah* during the period of the Hadrianic persecutions in Palestine.[124] But why the transfer of the *šemaᶜ* verse should necessitate the transfer of the *qeduššah* as well is never adequately explained by Finkelstein. The logical objection that today the two units are not absolutely contiguous, but are mediated by both the conclusion of the *yoṣer* benediction and the entire *ᵓahabah* benediction is "obviated" by assuming away the existence of these elements before the time of the Hadrianic persecutions![125] Once again, Finkelstein's conclusions follow more readily upon his own presuppositions than upon the data themselves.

We already have noted Finkelstein's *Tendenz* toward overspecification and hyperrigidity in dating the various component prayers of the Eighteen Benedictions. This *Tendenz* is also manifest in his treatment of the materials in the Passover *Haggadah*.[126] Here the methodological problems are compounded by Finkelstein's propensity for hazardously early datings. He asserts, for example, that not only the *midrash* on Deut. 26:5-9, which forms the main portion of the *Haggadah*, but also the two introductions to the *midrash*, cited by Rav and Samuel in b. Pes. 116a, as well as the *piyyuṭ, Dayyenu,* reflect polemics of the Ptolemaic and Seleucid periods and therefore are to be considered as pre-Maccabean in origin. The methodological difficulties of dating rabbinic texts on the basis of pre-rabbinic polemics which they allegedly contain have been dealt with by Heinemann,[127] who concludes that such dating is valid "only if the particular [passage] in all of its details and variants is appropriate to the background in question and is not appropriate to *any* other period or set of circumstances."[128] Even this caveat may be viewed by some scholars as insufficiently cautious. At any rate, Finkelstein's own reconstruction has been refuted point by point by Daniel Goldschmidt, in his *Haggadah šel pesaḥ.*[129]

Once again, Finkelstein's rigid philological approach is responsible for the majority of his conclusions. He asserts, for example, that the *midrash* must be of high antiquity since it has been preserved in all of the rites "in practically identical form, so that there can be little question of the original form of the text."[130] But Goldschmidt cautions that all of the manuscripts of the European rites are relatively late and points out that there are in fact many variations between the different texts of the *midrash*.[131] Moreover, Goldschmidt shows that the *midrash* is not a unitary composition written by Temple priests during the Ptolemaic period, but is a gleaning of exegetical comments which originated in the *bet ha-midrash*.[132] Finkelstein's recent attempt to support his early dating of the *midrash* by referring to the use of the midrashic method of the Dead Sea Scrolls[133] becomes irrelevant when one focuses on the considerable stylistic differences between the materials in the Scrolls and rabbinic materials. On stylistic grounds alone, the present formulation of the *midrash* cannot be dated any earlier than the Tannaitic period.

It also is his rigorous application of philological axioms which lies behind Finkelstein's sequential explanation of the two versions of the introduction to the *midrash*: "so fundamental a change in the ritual as the substitution of B for A would have come about, in all probability, only as a measure intended to please the imperial Seleucid government. . . . It would have been impossible for a scholar of the third century of the Christian Era, no matter how illustrious, to have substituted a formula of his own creation for the well-established introduction, 'We were Pharaoh's bondmen, etc.' . . ."[134] It is more reasonable to accept Goldschmidt's opinion that there simply were two current alternate versions, neither of them of high antiquity.[135] Finkelstein's historical reconstructions also attach great importance to minor variations in phraseology (another sign of his essentially philological orientation), particularly when these are deviations from a biblical text. Thus, "the substitution of the word *misham* ('from there') for *mimizraim* ('out of Egypt') apparently intended to clarify a possible ambiguity, which might have been particularly disturbing when Palestine was under Egyptian domination."[136] Goldschmidt, however, correctly notes that such variations by and large are not significant but instead are characteristic of liturgical materials.[137]

While most scholars have rejected Finkelstein's Seleucid *terminus a quo* for the liturgical poem, *Dayyenu*, they nonetheless have accepted his *terminus ad quem*, the year 70 C.E., since the final line gives thanks for the building of the Temple, which seemingly would have been less appropriate after its destruction.[138] This certainly is a plausible hypothesis, but need not be considered as proven beyond all doubt in view of Gedaliah Allon's demonstration that the version of *mah niŝtanah* in M. Pes. 10:4 which previously had been assumed on the basis of its "appropriateness" to be pre-70, actually is more appropriate to the generation of R. Gamaliel II and his fellows at Yavneh.[139]

The foregoing methodological analysis of Louis Finkelstein's liturgical studies points to a glaring need for more caution and less rigidity in approaching very old materials, such as those which are under examination in the field of classical Rabbinism.

Liebreich

Methodological rigidity and overspecification also characterize the liturgical scholarship of Leon J. Liebreich (1899-1966). Like Finkelstein, Liebreich tends to seize upon an assumption or operational procedure which has a certain *general* validity, or specific validity within a rather circumscribed area, and apply it with relentless consistency "across the board" without previously bothering to ascertain the methodological correctness of such an application.

He attempts to show, for example, that the order of Psalm verses and other biblical citations which are contained in such originally *nonstatutory* liturgical rubrics as the *qeduššah desidra*ʾ [140] and the *pesuqe dezimra*ʾ [141] can be accounted for with the same precision as the structure of the *šema*ᶜ or the Eighteen Benedictions. Such a demonstration necessarily presupposes the same authoritarian historical model assumed by all of Liebreich's predecessors; for if the order of the biblical citations never was absolutely fixed, then any attempt to rationalize their present order is itself unjustified. In fact, there is ample evidence from the amount of variation in all of the rites, and as Heinemann points out,[142] particularly in the Genizah fragments, to call into question any original "fixity" within these rubrics. While Liebreich acknowledges this variation, he nonetheless describes it in *philological* language, viz., in terms of additions and omissions, although he does not attempt to rationalize these changes.[143]

Throughout, the assumption of fixity accounts for Liebreich's operations. But the fact that, like Finkelstein, he must resort to artificial and extrinsic explanations and only rarely can produce convincing intrinsic evidence casts doubt on the validity of most of his conclusions. Thus, Liebreich notes, for example, that verses from the Book of Chronicles will frequently precede Psalm verses in the *tahanun, qeduššah desidra*ʾ,[144] and *pesuqe dezimra*ʾ [145] rubrics. He rationalizes this phenomenon as the practice of "establishing a link between David, the originator of psalmody, and his Psalter which provided the material for psalmody,. . . since the Book of Chronicles contains, among other matters, an account of the life of David with special stress on the Davidic origin of all the arrangements and liturgy of the Temple, and the Book of Psalms is traditionally of Davidic authorship. . . ."[146] Such an explanation obviously is extrinsic to the sense of the verses themselves within their liturgical context, and the phenomenon in question more properly may be regarded as a matter of coincidence; once again, we must bear in mind the caveat that not every detail is necessarily significant.

To explain both the occurrence and the proximity of certain verses in the various rubrics, Liebreich proceeds to "discover" an elaborate system of verbal "tallying," by reference to *Leitworte*.[147] This "discovery" is based on the observation that certain words or Hebrew roots recur in various verses. There is no question that in certain well-delineated types of cases this method can be helpful in accounting for the *clustering* of a number of biblical citations. Thus, for example, the similar use of the Hebrew root *bth* in Jer. 17:7, Isa. 26:4, and Ps. 9:11 (where the root is integrally related to the sense of the verses), is undoubtedly the correct explanation for their "clustering" in a liturgical context, as Liebreich points out.[148] The same phenomenon occasionally will occur when the root in question is less integrally related to the primary sense of the verses,[149] but the validity of the explanation depends on the contiguity of the verses.

Liebreich, however, makes extensive and rigorous application of this observation in order to account for the location of verses which are not at all contiguous and which even occur in different rubrics. Thus, verses which are found in the *tahanun* rubric can "explain" the occurrence of certain verses in the *qeduššah desidra²* by way of verbal tallies.[150] But the distance between the verses makes an actual "literary" dependence extremely improbable. While Liebreich has correctly noted that the verses in the *qeduššah desidra²* context are by and large "*tahanun*-type" verses, he has ignored the fact that so are the majority of verses which appear in all of the non-statutory rubrics. Indeed, the identical verses frequently will recur throughout the liturgy.[151] Under the circumstances, it is more reasonable to eschew the hypothesis of literary dependence or "direct influence" as too rigid, and to assert instead that there existed a standard liturgical "reservoir" of biblical citations which were felt to express admirably the supplicatory mood of the worshipper and hence came to pervade the liturgy. Verbal "tallies" in this case would be an *outcome* of the process (since all of these verses employ a similar "liturgical" vocabulary), rather than its starting point.

Liebreich's use of the "verbal tally" theory is exaggerated in two other respects as well. First of all, the words which are observed to "tally" frequently are insignificant and the "tallies" themselves more coincidental than intentional. Thus the Tetragrammaton and such standardly recurring words as *l²olam* ("forever") do not consitute significant tallies.[152] Even more artifical is Liebreich's "discovery" of so-called "hidden" tallies between the verses from Psalms and Micah in the *qeduššah desidra²* lection and the "Thirteen Attributes" of Exodus 34:6-7. Again, we must note that the sense of the passages in question is identical, and hence the similarities of vocabulary.[153] Moreover, the Micah passage in its biblical context echoes the "Thirteen Attributes." "Hidden" tallies, however, are primarily suspect on methodological grounds, viz., the more recondite the tally, the less likely is its objective validity.

In trying to account for the groupings of verses and complete Psalms in the *pesuqe dezimra*ʾ rubric, Liebreich must avail himself of an additional hypothesis, which not only is superimposed onto the data from without but is not even fully intelligible on its own terms. Liebreich notes correctly that the biblical prototypes for the rabbinic liturgical *berakah* formula are found in the Chronicles passages which are included in the *pesuqe dezimra*ʾ lection, but the fact that mention is made of God's Name and Kingship in this lection is surely more a *by-product* of the selection of citations than their determining factor.[154] The rules of the liturgical formula, moreover, are applicable only to the statutory elements of the liturgy, as Heinemann has demonstrated,[155] and these include the necessity to make mention of God's Name and Kingship. That the grouping of the two lectionaries of verses in the *pesuqe dezimra*ʾ, viz., *hodu* and *yehi kabod,* was determined by a desire "to accentuate the primacy of *malkut* over *berakah wehazkarat ha-šem*"[156] or *vice versa,* has absolutely no basis in the data themselves and is simply another example of a "hidden agenda," the very rationale for which, this time, is not even *suggested* by Liebreich.

Another characteristic of Liebreich's liturgical studies is his over-emphasis on the biblical antecedents and prototypes of rabbinic prayer. Here again, he pursues a basically valid observation with too great rigor. There is no question, on the one hand, that biblical idioms, allusions, and citations regularly are used in the rabbinic prayers and, on the other, that the themes of these prayers frequently are found in biblical prayers as well. But it is quite a different matter to assert *direct* literary dependence in all cases, particularly with regard to thematic parallels, as does Liebreich.[157] Such an assertion, again, seems to be traceable ultimately to a predominantly philological orientation. Thus, Liebreich is both justified and correct in noting that certain liturgical passages, such as *bareku, baruk šem kabod* . . . , and a number of phrases in the different versions of the Sabbath *qeduššat ha-yom* benediction, reproduce almost word for word the phraseology of the Prayer of the Levites in Neh. 5, and thus almost certainly are patterned after this prayer.[158] But direct literary borrowing only can be ascertained with respect to *precise formulations.* It is more difficult to prove that the entire thematic sequence of the *šema*ᶜ and its benedictions as well as the *tefillah* is "structurally . . . patterned after the Prayer of the Levites"[159] in Neh. 5. This is all the less probable since Neh. 5 itself is merely one example of an *entire genre* of biblical prayers.[160] The thematic constellation of Creation-Revelation-Redemption is not peculiar to Neh. 5, but occurs as well in the Psalms. The affinity which the *šema*ᶜ benedictions display to this prayer, then, are better characterized as a *generic* affinity rather than as direct literary borrowing. Liebreich himself approximates such a notion when he admits, for example, that "the liturgical principle that laudation shall precede supplication . . . [is] exhibited in Neh. 9

as well as in other prayers of the Bible and Apocrypha, and [is] enunciated in rabbinic literature. . . ."161

Nor can the use of particular words and roots in similar contexts always be cited as examples of direct literary borrowing, as Liebreich would claim with regard to both the terminology used to describe the destruction of the Egyptians in the third *šema*ᶜ benediction and the appeals to God's compassion in all three benedictions. It is more reasonable to regard such language as *formulary* and to assume that such phrases were stock liturgical idioms probably at the time of the composition of the Nehemiah prayer and certainly during the rabbinic period.162

This same approach is encountered in Liebreich's analysis of the Festival *yaᶜaleh weyabo*ᵓ prayer which he claims is "intimately connected" with Num. 10:9-10.163 Here, too, the assumption of stock liturgical idioms is more appropriate than a rigid philological explanation. Liebreich submits this prayer to the standard type of philological analysis which assumes original simplicity, *et al.*, and concludes that "the Palestinian form is, if not the original, certainly the closest approximation to the original, text of this liturgical composition."164 He continues:

> In using the word "original," it is important to observe that we do not lose sight of the fact that, like all early prayers, the prayer under consideration for centuries circulated orally. In view of the oral transmission of the prayer, therefore, "original" does not necessarily have reference to the precise wording or phraseology. At the same time, the Palestinian recension of *yaᶜaleh weyabo*ᵓ does preserve the original text of this prayer in the sense that, *no matter what textual variations it might have been subjected to*, from the standpoint of its structure and contents it consisted of a fixed introduction, two supplications, and a conclusion.165 (Italics mine.)

In fact, it is doubtful that even this much of an "original text" can be posited. It is worth noting that Liebreich does not so much deny the existence of an original formulation as he does the possibility of *discovering* it through standard philological analysis. And again, it is the presuppositions of classical philology which lead him to conclude that,

> . . . in the main, the text of the Palestinian recension of [*yaᶜaleh weyabo*ᵓ] remained static. On the other hand, the Babylonian recension . . . , by virtue of the liberties taken with the text, continued for some time to be fluid. This is attested to by a number of variants in a version of the Babylonian [*yaᶜaleh wehabo*ᵓ] [!]. Here are included not only a prayer for life, but also prayers for recovery from illness, for subsistence, and for redemption from exile.166

Nonetheless, Liebreich occasionally displays a fine awareness of the relationship between formal, stylistic characteristics and liturgical function. His analysis, for example, of the *qeduššah desidra*ᵓ passage which begins, *baruk* ᵓ*elohenu*, approximates a form-critical approach. He notes both the *stylistic* similarities between this passage and the benedictions which surround the reading from Scripture, as well as the various testimonies in the rabbinic sources which show that this passage *actually functioned* as a "Scripture benediction." The analysis as a whole is strikingly similar to that of Heinemann.[167]

Liebreich notes as well that *baruk* ꜣ*elohenu* does not conform to the rules of the liturgical *berakah* formula, but his explanation of this phenomenon as a "compromise" between those who would recite a statutory Torah benediction at the conclusion of a non-statutory lection of verses (a practice attested to in several Genizah fragments) and those who "must have" opposed this practice[168] is a case of circular reasoning and is not at all supported by the sources. First, we frequently find customs attested to in the Genizah fragments which deviate from (Babylonian) halakic norms.[169] Second, the assertion made here that the practice in question was regarded by *someone* as a deviation is not attested to in any source. Finally, there is absolutely no evidence which connects such a hypothetical controversy with the passage, *baruk* ꜣ*elohenu*. As a rule, any scholarly argument which rests solely on the assertion that something "must have been" the case automatically should be viewed as suspect. It is, in fact, Liebreich's authoritarian historical model, according to which the passage in question "must have been" instituted from above, which lies behind such an explanation. Heinemann's account[170] that the rules of the liturgical *berakah* formula were never successfully extended to the non-statutory rubrics of the liturgy is more plausible in this case. In addition, he has shown that the use of an epithet for the Tetragrammaton is characteristic of *bet-midrash* prayers.[171]

Liebreich also approaches form-criticism in isolating a particular genre of prayers in which a stereotyped opening form seems to be related to a particular liturgical function. Those prayers which begin with the word, ꜣ*attah* ("Thou hast . . . ," "Thou dost . . ."), are viewed by him as prayers of affirmation "in which the worshipper addresses God, affirming his belief in the validity of the ideas expressed therein; and since devout belief is tantamount to personal commitment or acceptance, this type of prayer is basically an article of faith, and, taken together all prayers of affirmation in the liturgy add up to a creed."[172]

In general, Liebreich's work testifies to the methodological dangers which are inherent when certain valid observations and methodological procedures are applied too rigorously and generalized too hastily.

Karl

Zwi Karl (1873-1959) was once described by a friend and colleague as possessing all of the qualities of a typical Galician Jewish *maskil* of the previous century.[173] In his scholarly writings, too, "he remained a product of his schooldays, and the influence of Graetz is evident in many of his studies; this was a generation whose *forte* was in uncovering, ploughing, harrowing, and sowing; but which never attained to maturation and ripening."[174] This certainly is an apt characterization of Karl's liturgical studies, which might at best be called "pseudo-critical." Although published in 1950, Karl's *Meḥqarim betoledot ha-tefillah* has hardly progressed methodologically beyond Zunz, and in certain cases lags terribly behind him. Karl makes few references to scholarly literature, and then only when it suits his purpose.[175] He also fails to demonstrate any acquaintance with the materials in non-Talmudic sources. In his general approach to the origin and development of the various prayers, he relies much too heavily on the norms of the (frequently later) *halakah*. Many of his results, then, should properly be regarded as Talmudic *ḥiddušim* rather than as scholarly conclusions.

While it is true, for example, that rabbinic *ʾaggadot* sometimes contain "a grain of historical truth,"[176] Karl characteristically rationalizes such *ʾaggadot* in true apologetic form. Thus, the dictum in b. Meg. 17b which states that "one hundred twenty elders, among whom were several prophets, instituted and arranged the Eighteen Benedictions in their proper order," should "properly" be understood to mean that a number of the benedictions contain idioms or entire petitionary phrases which were originally uttered by various literary prophets, etc.[177] So, too, the origin of a particular prayer may frequently be traced back to a Toraitic commandment. The *qedušš at ha-yom* benediction on Sabbaths and Festivals, for example, was instituted on the basis of the Toraitic commandment to "proclaim the festivals of the Lord at their appointed seasons" (Lev. 23:23).[178] Karl's inability to free himself from such *post facto* rationales which are characteristic of the traditional halakic literature is manifest here.

Particularly idiosyncratic is Karl's assertion that the *tefillah* was instituted by R. Gamaliel the Elder (who lived during the last decades of the Second Temple period). He supports this theory by referring to the Tannaitic dispute in M. Ber. 4:3, where the issue debated by R. Gamaliel II, R. Joshua, and R. Aqiba, viz., whether or not every individual must recite the daily Eighteen Benedictions, would seem to presuppose the prior existence of such a prayer.[179] But the assertion rests primarily on the presupposition of an authoritative "institution" of this prayer at a particular time. The standard explanation, according to which the Eighteen Benedictions were "edited" at Yavneh under the supervision of R. Gamaliel II, is more reasonable.

Karl, like his predecessors, attempts to pinpoint the origin of each of the Eighteeen Benedictions and the circumstances which led to its introduction. He, however, seems to view *all* of the petitions as referring to national needs; thus, the benediction for healing was instituted at a time of plague, etc.[180] Although he recognizes that the benediction for redemption, *goʾel yiśraʾel*, is thematically appropriate to almost any epoch in Jewish history, he sees nothing wrong in assigning it provisionally to the days of Ezra, when the people were already sighing for redemption![181] Karl's penchant for such remarkably early dating is more a product of his Talmudic mindset than it is of any serious historical considerations. According to Karl, Simeon *ha-Pakoli* "gathered together all of the various benedictions which were recited on different occasions, chose seventeen [!] of them, and arranged them in their familiar order. . . . At the same time, . . . Samuel *haQatan* instituted *birkat ha-minnim* and the *tefillah* became a prayer of eighteen benedictions."[182] Karl thus follows Elbogen's explanation of b. Ber 28b.

In dealing with prayer texts, Karl accepts all of the assumptions of the philological method. Thus variation is understood to be a sign of lateness[183] and must be accounted for sequentially.[184] The latter assumption is particularly problematic in Karl's analysis of the *pesuqe dezimra*ᵓ. Although he is aware that "the order of the Psalms is not fixed, but varies from rite to rite,"[185] he nonetheless attempts to account for additions and omissions. Assuming a monolinear development, he must show "why" Saᶜadya characteristically omits or abbreviates certain elements which are found in ᶜAmram, whose *Seder* was chronologically prior and hence more "original."[186] Thus, in order to explain why Saᶜadya omits Psalms 146 and 147[187] after ᵓašre (Ps. 145) while ᶜAmram includes them, Karl must resort to a tenuous theory according to which Palestinian Jews who recited the *pesuqe*ᵓ *dezimra*ᵓ, before arriving at the synagogue (in public?) did not want to arouse the ire of the Romans by mentioning *inter alia* either God's Kingship (in Ps. 146), or the hope that He will rebuild Jerusalem and gather the dispersed among His people (in Ps. 147).[188] This is, of course, a variation on the traditional (Babylonian) "persecution" theory accounting for changes in the liturgy. But Goldschmidt[189] has shown that the prayer texts in ᶜAmram's *Seder* are not reliable, having been altered by medieval copyists to conform with the prevailing local usage. Moreover, we have ample proof from the Genizah fragments that this rubric of the liturgy was never completely fixed, and such variation between ᶜAmram and Saᶜadya in principle, then, should not surprise us.

In the Preface to his book, Zwi Karl expresses the opinion that "the methods which I have employed in my investigation are likely to be useful to those who will follow me and should help them in furthering the work in this field, in which there is still much opportunity to make a significant contribution."[190] Although Karl occasionally has some interesting and unusual insights, this self-appraisal of his methodology is much inflated.

Goldschmidt

Ernst Daniel Goldschmidt (1895-1972) was trained as a classical philologist and served as Librarian of the Prussian *Staatsbibliothek* in Berlin from 1926 until 1935, when he was removed from that position by the Nazis. In the same year, he received an invitation from Schocken *Verlag*, the noted Berlin Jewish publishing house, to undertake a new, annotated edition of the Passover *Haggadah*. And so the philologist Goldschmidt entered the field of Jewish liturgical research. His several *Haggadah* studies, ranging from 1936 to 1960,[191] subsequently established him as the foremost authority in that area, while his critical editions of the Ashkenazic *seliḥot*[192] (1965), *kinot* (1968),[193] and High Holy Day *maḥzor*,[194] as well as his editions of Maimonides' prayer rite[195] and *Seder Rab ʿAmram*,[196] are of inestimable worth both in themselves and as bases for future research.

It is Goldschmidt's 1960 *Haggadah šel pesaḥ wetoledoteha* which is particularly relevant to our survey at this point, since it not only set out to refute Finkelstein's extravagant conclusions point by point,[197] but also called forth an extremely important interchange between Goldschmidt and Heinemann on the very questions of methodology with which we deal here.[198]

As regards his critique of Finkelstein,[199] it is worth noting that Goldschmidt objects only to certain *exaggerations* in Finkelstein's use of the philological method (all of which ultimately derive from his rather idiosyncratic historical thesis), but *not* to the underlying method itself. Thus, Goldschmidt rejects Finkelstein's conclusion that the *beraita*ʾ of the Four Sons in its original form dates from the Ptolemaic period and was first revised under the Seleucids,[200] but agrees that the current version is a conflation of several earlier ones and that the original version can be arrived at, and the process of its development reconstructed, by a synoptic analysis of the extant variants.[201] In fact, the version which Finkelstein deems to be "original" is reduced one step further by Goldschmidt.[202] The passage in question, it should be recalled, is not a prayer text, but a piece of rabbinic exegesis from the *bet ha-midrash*. While it is true that this area of rabbinic literature (or at least its halakic component) is in general more susceptible of classical philological analysis than are the prayer texts, the precise delineation of the extent to which the philological method justifiably may be applied here nonetheless remains a crucial methodological problem which only recently has begun to receive some attention,[203] but by no means has been solved.

Goldschmidt, however, also submits the prayer texts in the *Haggadah* to philological analysis. On the one hand, he allows that all of the manuscripts in our possession are relatively late and that the *Haggadah* as we now have it was compiled in the Geonic period.[204] This being the case, it follows that an "original text" cannot always be reconstructed. Even the criterion of commonality to all rites is not ultimate, since all rites, in certain cases, display the same corruptions.[205] On the other hand, Goldschmidt views the short version of the *yoṣer* benediction in Saʿadya's *Siddur* as original,[206] holds that certain passages in the *haggadot* of Saʿadya and the Genizah fragments preserve "the original form,"[207] and proceeds to reconstruct the original texts of such passages as *lefikak*,[208] *yehaleluka*,[209] and *nišmat*.[210] This last instance is particularly instructive, for in it we find the seeds of the somewhat "revised" philological approach which Goldschmidt advocated ten years later in the Introduction to his *maḥzor*. In the body of his study, Goldschmidt accounts for the present state of the *nišmat* passage in classical philological terms, as an original "core" text to which additions subsequently were made (some of them in the form of whole paragraphs which previously had their own independent existence). But in the addenda, submitted while the book was already at the press, the present text is conceived as a conflation of numerous brief and originally interchangeable versions of *birkat hašir* (each of which concluded with a closing eulogy formula) to which the usual sort of expansions were added in time.

Heinemann, both in his book[211] and in his review of Goldschmidt's *Haggadah*,[212] takes particular exception to the latter's analysis of *nišmat*, and the assumption of simplicity which lies behind it:

> Brevity is not a necessary stylistic element of prayer in general, nor of ancient prayers in particular. On the contrary, repetitions and the heaping up of synonyms are quite naturally found in this area, especially in festive prayers of praise composed in a hymnic style.[213]

Heinemann also objects that "could have been" does not prove "was in fact." Thus, the observation that a particular passage by its literary nature *could* have served as a complete benediction does not prove that the passage *had* ever existed in this form.[214]

But Heinemann's own description of *nišmat* as "the most exalted and eloquent prayer in the hymnic style to be found in the statutory liturgy," viz., as a unitary composition,[215] is also susceptible to some criticism, if not in principle, then in fact. In two lengthy footnotes in the Introduction to his *Maḥzor layamim ha-noraʾim* (1970), Goldschmidt responds to both the specific objections of Heinemann as well as to his general methodological approach.[216] Heinemann's characterization of *nišmat* as a unitary composition, he notes correctly, is itself an assumption which has not been supported with evidence. On the contrary, the independent existence of two of the longer sections, *ʾillu finu* and *yištabaḥ*, is attested to in the sources.[217] This phenomenon, of course, is open to two possible interpretations: either the two sections constitute "excerptions" from *nišmat*, or the present *nišmat* text represents a "conflation" of several previously interchangeable versions. Goldschmidt, whose orientation is philological, prefers the second explanation. But even if we should substitute a language of oral traditions and growth for the strictly "literary" philological language of Goldschmidt, his psychological process model seems eminently reasonable in this case, since "conflation" is frequently attested to in the sources.[218]

But how, indeed, are we to describe the prayer texts of the contemporary rites—in the language of oral traditions, or in the language of "literary" compositions, or in some combination of the two? This is the fundamental methodological point on which Goldschmidt challenges Heinemann. Goldschmidt the classical philologist, of course, must defend his method, but in the process he suggests a somewhat revised model which incorporates many of Heinemann's basic historical insights. Goldschmidt accepts Heinemann's conclusions regarding the state of the prayers during the Mishnaic and

Talmudic periods, before they were committed to writing. At this time a number of alternate "original" versions existed. Rather than choosing between such alternate versions, the Amora²im and the Geonim frequently tended to conflate them, or to assign their recitation to different occasions.[219] But the texts which are found in the contemporary rites, Goldschmidt asserts, are literary compositions and as such are susceptible to philological analysis.[220] He supports this assertion by pointing to the *poetic* style of the current versions of many of the statutory prayers, which display meter, *parallelismus membrorum*, etc. The "simpler" and probably more "prosaic" wordings which had existed before the prayers were committed to writing have not been preserved, and consequently we can draw no conclusions about them.[221] But Goldschmidt himself effectively calls this "proof" into question when he indicates that "we know that the early spontaneous prayers of many peoples took a poetic form and that, at all events, the metered form is relatively frequent in these prayers, while prose is rare."[222]

Ultimately, Goldschmidt remains firm in his philological assertion that "a mistake is still a mistake and an addition is still an addition," even if they occur in all of the contemporary rites.[223] Nonetheless, he has opened the door on an intriguing, crucial, and somewhat bewildering problem to which we shall return below, namely, the precise nature of the relationship between the texts in the later, written rites, and the oral prayers of the Talmudic period. In between these two stages lies the Geonic period, which now must loom large in future liturgical research.

With Goldschmidt we have completed our survey of the results obtainable when the methods of classical philology are applied to the field of Jewish liturgical studies. We nonetheless must take into account a similar application in the area of Christian liturgical research, since certain Jewish scholars have been influenced by both its conclusions and its methodological repercussions.

Baumstark

The method of "Comparative Liturgy," which was pioneered and developed by the noted German Catholic liturgical scholar Anton Baumstark (1872-1948)[224] to subsume under one "intelligibility principle" the manifold variations between the different non-Protestant Christian rites, is essentially a philological method. Bernard Botte, who was responsible for the revision of Baumstark's seminal volume, *Comparative Liturgy*, emphasizes the philological nature of this method:

> In the introduction to this book he [Baumstark] alludes to linguistics, and the title which he chose for his work naturally suggests the analogy of Comparative Grammar. The Comparative Study of the Languages of a single group enable us to describe the laws governing their evolution and to reconstruct the primitive system from which they derive, even when no other vestiges of it survive. In the same way,

> comparison of the different liturgies enables us to formulate the laws of their
> evolution and to disengage their primitive elements. . . . We are also reminded of the
> Comparative Study of Religion ('Comparative Religion'), which exercised an
> influence on Baumstark. But we should notice that it is the philologists who, above all
> others, have employed this method.

In analyzing the liturgical texts of the various Christian rites, Baumstark
makes rigorous use of the same philological operations which we have seen
employed in the study of Jewish liturgy. As regards both prose texts and
hymns,

> . . . the first task in the Comparative Study of the liturgical texts is of a purely
> philological kind. We must begin by finding out their history and as far as possible
> reconstructing their primitive state on a critical basis. This task is particularly
> necessary when a text is preserved in different recensions and (a case of very frequent
> occurrence) in different languages . . . . It will often be necessary to set out from
> Oriental versions in order to reconstitute the primitive form of an original Greek
> text.[226]

Baumstark's textual analysis frequently suffers from the same type of
historical reductionism we previously have encountered. His typical question
is, "Where did this innovation *come from*?"[227] (Italics mine.)

The Comparative Method, however, also is applied to larger liturgical
units and structures, ceremonies, customs, liturgical actions, etc., on the
assumption that one rite or group of rites can explain another, and particularly that the Eastern rites frequently can elucidate Western usages. In his
approach to these areas as well, some of which are decidedly non-literary,
Baumstark's underlying orientation is philological, while his historical model
is simple-evolutionary. Thus,

> . . . these structures, both in their fully developed forms and at every given stage in
> their evolution, are very often the result of a highly complex process. To show the
> tendencies which govern their growth, to separate the primitive *strata* from more
> recent ones, to reconstitute them in their often completely unrecognizable primitive
> forms, is the task of the historian of Comparative Liturgy.[228]

Philological criteria are here being employed on a broader scale.

The basic philological assumptions with which we have had ample
occasion to deal above are put forth by Baumstark in the form of actual *laws*
of liturgical development. Thus, liturgical development proceeds from
"variety to uniformity" (notwithstanding a certain "retrograde movement"
which accounts for "local peculiarities"),[229] and from "austerity to richness"
(viz., from simplicity to complexity, again allowing for certain "retrograde
movements").[230] So, too, "primitive conditions are maintained with greater
tenacity in the more sacred seasons of the Liturgical year."[231] While such
observations frequently may prove to be useful tools, Baumstark ascribes to
his method the certainty of an exact science: "It is only [our] subject matter

which belongs to Theology. But the student's treatment of it does not differ in principle from the comparative procedure in use in the exact sciences. . . . In its method, then, the Comparative Study of Liturgies approximates to that of the natural sciences."[232] This being the case, Baumstark's approach to his materials is deductive:

> By the law which requires that liturgical evolution should proceed from the simpler to the more complex, we shall deem the more austere the more primitive. Moreover, we shall have to regard as primitive phenomena which are found with the same meaning, the same function, and in the same area, in all Christian Rites, or at least in a sufficiently large number of such Rites, and especially so if they have parallels in the Liturgy of the Synagogue. We shall pronounce the same verdict where anything has a Jewish parallel, even when it is limited to a few Christian Rites or it may be only to one. On the other hand, we shall consider as recent all phenomena peculiar to a single Rite or to a few Rites, but without parallel of any kind in the Synagogue [why not, perhaps, on occasion as vestiges of *old* local customs?]. The same verdict must also be pronounced on those which, although absolutely or almost universal, change their meaning, place, or function from one Rite to another.[233]

The hazards of such a rigid approach to the sources, the greatest of which is the tendency to force the data to conform to a preconceived schema, have been thoroughly articulated by Bernard Botte in his Foreword to Baumstark's book. On the one hand, so-called linguistic and historical "laws" can never apply with the same force as "natural laws," since in the former case any determinism is always mitigated by the nature of the subject matter; on the other hand, hypotheses can never in and by themselves be identified with historical reality.[234]

Heinemann[235] has noted correctly that the non-textual aspects of Baumstark's method are not appropriate to the study of Jewish liturgy, which does not display the requisite variety of basic structures and variation between rites as does the Christian liturgy. In addition, Baumstark's "laws" of liturgical evolution only partially describe the development of the Jewish liturgy, while his philological approach to textual analysis is subject to the same objections which previously have been raised.[236]

Baumstark's evaluation of the relationship between the Christian and Jewish liturgies, together with the methodological results of this evaluation, are significant for our study since they parallel those of Kohler and influenced those of Spanier and, to a certain extent, of Heinemann. Baumstark writes:

> There is a rather curious tendency among Israelite scholars to underestimate [!] the age of certain Jewish liturgical texts, rather than the reverse. In view of the uncertainty in questions of chronology, the problem of the relationship between the Christian and Jewish Liturgies often resembles an equation with two unknowns. But mathematics should be capable of solving these equations as well as the others! [Note the allusion to the pure sciences once again—Botte here expresses his reservations, and rightly so.] Where Christian and Jewish usages agree, they must have their common source in a still more primitive basis in the Synagogue liturgy and of this source it is perfectly possible that Christianity is the more faithful witness.[237]

We have previously pointed out some of the dangers inherent in such an approach.[238] It is certainly unwise as well to posit as a general rule that the existence of a Christian parallel for a particular Jewish liturgical phenomenon automatically indicates an early date for the latter. Each case should rather be judged on its own merits. By and large, we should be on safer ground dealing with parallels of content, order, structure, and stereotyped phraseology (sometimes) than in matters of precise formulation.

Baumstark's own application of these guidelines leaves much to be desired. Although possessed of a phenomenal knowledge of Christian liturgical materials, he demonstrates his relative ignorance of Jewish liturgy in its historical development (notwithstanding his familiarity with Elbogen's book).[239] On the basis of supposed Christian parallels, he argues, as we would expect, for early datings of certain Jewish liturgical customs which are known to be *relatively late*. For example, Baumstark accounts for the universality of the recitation of the last three Psalms (the *laudes*) in the Morning Office as having been "inherited from the worship of the Synagogue." Referring to Elbogen's citation of the dictum of R. Yose bar Halafta⁾ in b. Shab. 118b, he concludes: "The fact is that this recitation of the last three Psalms came originally from the Morning Prayer of the Sabbath, a place which they certainly occupied already in Our Lord's time [!] and to which the Synagogue was to add later the three preceding ones."[240] The conclusion is absolutely baseless. The six Psalms are mentioned explicitly only from Geonic times onward,[241] while the Talmud makes explicit reference only to Ps. 145 (b. Ber. 4b).

Moreover, it is extremely doubtful that the Talmudic passage in question refers to the recitation of the last six Psalms.[242] The early dating to the time of Jesus is preposterous, since the *pesuqe dezimra⁾* rubric in *any* form is first attested to only in the Amoraic period! Baumstark's hypothesis that "the Jews have changed the order of the service" by reciting the *pesuqe dezimra⁾* Psalms at the remove from the biblical lections also is without foundation. The sources uniformly tell us that this rubric always preceded the morning service proper. Baumstark here "discovers" a non-existent parallel and then concludes that the Christian liturgy has preserved the original custom![243] Moreover, the Eighteen Benedictions is not properly an "intercessory" prayer, as Baumstark would have it, nor is the *qaddiš*, strictly speaking, a litany.[244] His understanding of the *yoṣer* benediction is also based on a number of false analogies.[245]

Baumstark's analysis, then, gives us good reason to exercise the utmost caution in searching for parallels between the Jewish and Christian liturgies. Properly speaking, one should have a sound background in both fields before attempting to compare them.

II. FORM-CRITICAL STUDIES

Novel methodological approaches to the study of rabbinic literature, paradoxically, never have been originated by scholars in the field itself. The pattern of the past century and a half has been one of application and adaptation of methods pioneered and developed outside the world of Jewish learning. An appreciation of the use of form-criticism, then, requires an account of the origin and development of the method. We therefore must focus our attention for the moment on German Protestant biblical scholarship at the turn of the century.[246]

By the last quarter of the nineteenth century, the philological approach had reached its apex in the so-called "documentary hypotheses" of New and Old Testament scholarship. As early as 1838, C. H. Weisse had proposed a solution to the New Testament "synoptic problem" by positing the original existence of two literary sources—an *Ur-Marcus*, and "Q" (*Quelle*, "source"), the original source of the discursive materials in Matthew and Luke.[247] In 1878, Julius Wellhausen put forth a similar theory to account for various double readings and pronounced *Tendenzen* in the Pentateuch.[248] He proceeded to isolate four literary sources, labeled as J, E, D, and P, viz., Jahwist, Elohist, Deuteronomic, and the Priestly Code.

As the century came to a close, voices from several quarters, first in Old, then in New Testament scholarship, questioned the efficacy of such a distinctly literary approach to the materials. Scholars were becoming increasingly aware that these "literary" sources themselves had preliterary histories in an oral state of transmission. Moreover, both the Old Testament and Gospel narratives came to be viewed more properly as folk literature than as actual artistic, literary products. Thus, in 1895 Hermann Gunkel, who was to become one of the great pioneers of form-criticism, devoted a study to the examination of the mythic background of the Creation and Apocalypse accounts in Gen. 1 and Rev. 12,[249] taking into account the related myths of neighboring Near Eastern cultures. In 1901, he pursued this same approach in a full-scale commentary on the Book of Genesis,[250] articulating his basic reasoning more fully in the Introduction, *Die Sagen der Genesis (The Legends of Genesis),*[251] where he writes:

> . . . Previous writers have in large measure treated J and E as personal authors, assuming as a matter of course that their writings constitute, at least to some extent, units and originate in all essential features with their respective writers, and attempting to derive from the various data of these writings consistent pictures of their authors. But in a final phase criticism has recognized that these two collections do not constitute complete unities, and pursuing this line of knowledge still further has distinguished within these sources still subordinate sources.

But in doing this there has been a neglect to raise with perfect clearness the primary question, how far these two groups of writings may be understood as literary unities in any sense, or whether, on the contrary, they are not collections, codifications of oral traditions, and whether their composers are not to be called collectors rather than authors."[252]

Eighteen years later, Martin Dibelius, in *Die Formgeschichte des Evangeliums*,[253] made the same observation regarding the "Two-Source Hypothesis" of New Testament criticism:

Without a doubt [the synoptic Gospels] are unliterary writings. They should not and cannot be compared with "literary" works. . . . the literary understanding of the synoptics begins with the recognition that they are collections of material. The composers are only to the smallest extent authors. They are principally collectors, vehicles of tradition, editors. Before all else their labour consists in handing down, grouping, and working over the material which has come down to them. . . . The form in which we hear of the words and deeds of Jesus is due only in a certain degree to the personal work of the evangelist. Owing to a *philological* and theological tradition we ourselves have become accustomed to ascribe to the authors and their prejudices a large responsibility for the tradition as a whole, *just as if we were dealing with Belles Lettres.* . . . In reality the personal factors had but little significance in shaping tradition . . . and it is very doubtful whether much depended on the personal factor in the earlier history of the tradition.[254] (Italics mine.)

And as regards Q:

The present position of our research into the source Q warrants our speaking rather of a stratum than of a document. We clearly recognize the effort of the churches to gather together words of Jesus in the manner of Q, but we do not know whether the result of these efforts was one or more books or indeed any books at all.[255]

Gunkel and Dibelius have here advanced their methodological criticism another step. Folk literatures, they note, are by their very nature collective products, in the transmission of which the traces of any personal stylistic idiosyncracies of particular individuals will be so thoroughly mitigated as to disappear entirely.[256] The resulting styles and forms of transmission, then, are better characterized as sociological conventions rather than as literary or artistic designs.[257] At this point the philological method, which is designed to deal with authentic literary creations in the full sense of the word, loses its utility. A new approach must be formulated in order to account for the preliterary origins and development of oral, folk traditions. Such traditions arise not in a controlled, literary environment, but rather in the daily life situations of the people themselves.[258]

These general observations came to form the basis for a new methodological approach, pioneered by Gunkel and Dibelius in Old and New Testament studies respectively—the method of form-criticism (labelled *Gattungsforschung*, "genre research," by Gunkel, and *Formgeschichte*, "history of [literary] form," by Dibelius). First of all, they reasoned, we must attempt to get behind the printed page and into the actual *Sitz im Leben*, the "life situation," in which these traditions and materials originated. Thus Gunkel writes:

> Accordingly, we should attempt in considering Genesis to realise first of all the form of its contents when they existed as oral tradition. . . . If we desire to understand the legends better we must recall to view the situations in which the legends were recited.[259]

At the same time, stylistic analysis of oral traditions reveals a regular incidence of highly stereotyped patterns, forms and phraseology; these constitute the vehicle for the transmission of materials. The same holds true, Gunkel notes, of such poetic "devotional" literature as the Psalms. But if the role of the individual as such is so minimal in the formation and transmission of these collective materials that such stereotyped patterns have to be described as social conventions, then it is legitimate to inquire as to the function of such patterns in the particular milieu in which they first originated. For each literary genre, or group of stylistic characteristics, a function is to be sought, emerging out of a particular *Sitz im Leben*. This is the task and the method of literary form-criticism which, as Dibelius notes, proceeds simultaneously along two tracks: one literary-analytic, the other sociological-constructive. "The *constructive method*. . . infer[s] the process of development out of its conditions, and the *analytic method* . . . split[s] up and examine[s] what has been received." The two methods must "approximate to each other."[260] Gunkel expresses the same notion in slightly different terminology: "A common setting in life is . . . one of the distinguishing characteristics of songs belonging to the same literary type. Another distinguishing characteristic is the great number of thoughts and moods which these songs share, while yet another—a very distinctive characteristic—is the literary forms [*Formensprache*] which are prevalent in them."[261] The *Sitz im Leben* is to be identified by Dibelius' "constructive method," while the stylistic and formal characteristics are arrived at through conventional literary analysis. The conjunction of the two methods will identify a particular genre.

Since a particular genre emerges out of a specific *Sitz im Leben* and only later passes into written "literature," the search for examples of that genre cannot be limited to any particular book or body of literature, nor indeed to a too-narrowly defined sociological unit. Thus, Gunkel quite rightly points out that form-criticism of the Psalms must take into its purview all of the so-called "devotional" poetry in the Bible, not just those specimens which are found in the Psalter; that which is under examination is, in fact, the *entire range* of liturgical poetry in ancient Israel. Moreover, Israel's customs and stylistic conventions must be viewed as well within the broader framework of ancient Near Eastern civilization. Frequently, Egyptian and Babylonian liturgical poetry will display the identical or similar patterns.[262] Similarly, in analyzing the Gospel materials, Dibelius has reference to Greek, rabbinic, and Patristic parallels, and makes use of New Testament materials *outside* of the Gospels to reconstruct the *Sitz im Leben.*[263]

Form-criticism, like any other method depends on certain presuppositions and is not itself immune from criticism. First of all, in order for the method to be applicable, the collective axiom must hold, that is, we must be dealing with a literature on which the impact of the individual transmitter or formulator is minimal. Dibelius, for example, expresses his reservations about Eduard Norden's use of form-criticism in the latter's 1913 volume, *Agnostos Theos:*[264]

> This book was intended to deal with a type of speech of a soteriological character. Hence his researches were to a large extent on that level of literature where the individual taste of the author determined the final form of the material which had been handed down.[265]

The collective axiom itself rests on a particular assumption about the nature of ancient society in general and, in Gunkel's Psalm analysis, about Israelite society in particular, namely, that "the typical and formal dominate over the individual and personal, especially in the earlier periods of Israel's history."[266] While the assumption in general seems reasonable, Gunkel's particular formulation, which implies a certain model of historical process, involves him in certain difficulties, as we shall see below.

A second problem is that of circularity. The two components of the form-critical method, viz., the constructive and the analytic approaches, theoretically are supposed to act as methodological checks on each other, since each proceeds independently of the other.[267] Only when the results of the two approaches approximate each other can we view them as fairly certain. But if both approaches proceed simultaneously from the identical body of data, which occasionally is bound to occur, the methodological check is lost and we run the risk of circular reasoning. Jacob Neusner makes explicit mention of this problem:

> . . . These are the chief notions brought to the interpretation of the texts; they do not seem to me outrageous or far-fetched. But they do derive from the materials for the criticism of which they then are used, and this represents a circularity to be specified and admitted.[268]

A major area of controversy is that of the classification and identification of the genres themselves. It goes without saying that each body of material to which the method is applied will yield a different system of genres. This stems from the basic differences among the various groups of materials to which the genres intrinsically are related. A certain amount of adaptation necessarily will be required when we move from Psalms to Gospel narratives, or from New Testament to rabbinic literature.[269] There will, of course, be certain affinities also, as between the Psalms and the rabbinic liturgy, or (to a somewhat lesser extent) between New Testament and rabbinic narratives. Nonetheless, within each particular area, many of the classifications appear somewhat arbitrary. Thus, for example, despite Gunkel's numerous claims to objectivity,[270] his particular classification scheme has been criticized by both Sigmund Mowinckel[271] and Claus Westermann.[272] Dibelius and Rudolf Bultmann disagree over the identification of certain genres in the Gospels,[273] while Heinemann criticizes Spanier's classification-scheme[274] and in turn has been criticized by Liebreich for certain omissions.[275]

Another problem is the frequent overlapping of formal and stylistic characteristics between genres. A genre is not, of course, to be identified on the basis of a single recurring stylistic characteristic, but rather on the basis of an entire configuration of such characteristics which recur conjointly. Thus, Dibelius writes, "The categories will be described by us with a *number of landmarks whose totality makes clear their nature.*" (Author's italics.)[276] But many of Gunkel's Psalm-categories, for example, dovetail.[277]

These difficulties notwithstanding, form-criticism has proved to be immensely helpful in solving certain problems with which the philological method is unable to cope. In what follows, we shall basically concern ourselves with particular applications of the method, which served as paradigms for its use in the study of Jewish liturgy.

Gunkel

The fame of Hermann .Gunkel (1862-1932) rests primarily on his pioneering form-critical analysis of the Psalms. By paying close attention to the language of the Psalms themselves as well as to the descriptions of cultic actions and formulae in the narrative books of the Bible, and by comparing both with cultic materials and liturgical poetry from the neighboring Egyptian and Mesopotamian civilizations, Gunkel came to the conclusion that the Psalm literature had its original *Sitz im Leben* in the ancient Israelite cult.[278] Various liturgical moods and settings yield different types of responses. Gunkel's analysis of the styles, diction, and content of the Psalms yields such broad liturgical literary genres as "Hymns," "Laments," "Thanksgiving Songs," "Penitential Psalms," "Royal Psalms," etc., with various subdivisions determined by the person, whether plural ("Community") or singular ("Individual").[279] Content, mood, style, and person are thus Gunkel's primary criteria for genre identification. Each large genre is typified by its own particular diction as well. Gunkel's attention to small details of style is especially significant and became prototypical for all subsequent form-critical studies. It is interesting to compare Gunkel's stylistic analysis of the "Hymns," for example,[280] with Heinemann's analysis of the rabbinic statutory prayers.[281] The similarities in diction should not surprise us, since much of the language of the rabbinic liturgy is directly lifted out of the biblical literature or is patterned on it, as we already have noted.[282]

Nonetheless, many of the genres Gunkel isolates seem somewhat arbitrary because they frequently dovetail in matters of diction, style, mood, and content. Thus, the line between "Hymns" (i.e., Psalms of Praise) and "Thanksgiving Songs" is often a very thin one.[283] This factor alone may account to a large extent for the numerous "mixtures" of genres which Gunkel finds.[284] In any case, it has brought Claus Westermann to question Gunkel's definition of the "Hymns," and ultimately his entire basis for classification.[285] One wonders, then, whether Gunkel's system of genres perhaps is not a bit too rigid and does not manifest a tendency toward reductionism.[286] At least some of the "mixed types" need not necessarily reflect a historical "degeneration."[287]

One category in particular which Gunkel claims to isolate raises many questions, viz., the so-called Non-Liturgical or "Spiritual" Psalms. These include such subcategories as "Spiritual Laments," "Spiritual Poems," "Spiritual Laments of the Individual," "Spiritual Songs," and "Spiritual Thanksgiving Songs," and constitute the great majority of the Psalms in the Psalter.[288] Nonetheless, they make use of practically the same diction as their "non-spiritual" counterparts, and are distinguishable only by virtue of their greater *Frömmigkeit*—"religiosity," or "piety":

> Here, and in the Wisdom Literature, is the place where individuality is expressed in the Old Testament. . . . Here a kind of piety which has freed itself of all ceremonies expresses itself, a religion of the heart. Here something wonderful has happened. Religion has cast off the shell of sacred usage, in which until now, it has been protected and nurtured: it has come of age.[289]

In both of these passages we detect a theological bias typical of German Protestant scholarship, and indeed, the sentences which immediately follow leave no room for doubt:

> These songs, above all, are the prototypes of Protestant hymnody. From the standpoint of poetry, they are not always outstanding; but from the standpoint of religion, they are the imperishable treasure in the Psalter. . . . These Spiritual Songs, as much as anything else in the Old Testament, stand closest to the Gospel.[290]

Gunkel's historical model of the development of the Psalm literature is directly traceable to this theological bias and is essentially identical with that of his nineteenth century predecessors. According to Gunkel, the cult is the original *Sitz im Leben* of all Israelite psalmody. But it is inconceivable to him that such fervent, individualistic piety as is manifest in the "Spiritual Psalms" could have originated in a cultic setting. These, then, must be later, secondary developments which were composed outside of the cult "through the influence of the prophetic spirit"[291] and subsequently taken back into the cult in the post-exilic period, where they served as a "refuge" for "genuine religion . . . in a time when religion was beginning to show signs of ossification [!]."[292] Here, then, is the simple evolutionary model of religious development, which "progresses" from primitive, formalized cult to spiritual, individual piety. Sigmund Mowinckel was the first to point out the inconsistencies in Gunkel's genre analysis which proceed from this bias:

> And what are Gunkel's arguments for this departure from his own sound fundamental position? They are, in fact, just the same as with the older school: the asserted incompatibility between the personal religious note in so' many of the Psalms, and the 'impersonal' character of the 'liturgical formula.' In other words: the newer Protestant lack of understanding of cult and of its real essence. If Gunkel and his followers were right at this point, exactly the same argument should be valid against the psalmists' strong dependence on all the conventional forms of the old cultic style.[293]

He argues instead that the "stereotyped phrase may express a personally experienced and genuine religion"[294] for both poet and worshipper. Mowinckel, building on these observations, goes on to advocate a "cult-functional" approach to the Psalms, all of which he views as having their origin in the cult.[295]

All subsequent Psalm research has been a reaction, one way or the other, to Gunkel's form-critical approach and to his particular application of the method.

Dibelius

The "constructive method," viz., the reconstruction of the historical-sociological *Sitz im Leben*, also looms large in the form-critical researches of Martin Dibelius (1883-1947), who was the first to develop this approach in the field of New Testament, and particularly Gospel, studies.[296] Dibelius' work is predicated on the analytical and synoptic studies of previous New Testament scholars (who made considerable use of philological tools),[297] but seeks to get behind the "synoptic problem" and to examine the historical factors which both called the primitive traditions into being and gave them their form:

> An analytical method which starts from the text and goes back to the sources and isolated elements of tradition is not satisfactory. Rather one requires a constructive method which attempts to include the conditions and activities of life of the first Christian Churches. If we leave this work on one side, the sources and the small details which are brought forward by the analytical method hang in the air, and their sociological relationships, or 'Sitz im Leben,' is [*sic*] not clear. Naturally in each method the independence of their way of thought must be preserved, synthesis and analysis must not so much condition, as meet each other.[298]

It is with the "constructive method," then, that Dibelius begins, attempting to build a historical model of the early Christian community to account for the forms in which its earliest traditions were crystallized. By comparing the Pauline epistles with the accounts of preaching in the Book of

Acts (both extra-Gospel sources), Dibelius concludes that the original *Sitz im Leben* of the Gospel tradition must lie in such sermons, i.e., must lie in the conscious, outer-directed, propagandistic activities of the early Christian fellowship, which included teaching, preaching, and proselytising: *"missionary purpose was the cause and preaching was the means of spreading abroad that which the disciples of Jesus possessed as recollections."*[299] The tradition, therefore, was tendentious from its very outset.

It is clear from both the Pauline epistles and the Book of Acts, asserts Dibelius, that the primary message, or *kerygma*, of the primitive Greek churches was of salvation through the atoning death of the Christ and that the life of Jesus was only significant to the extent that it provided examples, or paradigms, for the preacher's message.[300] Only gradually, when the *Parousia* began to appear less and less imminent and the Church began to "enter into the world," did the life of Jesus come to attain a greater importance. Dibelius then analyzes the extant Gospel materials and isolates the different *genres*, each with its own distinguishing set of formal characteristics, which correspond to the different phases of his historical model. He proceeds from the most primitive Sermonic Paradigms to Folk Tales about Jesus the "miracle worker" or thaumaturge (narratives which exist for their own sake and have both Greek and rabbinic Jewish parallels), to Legends about Jesus' disciples and associates.

Dibelius' own summary of his results is instructive:

> The fortune of primitive Christianity is reflected in the history of the Gospel-Form. The first beginnings of its shaping hardly deserve to be called literary. What Form was present was determined by ecclesiastical requirements arising in the course of missionary labor and of preaching. The Passion story, the most significant piece of tradition for Christian faith, was told relatively early as a connected story. Moreover, isolated events from the life of Jesus, suitable for sermons, were told in short stories, and sayings and parables were used especially for a practical purpose. But pleasure in the narrative for its own sake arose and seized upon literary devices. The technique of the Tale developed, and lent meanwhile a fully secular character to the miracle stories. In addition, legendary narratives full of personal interest in the persons of the sacred story joined themselves to the periphery of the tradition. One told of these persons in the same way as similar narratives from the surrounding world spoke of other holy men. Already between the lines of the Gospel-Form one can see the faith of Christendom moved from its fundamental strangeness in the world and its self-limitations to the religious interests of the Church, to an accommodation to the world and to harmony with its relationships.[301]

The simple evolutionary nature of Dibelius' schema is manifest here. It would be possible to call this process model into question, however, without automatically casting doubt on the validity of the generic classifications since these latter are also distinguishable on stylistic and formal grounds. One could inquire, for example, whether the narrative style of the Tales necessarily must be viewed as secondary to the Paradigms. A case might be made for coextensive primacy on psychological and anthropological grounds, viz., that such a style is more "instinctual" than "artificial." At any rate, we should recall that historical development does not always proceed according to neat, logical schemas.[302]

The influence of Dibelius' evolutionary model is also discernible in his treatment of the problem of historicity, viz., of the relative historical reliability of materials which were transmitted in a particular form. Thus, the Tales as a whole are relatively unreliable, on account of their greater stylization and conformity to a fixed secular pattern.[303] On the other hand, the determination of "the relative dependability of the Paradigms rests upon the fact that they belong to the same sociological stratum as the earliest preaching."[304]

Dibelius wavers on the general question of historicity. The form-critical method demonstrates that most traditional materials have been substantially conditioned by the form in which they ultimately were cast. Nonetheless, Dibelius wants to hold on to the "historical kernel." Thus, on the one hand,

> it should cause no surprise if in the Paradigms we were to come across sentences or at least words of Jesus of whose historical reliability there is doubt. They are not proved to be genuine by the fact of relatively primitive tradition, and on the other hand the paradigmatic nature of the matter is not spoiled by such unhistoric traits. For both aspects belong together. Tradition of this nature, the oldest anywhere to be found among Christians, conditions unhistorical changes of the words of Jesus.[305]

Although the Passion story, for example, was both "written for the edification . . . of Christians,"[306] and patterned in its details after Scriptural verses,[307] Dibelius nonetheless takes up the question of eyewitnesses[308] and concludes that "we cannot always, nor at once, reach a verdict about the historicity of a motif by showing it had an Old Testament basis."[309] Similarly, although Dibelius recognizes that the discursive material of the "Q" stratum contains many early Christian exhortations which do not go back to Jesus, he asserts that collections of Jesus' words were made at an early date and that "Q," while showing "traces of a more advanced development,"[310] includes some of these genuine words of Jesus. That these *logia*, parables, *et al.*, were perceived by the early Christian community as authentic words of Jesus and were handed down as such is certain; that they actually *are* sayings of Jesus and, more particularly are the *ipsissima verba*, seems far less likely, especially in view of the fact that the "direct" line of transmission was through the Palestinian Judeo-Christian community, about whom we know practically nothing, and was in Aramaic.[311]

The two streams of the tradition, the narrative and the discursive, were transmitted in different ways, according to Dibelius: *"the tradition of narrative and the tradition of words are not subject to the same law."*[312] He draws an interesting analogy to the transmission of the *haggadah* and the *halakah* in rabbinic Judaism, where the wording of the former was allowed to vary, while great stress was laid upon the exact formulation of the latter.[313]

But more than this, he would posit a certain historical connection between the two, since "for a Christian formerly a Jew, the differentiation between the Haggadic and the Halakhic parts of his new Christian tradition would be easy from the first."[314]

While searching for Greek and Jewish parallels to Gospel Paradigms, Legends, and Tales, Dibelius applies his form-critical methodology, briefly but very significantly, to rabbinic literature, and particularly to the Talmudic *haggadah*. In so doing, he touches on many of the issues and identifies many of the problems which are now becoming increasingly important as form-criticism begins to be applied systematically to rabbinic literature. Thus, Dibelius raises the question of redaction and identifies some of the criteria for the association of various pericopae, in which "we catch sight of precanonical connections amongst the rabbinic stories."[315] He deals with the phenomenon of the transformation of popular folk tales or narratives by the rabbis, who, by shifting their emphasis or "leading idea," have refashioned them into legal *exempla*. Moreover, Dibelius puts his finger on what is perhaps the most basic difficulty inherent in a form-critical treatment of this material, viz., the problem of categorization:

> The *Halakhic stories* occupy a large space in the Talmud, and can scarcely be brought under *one* type by their Form. . . . Every attempt to deal with the Formgeschichte of the rabbinic narrative material is subject to the difficulty of deciding the categories. . . . For decision about the category follows upon the determination of the leading interests,[316] and this again must be taken from the Form of the story. If the Form is not preserved by the editors of the tradition, if it is broken up, if the original leading interest is replaced by another, then the original Form can only be regained by reconstruction,[317] and the certainty about the process of the event is considerably lessened thereby.[318] (Author's italics.)

The particular direction which form-criticism takes in its use by Dibelius points to the vital importance of the particular historical model which the scholar employs for his reconstruction of the *Sitz im Leben*. Dibelius' researches have proved to be seminal not only for all subsequent New Testament scholarship but also, and more to our point, for recent scholarship in several branches of rabbinic literature.[319]

Spanier

While Gunkel and Dibelius provided the methodological foundations, it was Arthur Spanier (1889-1944) who provided the impetus for a systematic application of form-criticism to the Jewish liturgy. As early as 1934, Spanier was drawing attention to formal and stylistic characteristics of the prayers which largely had been ignored in previous philological studies. The predominance of the liturgical *berakah* and its particular stylistic features now became a primary object of study. Spanier also was the first to attempt a

generic classification of the prayers in which formal and stylistic characteristics were to be identified.[320] In all of these respects, he laid the groundwork
for Heinemann's subsequent research. Moreover, he was the first to raise
certain issues to which Heinemann later addressed himself at great length,[321]
and was the first scholar seriously to question the appropriateness to Jewish
liturgical studies of the pure philological method.[322] But these basic insights
never were integrated by Spanier into an overall approach to the liturgy; that
remained for Heinemann to do.

Spanier's four articles on Jewish liturgy, which appeared between 1934
and 1939 in the *Monatsschrift für Geschichte und Wissenschaft des Judentums*, deal primarily with three areas: formal and stylistic analysis of the
prayers,[323] Jewish-Christian liturgical parallels,[324] and an alternate approach
to the normative philological method in analyzing the development of the
prayer texts.[325] We shall take up each of these areas in turn.

Spanier's essays in form-criticism are, as Heinemann rightly points
out,[326] somewhat simplistic. Properly speaking, they really are not "form-
critical" at all, in the sense in which we have come to characterize the method,
since they make no use of the "constructive approach," i.e., there is no attempt
to identify a historical or sociological *Sitz im Leben*. Rather, genre
identification is based on literary analysis alone. Here, too, there are
problems. Spanier's classification-scheme essentially is that of the later
rabbinic tradition, as he himself points out. Thus, the statutory prayers, and
particularly those in the major "series of benedictions" (the *tefillah*, the Grace
after meals, the *šema^c* benedictions, and the *haftarah* benedictions) may be
subsumed under the thematic-modal categories of Praise-Petition-Thanks-
giving/Acknowledgment.[327] But these categories, and the halakic-formal
rules which are derived from them by the Tosafists, for example, originally
were applied *ex post facto*. Thus, it should not be surprising that there are
numerous exceptions to the "rules."

Spanier's own attempt to describe the various genres in terms of their
stylistic characteristics rests much too heavily on these later halakic
distinctions and suffers thereby. Thus Spanier claims that the opening
berakah formula is characteristic only of the Prayers of Praise (*Preisgebete*).
His determination that neither the Prayers of Thanksgiving (*Dankbene-
diktionen*) nor the Prayers of Acknowledgment (*Bekenntnisbenediktionen*:
prayers recited after a biblical passage) were to make use of the *berakah*
formula rests exclusively on *later* halakic sources (*Shulḥan ^cAruk, ᵓOraḥ
Ḥayyim*, 6, 3; *Tosafot* on b. Pes. 104b), which are not always reliable guides in
these matters. The two so-called "exceptions," viz., the benedictions which
follow the Torah and *haftarah* readings, suffice to indicate the inadequacy of
the "rule."

Spanier further characterizes the *Preisgebete* as making ex   .ve use of
the third person style of address to God (*Er-Stil*), while the o.ner types of
benedictions make use of the second person style (*Du-Stil*).[328] But here again

there are notable exceptions for which Spanier can only account very feebly. The second and third benedictions of the *tefillah* make use of the *Du-Stil* although they are *Preisgebete*.[329] Yet, in another article, he asserts just as flatly that "die kategorische Du Prädikation am Anfang der Benediktion gehört also zum Stil der Preisgebete[!]."[330] Moreover, Spanier now claims that the fourth benediction of the *tefillah*, the first of the petitionary prayers, has assimilated the ꜣ*attah* from the preceding Benedictions of Praise. It is evident that both of these contradictory schemas are much too rigid and that, in fact, the *Du-* and *Er-Stile* are pervasive in the liturgy and not exclusive to any particular type of prayer.

Spanier, at least in his first three articles, does not question the validity of the philological method or any of its assumptions. On the contrary, he refers to the original brief forms of both the *yoṣer* and *haškibenu* benedictions.[331] In fact, his stylistic analysis of the prayers is actually intended to serve as an *additional* criterion for *philological* operations. Thus, the intrusion of the *Er-Stil* in a prayer such as ꜣ*emet weyaṣib*, in which the *Du-Stil* predominates, is viewed as corroborative evidence for identifying a later insertion. The same holds true for the intrusion of the *Du-Stil* in ꜣ*emet we-emunah*, where the *Er-Stil* predominates.[332] But *why* either of these prayers should be characterized by one style or the other is something which Spanier never explains.[333] Once again, as in the analyses of Finkelstein and Liebreich, the stylistic criterion is external to the sense of the prayer and is never related functionally to its context.[334]

Spanier also follows Kohler and Baumstark in stressing the importance of early Christian liturgical parallels for a proper understanding of the development of the Jewish liturgy. He notes, for example, the preservation of the biblical "doxological eulogies" in the early Christian prayers, whereas this form, which is characterized in the Mishnah (M. Ber. 9:5) as proper to the Temple usage, ultimately disappeared from the rabbinic prayers.[335] Whether this phenomenon is to be accounted for by the theory that the Christian doxologies preserve a current, living Jewish custom which was "assimilated" to the Christian liturgy, as Spanier and Baumstark claim, or by assuming that the stereotypic doxological patterns were rather patterned after those in the Psalter, would seem to be an open question.

Spanier further points out that the stereotyped *ki-*ꜣ*attah* phrase, which in the Jewish liturgy usually functions as a "rationale clause" following on a petition and as a transitional phrase immediately before the concluding eulogy, frequently occurs in the early Christian liturgies as the concluding eulogy itself. From this he infers that such a usage originally must have been common in the Jewish prayers as well.[336] Following Baumstark, he is led by this to conclude that the form of the concluding eulogy in the Jewish benediction originally had not been fixed, but that many patterns were in use, some of which ultimately were preserved in the early Christian liturgies. He does not, however, concur with Baumstark's thesis that the ultimate predominance of the relatively simple eulogy formula (which became typical in the Jewish liturgy) was connected with anti-Christian tendencies.[337] The model of original multiplicity proposed here by Baumstark and Spanier corresponds to that of Heinemann, who, for this reason, accepts their thesis regarding the Jewish origin of these Christian formulae.[338] The theory certainly is plausible, and there is no question that the stylistic parallels are real and that dependence is extremely likely. Nonetheless, a bit more caution should be exercised here. We should not deny to the early Christian community any liturgical creativity. It is at least as possible that the use of Jewish elements—stereotyped patterns and expressions—in early Christian prayers was quite free and that the "original" Jewish contexts have been violated to suit Christian needs and tastes. Thus, the use of the ki-ʾattah pattern as a eulogy in Christian prayers does not in and of itself prove that the pattern once had been so used in Jewish prayers as well.

If Spanier's conclusions regarding Christian and Jewish eulogy-formulae are at least plausible, his suggestion that the Greek version of the ʾabot benediction which is preserved in the early Christian *Apostolic Constitutions* can tell us a great deal about the "original" Hebrew form and wording of this benediction is very far-fetched. On the one hand, Spanier claims that this version dates from a time when the wording of the *tefillah* was not yet fixed; on the other, he seeks to draw normative conclusions from the Greek wording of this benediction. He observes, for example, that the liturgical *berakah* formula does not appear at the beginning of the ʾabot benediction in the Greek version, but rather at the beginning of the *geburot* benediction. From this he draws the conclusion that the Hebrew version originally must have conformed to this style.[339] But such a conclusion is extremely hazardous. First of all, we should not expect a Greek Christian text to conform to the rabbinic rules for liturgical *berakah* formulae and series of benedictions. Secondly, to argue that since the Greek version does not conform to such rules, the Hebrew version also originally must have approximated to its style is highly tenuous.[340]

On the basis of a comparison between the Greek version and the later Hebrew version in the Ashkenazic rite, Spanier concludes that the ʾabot benediction was not originally a Prayer of Praise at all, but rather a Petitionary Prayer. This he infers primarily from the Hebrew phrase, *wezoker ḥasde ʾabot* ("who remembreth His covenental loyalty to the Patriarchs," according to Spanier's understanding of this phrase), and from the Greek eulogy, "Shield of the *descendents* of Abraham," which he holds to be original. Aware that the Palestinian version in the Genizah fragments (in which the "petitionary" phrase in question is lacking) contradicts his theory outright, Spanier chooses to regard the Greek version as more authentic.[341] Such an appraisal is highly questionable, to say the least. Furthermore, he holds that the prayer in Ben Sira, 51, faithfully reflects an early form of the *tefillah* in which the ʾabot benediction follows upon the various national petitions. This, too, is highly speculative. Finally, since he conceives the Greek eulogy to have been the original, he must account for the origin of the present eulogy. The latter, he claims, was derived from an ancient form of the Thanksgiving benediction which was recited in the Temple (although the verbal affinity is rather with the Thanksgiving benediction that is found in the modern Ashkenazic rite [!] and is itself comprehensible in terms of stock liturgical phraseology). This is the maze into which Spanier is led by too rigorously pursuing parallels between Christian and Jewish prayer texts.

In his first three articles, Spanier largely adheres to the basic assumptions of classical philology and to the authoritarian historical model it implies. But in the last volume of the *Monatsschrift* in 1939—when his own fate, ironically, and the fate of German-Jewish scholarship had already been sealed—Spanier published a brief but remarkably insightful article which was to serve as the springboard for a major attack on the philological method, primarily on its underlying historical model. He writes:

> Man ist vielfach gewöhnt, die Entwicklung der jüdischen Liturgie sich im Bilde eines stetig wachsenden Organismus vorzustellen. Es ist ein weitgehend anerkannter Grundsatz, dass lange Gebete auf kürzere Formen zurückzuführen seien und dass die Vielfältigkeit, die sich in den verschiedenen Riten ausprägt, auf eine ursprüngliche Einheitlichkeit zurückweise. Der Philologe pflegt, wenn er verschiedene Handschriften oder gar verschiedene Rezensionen ein und desselben literarischen Werkes vor sich sicht, den 'Archetypus' zu suchen, und er überträgt diese Forschungsweise unwillkürlich auch auf liturgische Texte.
>
> Dennoch fragt es sich, wie weit das mit Recht geschieht, Dass *letzten Endes* auch auf unserem Gebiet die Einheitlichkeit vor der Mannigfaligkeit liegt, soll natürlich nicht in Frage gezogen werden. Nur dürfte die Entwicklung in ihrem Verlauf nicht immer so gradlinig gewesen sein, wie es vielfach—nicht so sehr in der Theorie, aber doch in der Praxis der wissenschaftlichen Einzelarbeit—angenommen wird.
>
> Gewiss wird, nachdem die ersten Anstösse zum Werden des Gemeindegebetes gegeben waren, ein üppiges Spreissen und Blühen eingesetzt haben. . . . Dem Betenden oder Vorbetenden war in jener Zeit von der Überlieferung ein reicher Schatz von Möglichkeiten geboten, mit dem er schalten und walten durfte.[342]

Thus, Spanier calls into question both the monolinearity of the philological-historical model and the validity of the *Urtext* assumption. He also notes the difference between theory and practice which, as we have noted, came to characterize so much of Jewish liturgical scholarship (Elbogen is the classic example). And he proposes the historical model of primary multiplicity, which must also now be applied in practice (although he still cannot liberate himself entirely from the notion of ultimate original simplicity). Only later, he asserts, was relative uniformity achieved both in Palestine[343] and Babylonia, as a result of the work of the rabbis.

The traces of this development, Spanier asserts, may be found in the Talmudic literature. Thus he rightly notes that the Mishnah, with one exception, does not refer to any prayer-formulae, but rather to the general content and order of the benedictions. The Tosefta refers to various subjects and themes which must be mentioned in various benedictions. Only in the Talmuds are actual prayer-formulations cited,[344] and here we find the fourth-century *°amora°* Rav Papa recommending that various alternate formulae be *combined.* On these grounds, Spanier offers a revised model for understanding some of the passages which classical philology would identify as "insertions." He proposes instead that many of the texts of the Ashkenazic rite (which, like all of the European rites, is descended from the Babylonian rite) should be viewed as conflations of previously alternate versions of the same prayer. Thus, many double readings can be identified in the prayer texts. In essence, Spanier is here proposing a revised philological model.[345]

Some of Spanier's observations are undoubtedly correct. Thus, it is likely that the Palestinian eulogy formula, *ṣur yiśra°el wego°alo*, is a conflation of *ṣur yiśra°el* and *go°el yiśra°el*, on the model of b. Ber. 59b and 60b. It is almost certain that passages such as *wekol ha-ḥayyim* and *we°al kulam* in the Thanksgiving benediction of the *tefillah* are originally alternate versions, since both are self-contained entities fulfilling the same function as transitional clauses before the eulogy. On the other hand, this method is prone to reductionism and occasionally may break up legitimate instances of *parallelismus membrorum* in the text. Spanier appears to be doing this in his treatment of the prayer for Healing and the first phrases of the Thanksgiving benediction.[346]

On the basis of the relevant passages in the Talmudic literature, Spanier concludes that philological analysis can take us back no further than the third or fourth century, since before this time there were no fixed formulae. Any attempt, then, to isolate pre-70 passages in the extant prayer texts automatically is to be declared invalid on methodological grounds.[347] Spanier has here taken a giant leap in the right direction, but his dating still seems much too early. Properly speaking, philological analysis, when it can be applied, can probably take us back to the Geonic period at the very earliest, as we shall note below.

In Spanier, then, we find all of the elements which later were to bear fruit in Heinemann's researches.

Heinemann

From a methodological point of view, Heinemann's study, *Ha-tefillah bitequfat hatanna°im weha°amora°im*, is the most significant and suggestive work in the field of Jewish liturgy since Elbogen's *Der jüdische Gottesdienst*, and also constitutes the first full-length, comprehensive monograph on the liturgy since the latter work appeared in 1913. Upon publication, it was hailed for its "fresh . . . and novel approach,"[348] although adherents to the philological method took issue with some of its conclusions as well as with the approach in general.[349]

A full two chapters of the book are devoted exclusively to a discussion of method, in which the author criticizes the excesses of the historical-philological approach and articulates his own model and assumptions.[350] Although Heinemann purports not to deal primarily with historical problems,[351] it is in fact the historical model he proposes which constitutes a most intriguing (and problematic) innovation on his part. In place of the "centralized authoritarian" model assumed by his predecessors (including, for a time at least, Spanier),[352] he employs a decentralized, flexible model in which the prayers are to be viewed as authentic folk creations composed by the people themselves rather than as compositions instituted at some point in time by the rabbis.[353] Parallel occurrence of the same phraseology in several widely different contexts is then to be viewed as the natural use of certain stock phrases rather than as actual literary borrowing.[354]

Unfortunately, we know almost nothing about the origin and early history of the synagogue as an institution,[355] while all of our information on the formation of the statutory prayers comes from rabbinic sources, which themselves have a prehistory. Neither the exact relationship between the rabbinic schoolhouse and the synagogue, nor the extent to which rabbinic authority actually extended over the masses in both Palestine and Babylonia during either the Tannaitic or Amoraic periods is clear from these sources. While Heinemann's general characterization of the synagogue as a popular folk institution over which the rabbis gradually came to exercise control[356] seems valid, it is not at all clear that the prayer texts and formulae, as well as most of the structures, which the rabbis set down in Mishnah, Tosefta, and the two Talmuds as "normative" necessarily originated with the masses and not within rabbinical circles themselves.[357] This does not, however, invalidate Heinemann's assumption of the original multiplicity, since the same diversity of formulation is amply attested to in the sources regardless of its ultimate provenance. Nor does this undermine his application of form-critical methods to the liturgy, which he justifies by referring to the popular, folk origin of the prayers. On the contrary, even the literature of the schoolhouse has proven itself susceptible to form-critical analysis.[358] It is to Heinemann's particular use of form-criticism that we now turn.

Heinemann's primary form-critical model is Dibelius, as we have noted above. Thus, he places a heavy emphasis on *Sitz im Leben*. In fact, most of Heinemann's categories embody the topological-sociological *Sitz im Leben* in their very designation—viz., Temple Prayers, *bet midraš* prayers, statutory synagogue prayers, non-statutory and private prayers. In the latter types, we catch a glimpse of still another criterion for categorization: the halakic status of the prayer. The fact that Heinemann's categories do indeed seem to describe the prayers adequately and relatively objectively is due in no small measure to the fact that they are intrinsically related to the prayers themselves; and the halakic status of a particular prayer is, as Heinemann demonstrates most conclusively, a crucial element in its style. The determination that a particular prayer does not conform completely to the rules of the liturgical *berakah* because the rules were never completely applied to it may seem a bit facile and perhaps circular in any one instance, but the preponderance of such cases, when coupled with the observation that none were *originally* statutory prayers, and when viewed in light of the numerous formulae in the Genizah fragments which do not conform to the Babylonian rules, seems to validate Heinemann's reasoning. The Genizah fragments certainly are sufficient proof that multiplicity, and not uniformity, was the original "rule," which prevailed for a very long time.

Heinemann's categories, however, are not all of the same order, as he himself acknowledges.[359] In addition to the major topological categories, Heinemann also isolates several stylistic-functional categories, which have a sociological basis viz., the "benediction by which a man blesses his fellow," the "invitational formula," the "response," and one category, the "courtroom pattern," which might best be characterized as stylistic. By and large, he tends to avoid the thematic-modal criteria used by Spanier (and also by Gunkel): "Praise," "Petition," "Thanksgiving," etc. It is obvious that, to a large extent, the criteria for categorization will depend upon the particular *Gestalt* of the scholar himself, and upon his own personal "feeling" for the material. Thus, Heinemann writes: "The categorization scheme which we have applied . . . has not been theoretical or systematic, but rather functional in nature—nor have we intended it to be exhaustive."[360] This is as it should be, since a theoretical or systematic schema usually will end up by forcing the data into its mold. On the whole, Heinemann's assumptions do not appear unreasonable, while his conceptual scheme produces significant and plausible results.[361]

Nor does Heinemann entirely forsake the philological method. His lengthy excursus on the probable origin of the liturgical *berakah* formula, for example, makes use of both stylistic and philological criteria.[362]

In demonstrating the original fluidity of the prayer formulae which remained in force throughout the Talmudic period, Heinemann has rendered a great service to the field of Jewish liturgical studies. Nonetheless, his work stops short (as he himself acknowledged)[363] of what now must be regarded as the crucial epoch for the subsequent development of the liturgy, i.e., the Geonic period. To future scholars in the field of Jewish liturgy will belong the task of taking up where Heinemann has left off.[364]

III. CONCLUSION

What, then, are the major historical problems which still confront us? There seem to have been three crucial turning points in the early history of the liturgy. Two of these undoubtedly will remain obscure, since we have no adequate source material with which to unlock their secrets. The third, however, may yet generate fruitful scholarship.

The first problem is to account for the origin of the synagogue itself. Here we are faced with a wealth of conjectures and almost no facts. The origin of the synagogue has been dated as early as Deuteronomic times[365] and as late as the Maccabean period,[366] with the traditional scholarly consensus arguing for an exilic or post-exilic dating.[367] All of these datings are equally speculative. But of equivalent importance is the manner in which the synagogue originated, that is, the sociological background, forces, groups, etc., which brought it into being. Were we to know how and for what purpose and under what leadership the synagogue originated, we would be better able to employ an appropriate historical model to describe its early development and the early development of the liturgy. The problem is all the more enticing since, almost certainly it never can be solved; there are simply no data available. Further work on this problem must, then, inevitably prove to be futile.

The second crucial turning point in the history of the liturgy, and, for that matter, in the history of Jews and Judaism, was the destruction of the Second Temple in 70 C.E. and the activity of the rabbinical consistory at Yavneh. What actually transpired at Yavneh? How was the statutory liturgy, and particularly the Eighteen Benedictions, shaped here? Was there in fact a prayer of Eighteen Benedictions before 70, or was the number fixed by Rabban Gamaliel II and his circle at Yavneh? To what extent are the basic rubrics and formulae rabbinic or popular in origin? If the number eighteen was fixed at Yavneh, how do we suddenly arrive at nineteen benedictions in Amoraic Babylonia? Again, these are questions which probably never will be answered to our complete satisfaction because the data are sparse, ambiguous, and relatively late.

The third crucial juncture, as we noted above, is the Geonic period in Babylonia. At this time there was an attempt, not completely successful, to fix the wording of the prayers once and for all. What was the full scope and nature of that attempt? Here we must rely on Geonic responsa and on Genizah materials.[368] How are the texts of the later European rites related to Geonic texts? To pre-Geonic oral formulations? To Talmudic citations? Accepting Heinemann's model of original multiplicity, it seems that we should be trying to account for the basic similarities in the wordings of the European rites, more than their differences. How, precisely, did these rites spread and proliferate over Europe, Asia, and North Africa, and what is the exact nature of their interrelatedness?

There remains as well a very basic problem which was outside the scope of this essay, viz., to determine the exact nature of the early relationships between statutory prayer and *piyyuṭ*—how poetic versions of the statutory prayers themselves evolved into lengthy, artistic compositions with an independent *raison d'être*.[369]

Moreover, on a methodological level, the extent to which philological analysis can be applied to the prayer texts of the European rites still remains to be determined. Obviously, there *do* exist later additions and corruptions in the manuscripts and printed editions of these rites. Once the process of transmission ceases to be oral and becomes written, the materials become susceptible of philological analysis. Such analysis, however, in order to be valid, cannot be so rigid or so rigorous as some of the examples dealt with above. The final results ultimately will have to be more modest in their claims, since philology cannot take us back to the preliterary stage. The very nature, then, of the present prayer texts must be examined anew in order to determine how relatively early or late they actually may be.

These last areas seem to be fruitful for subsequent investigation. Here again, many of the answers may evade us, but there is a wealth of material to investigate and a host of new questions to put to the extant sources. There still are a large number of unpublished Genizah fragments, in which new answers and newer questions may come to light. In all of these areas of research, the basic problems of methodology and methodological adequacy will remain, even as new methods will be developed and existing methods refined. For in the final analysis, our knowledge of the past is forever bounded by the parameters of our own *"Sitz im Leben"* and by the finitude of our own thought processes.[370]

NOTES

[1]Bernard Botte, in his foreword to the third edition of Anton Baumstark, *Comparative Liturgy,* Oxford: 1958, p. viii.

[2]J. Heinemann, *Ha-tefillah bitequfat ha-tanna'im weha' amora'im. Tibah udefuseha,* 2nd ed., Jerusalem: 1966, p. 11. [henceforth: *Ha-tefillah*]. [*Prayer in the Talmud: Forms and Patterns,* English version by Richard S. Sarason, Berlin-New York: 1977].

[3]See below, p. 131ff.

[4]In MGWJ, LXXXIII (1939), pp. 142, 148-49.

[5]"Zur Formengeschichte des altjüdischen Gebetes," MGWJ, LXXVIII (1934), pp. 438-447; "Stilkritisches zum jüdischen Gebet," MGWJ, LXXX (1936), pp. 339-350; and see below, p. . 140ff.

[6]MGWJ, LXXXIII, p. 149.

[7]Daniel Goldschmidt, *Haggadah šel pesaḥ wetoledoteha* [henceforth, *Haggadah*], Jerusalem: 1960. See below, p. 124ff.

[8]Joseph Heinemann "*Haggadah šel pesaḥ wetoledoteha* lᶜ D. Goldschmidt," *Tarbiz,* XXX (1960–61), pp. 405–410. See below pp. 126–27.

[9]*Ha-tefillah,* pp. 11-15; 29ff. For a fuller appraisal, see Jakob J. Petuchowski, "A New Approach to Jewish Liturgy," *Judaism* XV, 1, (1966), pp. 114-120.

[10]The seeds for a critical, developmental approach to the liturgy before Zunz may be discerned to some extent in the carefully edited *Maḥzor* (1800-2) and *Siddur* (1823) of Wolf Heindenheim (1757-1832), which were based on the use of a number of manuscripts. Cf., Ismar Elbogen, *Der jüdische Gottesdienst in seiner geschichtlichen Entwicklung,* 4th ed., Hildesheim: 1962 [henceforth. Elbogen, Gottesdienst], p. 390.

[11]Zunz's late dating of the classical *piyyuṭ* has, however, been disproven. Cf., the remarks of Jefim Schirmann, in Elbogen, *Ha-tefillah be Yiśraʾel,* Jerusalem: 1972 (henceforth: Elbogen [Hebrew]), pp. 211-12 *et passim.*

[12]Leopold Zunz, *Ha-deraŝot beyiśraʾel,* ed. Hanoch Albeck, Jerusalem: 1954, p. 219. The passage appears in English in HUCA, XXXI (1960), p. 260; and cf., Samuel S. Cohon, "Zunz and Reform Judaism," HUCA, XXXI, pp. 251-276; also Elbogen, *op. cit.,* pp. 415-16.

[13]*Ha-deraŝot,* p. 218; translated by Cohon, *op. cit.,* p. 260.

[14]Cf., the introduction to the first edition of the prayerbook of the West London Synagogue, *Forms of Prayer* (1841), cited by Petuchowski, *Contributions to the Scientific Study of Jewish Liturgy,* New York: 1970, pp. XIV-XV, and Zunz's 1840 letter to Prof. H. Hurwitz in London, cited by Ludwig Geiger in *Liberales Judentum,* IX (1917), pp. 119-20. Cf., also, Elbogen, *Gottesdienst,* p. 437.

[15]Cf., Michael A. Meyer, *The Origins of the Modern Jew,* Detroit: 1967, pp. 158-60; especially Meyer's remark on p. 160: "In fact the young Zunz is best understood, I believe, not as a philosopher or historian (though there are in his works some philosophical elements and indications of historical conceptualization) but as a *philologist.*" (Author's italics.)

[16]*Ibid.,* p. 159.

[17]*Ha-deraŝot,* p. 179.

[18]*Ibid.,* p. 180.

[19]But see how Heinemann explains this phenomenon, *Ha-tefillah,* p. 39ff.

[20]*Ha-deraŝot,* p. 179.

[21]Israel Davidson, Simḥa Assaf, Issachar Joel, eds., *Siddur Rab Saᶜadyah Gaʾon,* Jerusalem: 1940, p. 13 in the text.

[22]Cf., for example, Elbogen, JQR (O.S.), XIX (1907), p. 235: "Zunz, following Rapoport, separated out from the *Yotser* the later elements and fixed its original wording at forty-five words. The Siddur of Amram Gaon shows that even this estimate overshot the mark." Cf., also Zwi Karl, *Meḥqarim betoledot ha-tefillah* [henceforth, *Meḥqarim*], Tel Aviv: 1950, p. 31; Daniel Goldschmidt, *Haggadah,* p. 32, note 13; and Finkelstein, REJ (O.S.), 93 (1932), p. 19ff., who for quite peculiar reasons rejects the eulogy as original!

[23]*Ha-deraŝot,* p. 178.

[24]Cf., Lawrence A. Hoffman, *Liturgical Responses Suppressed by the Gaonim in Their Attempt to Fix the Liturgy,* unpublished Ph. D. dissertation, Hebrew Union College, Cincinnati, 1973, p. 28ff., *et passim.*

[25]*Ha-derašot*, p. 179.

[26]Elbogen, *Gottesdienst*, p. 32.

[27]The *goʾel yiśraʾel* problem has been dealt with by almost every subsequent investigator of the Eighteen Benedictions. Cf., for example, the very interesting hypothesis proposed by S. D. Luzzatto, *Maboʾ lemaḥzor bene romaʾ*, ed. Goldschmidt, Tel Aviv: 1966, p. 18. Goldschmidt, *ad. loc.*, note 9, rejects this theory, while Heinemann, in Elbogen, [Hebrew], pp. 26–27, accepts it. Cf., also, Elbogen, *Gottesdienst*, pp. 30, 35–36, and notes *ad. loc.*; Kaufmann Kohler in HUCA, I (1924), p. 399. This question has no relevance for Finkelstein, JQR (N.S.), XVI (1925–26), p. 13ff., who uses an entirely different and highly artificial series of criteria for grouping (as we shall note below).

[28]*Ha-derašot*, p. 480, note 33. Both the particular wording of this benediction in the European rites, in which the phrase in question does at first glance give the impression of an "insertion," as well as the difference between the Palestinian and the Babylonian eulogy-formulae for this benediction were long used to justify the philological method, which assumes that the present text contains within it the "original" text. Cf., for example, Elbogen, *Gottesdienst*, p. 29; Kohler, HUCA, I, p. 406; Karl, *Meḥqarim*, p. 80; but cf. the rebuttal of Arthur Spanier, MGWJ, LXXXIII (1939), p. 149, note 8. Heinemann seems to accept a modified version of Zunz's position, namely, that the Palestinian version in the Cairo Genizah fragments "might have been used in the days of the Temple." Cf., s.v. "Amidah," *Encyclopaedia Judaica*, Jerusalem-New York: 1971, II, 842. Obviously, there is no way of proving such an assertion.

[29]Heinemann explains the development of the *tefillah* by positing a number of simultaneously originating and overlapping series of benedictions *(sidre berakot)* which were finally edited at Yavneh. See *Ha-tefillah*, p. 138ff. For his account of the relationship between the various *tefillot* recited on different occasions, see *ibid.*, p. 143 as well as his article, *"Tefillot ha-šabbat," Maḥanayim*, LXXXV-LXXXVI (5724), pp. 54-57.

[30]The "simple evolutionary" model used with great consistency by German Protestant scholars of the last century, usually in an attempt to demonstrate the higher "spirituality" (identified with *individual* piety) of Christianity over Judaism. As late as 1932, Hermann Gunkel was still making use of this model. See below, pp. 135–37.

[31]*Ha-derašot*, p. 179.

[32]Heinemann, *Ha-tefillah*, p. 33, note 18, holds that Zunz *did* subscribe to the notion of an *Urtext*, but he does not distinguish between the latter's treatment of the *šemaᶜ*, where there is unambiguous positive evidence, and his treatment of the *tefillah*, where the question is open. The examples of variant texts which Zunz cites (p. 481, note 37) are all to be found in the Talmudic literature. Nonetheless, Heinemann is probably correct, if only because the philological method to which Zunz adheres *presupposes* the existence of an *Urtext*. In this case, the *Urtext* of certain benedictions would simply not be attainable.

[33]Thus the *qeduššah deyoṣer* and the benediction for the restoration of the Davidic monarchy, which do not appear in the Genizah fragments representing the Palestinian-Egyptian rites, are nonetheless attested to in other Palestinian sources and those undoubtedly based on Palestinian custom; cf. *Ha-tefillah*, pp. 145-146.

[34]This is a particularly thorny problem, since (a) medieval copyists felt no compunction about altering the wording of prayer texts in ancient sources to conform to the contemporary usage of their own milieux (cf., particularly, Goldschmidt, *Haggadah*, p. 33, note 13, as well as his

edition of *Seder Rab ᶜAmram Gaᵓon,* Jerusalem: 1972, p. 10; on variants in the Talmud, cf., Elbogen, in JQR, XIX [1907], p. 242; and *Ha-tefillah,* p. 45, note 39), and (b) we cannot determine with precision the relationship between the citation in the Talmud of an opening word or phrase and the full texts which now begin with that word or phrase in the written *siddurim* of the various rites. A suggestive example of this problem is the fact that the second morning benediction before the *šemaᶜ* in the Italian, Sephardic, and Oriental rites begins with the phrase, *ᵓahabat ᶜolam,* while the continuation is similar to that version in the other rites which begins *ᵓahabah rabbah* (cf. Goldschmidt, in Luzzatto, *Maḥzor,* p. 83, and note 34 there; also Elbogen, *loc. cit.*).

[35]Cohon, in HUCA, XXXI, p. 276.

[36]Cf., Zunz, *Die Ritus des synagogalen Gottesdienstes,* Berlin: 1859, pp. 2-3. He also expresses there the rather peculiar notion that some of the variety is due to differences which existed "in älterer Zeit zwischen dem Dienste innerhalb und dem ausserhalb des Tempels."

[37]Reprinted separately with critical annotations by Daniel Goldschmidt; S. D. Luzzato, *Maboᵓ leMaḥzor bene romaᵓ,* Tel Aviv: 1966.

[38]Cf., Goldschmidt, *op. cit.,* pp. 13, 79.

[39]Luzzatto, *Maboᵓ,* p. 17.

[40]*Ibid,* and cf.,*Ha-tefillah,* p. 32, note 14.

[41]*Ibid.,* p. 18.

[42]*Ibid.*

[43]See *Ha-tefillah,* p. 29ff.

[44]Luzzatto, *Maboᵓ,* p. 20.

[45]*Ibid.,* p. 22.

[46]Cf., for example, Ezra Fleischer, *"ᶜIyunim bibeᶜayot tafkidam ha-liturgi šel suge ha-piyyut ha-kadum,"* Tarbiz, 40 (5731) pp. 41-63, who affirms the position of Luzzatto on this issue. See particularly, p. 46, and note 13 there, where he addresses himself to Heinemann's conclusions. The opposite view is held by Jefim Schirmann, in Elbogen [Hebrew], p. 211.

[47]Unless he were to assume that the "fixed" written wordings merely constitute traditional wordings which had previously been prevalent, but such an assumption would seem to contradict the thrust of his actual argument.

[48]Of much greater value is the recently published Hebrew translation which has been thoroughly revised and updated by Heinemann and other scholars, *Ha-tefillah beyiśraᵓel behitpaṭḥutah ha-historit,* Tel Aviv: 1972. For ease of cross-reference we shall refer exclusively to that edition in this section, which we designate as Elbogen [Hebrew].

[49]Particularly in his characterization of the late medieval period (Hebrew, p. 280), and in his treatment of the Kabbalistic influence on the liturgy (section 44) and of the modern period (sections 45-47).

[50]See the editors' preface to the *Einheitsgebetbuch,* which appears in English in Jakob J. Petuchowski, *Prayerbook Reform in Europe,* New York: 1968, pp. 206-213; particularly pp. 212-13.

[51]Elbogen [Hebrew], p. 13.

[52]*Ibid.,* p. 15.

[53]JQR (O.S.), XIX, p. 229ff.

[54]*Ibid.,* p. 231.

[55]*Ibid.,* p. 233.

[56]*Ibid.,* p. 234. In this particular context, Elbogen is referring to the gradual evolution of the *šema^c* and its benedictions in general. In *Gottesdienst,* this assumption leads to the conclusions that (a) the first benediction before the *šema^c,* which deals with the theme of creation, originally could have made use of the same wording in the morning and evening and hence the distinction between *yoser* and *ma^ʾarib* would be secondary (Hebrew, pp. 77, 187; it seems to us more reasonable to assume the contrary in this case, since sunrise and sunset would seem to evoke appropriately different responses, and since these two benedictions would more likely have been conditioned from the outset by their *function,* which is *occasional*), (b) the earliest prayers would not have contained distinctive wordings for the Sabbath and each of the Festivals (*ibid.,* p. 184; again the contrary seems to us to be more reasonable, for the same reason), (c) the petitions in the Eighteen Benedictions were originally quite general and then became more specific (*ibid.,* p. 184, p. 24, where "general" petitions are identified with the personal as opposed to the national petitions [!]).

[57]See above, note 22.

[58]JQR (O.S.), XIX, p. 236.

[59]Elbogen [Hebrew], p. 199.

[60]*Ibid.,* p. 24. These "circles" become basic to Kaufmann Kohler's analysis of the Eighteen Benedictions, as we shall see below.

[61]See above, p. 102, and note 26 there.

[62]See above, note 56.

[63]Kohler, HUCA, I, p. 401, notes correctly that *birkat ha-minnim* fits in well with this schema and that the incident described in b. Ber. 28b, which is the Babylonian Amoraic "explanation" for the presence of a nineteenth benediction, should be understood as the "revision" of an already existing benediction. This view is supported by Tos. Ber. 3:25. Cf., Heinemann, in Elbogen [Hebrew], pp. 31-32; and *Ha-tefillah,* p. 142ff.

[64]Cf., Heinemann, in Elbogen [Hebrew], pp. 26-27.

[65]Elbogen, [Hebrew], pp. 27-29. See above, note 63.

[66]See *Ha-tefillah,* p. 142ff.

[67]Elbogen [Hebrew], p. 29.

[68]JQR (O.S.), XIX, p. 715.

[69]Ibid., p. 716.

[70]Ibid., p. 717.

[71]Ibid., p. 718.

[72]So, too, does Heinemann understand this passage. See *Ha-tefillah*, p. 33, note. 18.

[73]Elbogen [Hebrew], pp. 32-33. The passage is cited by Heinemann, *ibid.*, p. 32, note 14.

[74]The examples are too numerous to cite in full. In the very same chapter see, for example, Elbogen [Hebrew], pp. 34, 38, 40, 41, 42, 43.

[75]Cf., for example, Elbogen [Hebrew], pp. 44, 57, *et passim*.

[76]Ibid., pp. 74, 75, 423, note 54.

[77]Ibid., p. 84.

[78]Ibid., p. 51.

[79]Ibid., p. 177.

[80]Cf., particularly, Kaufmann Kohler, *Jewish Theology Systematically and Historically Considered*, New York: 1918, Chapter LVII, which is entitled, "Christianity and Mohammedanism, the Daughter-Religions of Judaism"; also, *The Origins of the Synagogue and the Church*, New York: 1929 [henceforth: *Origins*], p. xxxiv.

[81]*Origins*, p. xxxiv. Cf., also, *Jewish Theology*, p. 445.

[82]*Origins*, p. 18ff.

[83]Ibid., p. 118.

[84]Ibid., p. 206ff.

[85]Ibid., p. 211ff.

[86]Ibid., p. 237, 238ff, 259.

[87]They are variously described by Kohler as "leaders" of the Pharisees (*ibid.*, p. 35) and "creators" of Pharisaism (p. 81), but more often are set in opposition to the Pharisees (pp. 37, 51, 59, 69, 70, 109-110, 136). They are characterized as the authors of the prayers and the *haggadah*, and as such are to be distinguished from the *soferim*, or Scribes, who formulated the *halakah* (pp. 28, 94; also HUCA, I, p. 389). Nonetheless, when it suits his purposes, Kohler will ascribe to them the introduction of distinctly Pharisaic doctrines (*Origins*, pp. 70, 81ff). What emerges from a thorough examination of all of the above passages is a distinct *Tendenz* on Kohler's part to dissociate the "spiritual" elements of rabbinic Judaism from the "legalistic" or "Pharisaic" ones (in the New Testament sense of the term). Both the Synagogue as an institution as well as its

liturgy, Kohler asserts, are "spiritual" and hence have a "Hasidean" rather than a "Pharisaic" origin. Moreover, that greater "spirituality" which the Church claims for itself, Kohler wishes to portray as an inheritance from the Synagogue which was in fact brought into the Church by the very same group that founded the Synagogue—viz., the Hasideans, or Essenes. The entire hypothesis, then, reduces itself to an apology designed to counter the thinly-veiled polemics against "Pharisaism" (viz., rabbinic Judaism) which were commonly put forth by nineteenth and early twentieth century German Protestant scholars (Bousset, Schürer et al.). Kohler, in effect, has accepted the critique of Pharisaism and has found a way of "getting out from under it" by identifying a *second* group which contributed the "spiritual" element to both Judaism *and* Christianity.

[88]Hyman G. Enelow, "Kaufman Kohler," *American Jewish Yearbook*, XXXVIII (1926-27), p. 259. The essay is reprinted as an introduction to Kohler's *Origins*. Cf., also, the criticisms of Elbogen, in *Gottesdienst* [Hebrew], pp. 22, 187, 388, note 1.

[89]Kohler, *Origins*, p. 57.

[90]In M. Tamid 5:1, we are told that the priests in the Temple recited only one benediction before the *šema*ᶜ. Elbogen, *Gottesdienst* [Hebrew], p. 19, arguing on functional grounds, maintains that this must have been the "Torah benediction" (viz., the equivalent of ᵓ*ahabah rabbah*). Kohler holds to the same view, but argues that the Torah emphasis is "priestly" in origin, and hence the Torah benediction in the Temple would have been *substituted* for the Hasidean *yoṣer* benediction (*Origins*, pp. 59-60). Heinemann, (*Ha-tefillah*, p. 145) holds that the Mishnah only informs us about the Temple usage, where their priests "apparently omitted the *yoṣer* benediction, since they recited their prayers before the rising of the sun." Even the latter explanation, it should be noted, is purely speculative. Cf., also, the somewhat idiosyncratic theory of Finkelstein, REJ (O.S.), 93 (1932), p. 16ff., who holds, among other things, that the *yoṣer* benediction was indeed primary and as such was also recited by the priests in the Temple.

[91]*Origins*, pp. 57-58.

[92]See the insightful analysis of Heinemann, *Ha-tefillah*, pp. 79f., 84f.

[93]HUCA, I, p. 398.

[94]*Ibid.*, p. 392.

[95]*Ibid.*, pp. 390-391, 401-2, 405-6. Heinemann's proposed solution to the problem (*Ha-tefillah*, pp. 142-43), that "those who customarily recited a separate benediction [in Palestine] for the Davidic restoration would combine two *other* benedictions into one as a matter of course," constitutes an improvement, but he, too, cannot successfully account for the variation between Palestine and Babylonia in this matter: "it is difficult to understand the departure from tradition involved in the ultimate institution of nineteen benedictions in Babylonia."

[96]*Origins*, p. 68; HUCA, I, p. 393.

[97]HUCA, I, pp. 396-97.

[98]*Ibid.*, p. 395. Spanier, too, "Die erste Benediktion des Achtzehngebetes," MGWJ, LXXXI (1937), pp. 71-76, expresses the same notion, only he bases his assertion (much too heavily) on the Greek version of the Seventh Book of the *Apostolic Constitutions*—a very Kohleresque rationale!

[99]*Ibid.,* p. 403.

[100]See the Spanier article cited above in note 98, and also below. Baumstark also endorses this procedure; see below, p. 129ff.

[101]HUCA, I, p. 395.

[102]*Ibid.,* p. 397.

[103]*Ha-tefillah,* p. 146.

[104]Louis Finkelstein, "The Development of the Amidah," JQR (N.S.), XVI (1925-26), pp. 1-43, 127-70.

[105]"The Birkat Ha-Mazon," JQR (N.S.), XIX (1929), pp. 211-62.

[106]JQR (N.S.), XVI, p. 1.

[107]J.R (N.S.), XIX, p. 224.

[108]Thus the two forms of the last benediction of the *tefillah* in the European rites are explained by assuming one to have been of Palestinian, the other of Babylonian origin (JQR [N.S.], XVI, p. 32). The numerous versions of the benediction for Jerusalem are to be accounted for along similar lines, but the explanation is further complicated by Finkelstein's dating criteria, which are responsible for his concluding that "the Babylonian *Amidah* in early times did not contain the prayer for Jerusalem, which therefore cannot be considered part of the original *Amidah*" (*ibid.,* p. 34). To this highly strained and artificial explanation, compare the relative *ease* and *clarity* of Heinemann's account, *Ha-tefillah,* p. 35ff. Finkelstein explains the variance between the Palestinian and Babylonian customs with regard to the weekday recitation of the *qeduššah* in the *tefillah* by asserting that "in Palestine the daily *Amidah* had been fixed by R. Gamaliel, and no additions could lightly be made, while in Babylonia the prayer remained in a fluid state for some time" (*ibid.,* p. 31). The totality of Finkelstein's assumptions, both philological and historical, lead him to conclude that "the Babylonian *Amidah* thus developed without the guidance of an authoritative center, such as controlled the growth of the Palestinian *Amidah.* Hence the numerous versions of the *Amidah* of the Dispersion, in which the texts differ from each other not only in matter of words, but sometimes even in the complete content of the paragraphs" (*ibid.,* p. 43)—a conclusion which flies in the face of all of the evidence and everything that we know about the course of liturgical development of the two countries! Cf., *Ha-tefillah,* pp. 182-83; and Hoffman, *Liturgical Responses, etc., passim.*

[109]As in Finkelstein's chronological explanation of the two introductions to the *midrash* (those espoused by Rab and Samuel) in the Passover *Haggadah,* "Pre-Maccabean Documents in the Passover Haggadah," HTR, XXXV, p. 293ff., particularly pp. 313-14. It is only the *a priori* inadmissibility of two different, simultaneously existing versions that necessitates the type of reconstruction which we find here. Daniel Goldschmidt, who, no less than Finkelstein, is a devotee of the classical philological method, nonetheless recognizes that these are merely two interchangeable versions which were current at the time of Rab and Samuel. See his *Haggadah šel pesaḥ,* p. 13ff.

[110]See *Ha-tefillah,* pp. 10, 12, 29ff., 32ff. Cf., also, Elbogen, *Gottesdienst* [Hebrew], p. 392, note 4.

[111]Arthur Marmorstein, *The Old Rabbinic Doctrine of God,* London: 1927, p. 70; and cf., Heinemann, in Elbogen [Hebrew], p. 389, note 1.

[112]Elbogen [Hebrew], p. 389, note 1.

[113]Finkelstein also misinterprets the *beraita*ᵓ, in Tos. Ber. 3:7 where *ha-poteaḥ* ("He who *begins* his prayer . . .") is most certainly *technical* language which refers to the liturgical *berakah* formula at the beginning of a "long" benediction.

[114]We thus concur with the observation of Elbogen that "solche Anrufungen wurden in allen Riten mit Leichtigkeit eingefügt" (*Gottesdienst,* p. 583 [Hebrew, p. 389, note 1]), as well as with Heinemann, who is "not convinced" that the presence or absence of such an address is not merely coincidental (*Ha-tefillah,* p. 118, note 37).

[115]JQR (N.S.), XVI, p. 11ff.

[116]*Ibid.,* p. 13.

[117]Unless, of course, we are dealing with highly stereotyped *magic* formulae, in which case such an *external* characteristic may become extremely significant. But this is certainly not the proper way to understand the petitions in the Eighteen Benedictions!

[118]JQR (N.S.), XVI, p. 14. Moreover, Finkelstein himself would seem to be vaguely aware of the futility of this kind of approach to dating since he himself admits, for example, that "the nationalist attitude of certain paragraphs might not be inconsistent with their origin at almost any period" (*ibid.,* p. 16), although he promptly proceeds to disregard his own *caveat* in the very same sentence!

[119]Cf., for example, the series of articles which ran in the *Journal of Jewish Studies:* J. G. Weiss, "On the formula *melekh ha-ᶜolam* as anti-Gnostic protest," JJS, X (1959), pp. 169-71; Cecil Roth, "*Melekh ha-ᶜolam:* Zealot Influence in the Liturgy?", JJS, XI (1960), pp. 173-76; Joseph Heinemann, "The Formula *melekh ha-ᶜolam,*" *ibid.,* pp. 177-79; E. J. Wiesenberg, "The Liturgical Term *melekh ha-ᶜolam,*" JJS, XV (1964), pp. 1-56; Joseph Heinemann, "Once again *Melekh ha-ᶜolam,*" *ibid.,* pp. 149-54. Heinemann has currently taken up again the question of the antiquity of *malkiyyot* in the New Year liturgy. See *Prayer in the Talmud,* pp. 94-97, n. 26. The results are disappointing.

[120]JQR (N.S.), XVI, p. 21.

[121]Thus, Zunz, *Ha-derašot,* p. 178; Elbogen, *Gottesdienst* [Hebrew], p. 22; Kohler, HUCA, I, p. 396; Heinemann, *Ha-tefillah,* p. 27.

[122]JQR (N.S.), XVI, p. 35.

[123]The same rigorous reductionism accounts for Finkelstein's peculiar account of the *berakah meᶜen šebaᶜ* (the "one benediction comprising seven") in the Babylonian and derivative rites (JQR [N.S.], XVI, p. 24ff.). That the *piyyuṭ, magen* ᵓ*abot* is a later insertion and that its framework constituted "the Sabbath *Amidah* of the time of its origin" (*ibid.,* p. 26), flies in the face of what we know about the usage and positioning of Palestinian *piyyutim* in the Babylonian and European rites. Cf., Ezra Fleischer, "ᵓ*Iyunim,* etc., " *Tarbiz,* 40 (5731), pp. 41-63; and Joseph Heinemann, "One Benediction Comprising Seven," REJ (N.S.), XXV (1966), pp. 101-11. In any case, the *composite* piece which Finkelstein analyzes is first attested to only in the Geonic period

(*Seder Rab ᶜAmram,* ed. Goldschmidt, p. 64; *Siddur Rab Saᶜadyah,* p. 114; but see the text in ᶜ*Amram,* p. 63, for private recitation, which is certainly nothing other than an alternate version of the *berakah meᶜen šebaᶜ*).

¹²⁴La Kedushah et les Bénédictions du Schema," REJ (O.S.), 93 (1932), pp. 1-26; cf. particulary, p. 5ff., pp. 14-15. Finkelstein relies heavily on the testimony of the eighth-ninth century Babylonian scholar Ben Baboi. But the "persecution" theory is a stereotypic Babylonian rationale.

¹²⁵*Ibid.,* p. 17.

¹²⁶Louis Finkelstein, "The Oldest Midrash: Pre-Rabbinic Ideals and Teachings in the Passover Haggadah," HTR, XXXI (1938), pp. 291-317; "Pre-Maccabean Documents in the Passover Haggadah," HTR, XXXV (1942), pp. 291-332, XXXVI (1943), pp. 1-38.

¹²⁷Joseph Heinemann, "*Haʾumnam ʾaggadot ḥašmonaʾiyot weʾanti-ḥašmonaʾiyot?*", *Molad,* 27 (1971), pp. 150-60.

¹²⁸*Ibid.,* p. 151.

¹²⁹Goldschmidt, *Haggadah,* pp. 16, 22, 24ff., 27, note 15; 30ff., *et passim.*

¹³⁰Finkelstein, in HTR, XXXI, p. 294.

¹³¹Goldschmidt, *op. cit.,* p. 33ff.

¹³²*Ibid.,* p. 37ff.

¹³³Finkelstein, *Pharisaism in the Making: Selected Essays,* New York: 1972, p. VI.

¹³⁴Finkelstein, HTR, XXXV, pp. 313, 304-5.

¹³⁵Goldschmidt, *op. cit.,* pp. 13-14.

¹³⁶Finkelstein, *loc. cit.,* p. 295.

¹³⁷Goldschmidt, *op. cit.,* p. 16, and notes 9 and 10 there.

¹³⁸Cf., for example, Goldschmidt, *op. cit.,* p. 50.

¹³⁹Gedalia Allon, *Toledot ha-yeduhim beereṣ yiśraʾel bitequfat ha-mišnah we-ha-talmud,* Tel-Aviv: 1955, I, pp. 164-65. So, too, Goldschmidt, *op. cit.,* p. 12.

¹⁴⁰Leon J. Liebreich, "An Analysis of *U-baʾ Le-Ziyyon* in the Liturgy," HUCA, XXI (1948), pp. 176-209, particularly p. 186ff.

¹⁴¹Liebreich, "The Compilation of the Pesuke de-Zimra," PAAJR, XVIII (1948-49), pp. 255-67.

¹⁴²*Ha-tefillah,* p. 14, and note 12 there.

¹⁴³Cf., for example, HUCA, XXI, pp. 189ff., 196-97, where Saᶜadya's version of the *qeduššah desidraʾ* is acknowledged to differ from the versions in the European rites, but is

considered to be more "original," "since the plan reflected in the selection and arrangement of verses in the lectionary is exhibited more fully" therein. But that "plan" is superimposed from without!

[144]HUCA, XXI, p. 186ff.

[145]PAAJR, XVIII, p. 159ff.

[146]HUCA, loc. cit.

[147]HUCA, XXI, p. 187ff.

[148]Ibid., p. 198. The two ʾašre verses (Ps. 84:5, 144:15) which are recited before Ps. 145 are another example of this phenomenon.

[149]It should be noted that in both the Bible itself (particularly in the books of literary prophecy) and in the Talmudic literature as a whole, numerous diverse pericopae are juxtaposed according to the Leitwort principle, which might better be described less mechanically as a kind of "free association" or "stream of consciousness" type of editorial redaction. In the Babylonian Talmud, for example, a particular story reported by Rabbi So-and-So, which is cited as a relevant illustration of a particular legal case, will call forth other stories handed down by the same Rabbi which are not at all relevant to the case at hand, but have been organized under the redactional heading of "stories handed down by Rabbi So-and-So." In a somewhat similar fashion, a particular Biblical citation which is used in a liturgical context may automatically call forth a second verse or cluster of verses with which it is freely associated. It should be noted, of course, that in most of the cases in which such free association is the "organizing principle," the connections between the pericopae or verses will be exclusively external.

[150]HUCA, XXI, p. 187ff.

[151]Examples of this are Ps. 78:38, 20:10, etc.

[152]Cf., for example, HUCA, XXI, pp. 192, 194-95.

[153]Indeed, the "Thirteen Attributes" at a very early date became paradigmatic for supplicatory prayers. An appeal to God's "Thirteen Attributes" constitutes the core of the selihot ritual—the supplicatory rite par excellence.

[154]PAAJR, XVIII, p. 257ff.

[155]Ha-tefillah, p. 63ff.

[156]PAAJR, XVIII, p. 261.

[157]Liebreich, "The Impact of Nehemiah 9:5-37 on the Liturgy of the Synagogue," HUCA, XXXII (1961), pp. 227-37.

[158]Ibid., pp. 228-29, 234-35.

[159]Ibid., p. 228.

[160]It is precisely here where the form-critical approach opens up new vistas and constitutes a

significant improvement over the philological method. Cf., Herman Gunkel, *Einleitung in die Psalmen,* Göttingen: 1933, pp. 4-5; and below, p. 133.

[161]HUCA, XXXII, p. 231.

[162]Heinemann's account of this phenomenon is particularly cogent; see *Ha-tefillah,* pp. 39ff.

[163]In "Aspects of the New Year Liturgy," HUCA, XXXIV (1963), p. 132ff.

[164]*Ibid.,* p. 131.

[165]*Ibid.*

[166]*Ibid.,* p. 175.

[167]Liebreich, in HUCA, XXI, p. 176ff.; cf., Heinemann, *Ha-tefillah,* pp. 166-67. Heinemann's analysis, of course, is much broader, since it is his aim to identify and characterize the entire genre of "*Bet Ha-midrash* prayers," of which *baruk ᵓelohenu* is merely one example. It is this generic-functional analysis which prompts Heinemann's assertion that the three distinct parts of this passage originally constituted three independent *Bet ha-midrash* formulae, while Liebreich concludes that "the Benediction must have contained them as a unit from the beginning, judging by the fact that they are invariably joined together in all extant rituals" (*loc. cit.,* p. 184). *Both* scholars here are actually resting their cases on philological assumptions— Heinemann on the assumption that passages which could have existed separately must have existed separately (an assumption with which he himself takes issue in his debate with Goldschmidt over *nišmat* [see below]); Liebreich on the assumption that a passage which is common to all rituals (here, a conjunction of stylistically distinct elements) must be original. In such a case it is difficult to decide between the two conclusions.

[168]Liebreich, *loc. cit.,* p. 185.

[169]Cf., Hoffman, *Liturgical Responses,* etc., *passim;* and *Ha-tefillah,* p. 12ff.

[170]Heinemann, *Ha-tefillah,* p. 63ff.

[171]*Ibid.,* p. 159.

[172]Liebreich, in HUCA, XXXIV, pp. 160-61. Such an approach may be said to approximate "normative" form-criticism only, as it is based on the observation of a *single,* isolated stylistic characteristic which is related to content, but not to any particular *Sitz im Leben* (topological-sociological). Cf., *Ha-tefillah,* p. 10, pp. 176-77, and p. 26, note 16.

[173]Asher Weiser, in Asher Weiser and B. Z. Luria, eds., *Pirsume ha-ḥebrah leḥeqer ha-miqraᶜ beyiśraᵓel, Sefer yod lezeker Ṣewi Karl,* Jerusalem: 1960, p. vii.

[174]*Ibid.*

[175]He will frequently refer to Elbogen for purposes of confirmation or refutation, but demonstrates no acquaintance with the significant literature which had already appeared by the late 1940's in scholarly journals, much of which has been analyzed above.

[176]Karl, *Meḥqarim,* p. 7.

[177]*Ibid.*, p. 68; and cf., pp. 62, 63, 142.

[178]*Ibid.*, p. 114. Examples of this particular approach are plentiful. Cf., pp. 28, 33, 44, 52, 82, 88, 119, 125, 126, 144, 145. Among these is the assertion that the prayer *ya'aleh weyabo'* is based on Num. 10—a claim which, as we noted above, p. 121, was accepted by Liebreich.

[179]*Ibid.*, p. 80. Heinemann, too, concludes from the routine usage of the term, "Eighteen Benedictions," by the Sages of the generation of Yavneh in this and other passages that "the custom of reciting precisely the eighteen benedictions must have crystallized sometime during the century before the destruction of the Temple (at the very latest)." See *Ha-tefillah*, p. 141, note 17 there. One may nonetheless inquire as to whether this "routine usage" is not rather that of the (later) *redactors* of the Tannaitic dicta in the Mishnah, perhaps that of Rabbi Judah the Prince himself. So, too, may not the explanation of the twenty-four benedictions recited on fast days before the destruction of the Temple as "the daily eighteen plus six" (M. Ta. 2:2—another piece of supporting evidence cited by both Karl, *loc. cit.*, and Heinemann, *ibid.*, p. 140, and note 10 there), possibly be a Tannaitic anachronism? Cf., Kohler, HUCA, I, p. 394.

[180]Karl, *op. cit.*, p. 64.

[181]*Ibid.*

[182]*Ibid.*, p. 68.

[183]*Ibid.*, p. 66, 100, 140, 144.

[184]*Ibid.*, pp. 39, 45, 49, 50-51, 76.

[185]*Ibid.*, p. 54, note 52.

[186]*Ibid.*, pp. 45, 49, 76.

[187]In *Siddur Rab Sa'adya*, text, p. 33, however, only Ps. 146 is omitted.

[188]*Ibid.*, p. 45.

[189]Goldschmidt, *Seder Rab 'Amram*, Introduction, p. 10.

[190]Karl, *op. cit.*, p. 7.

[191]*Die Pessach-Haggada*, herausgegeben und erklärt von E. D. Goldschmidt, Berlin, 1936, 1937; *Seder Haggadah šel pesah 'al pi minhag 'ashkenaz wesefarad, mugah umebo'ar 'al yede* D. Goldschmidt, Jerusalem: 1947; *Haggadah šel pesah wetoledoteha*, Jerusalem: 1960.

[192]Daniel Goldschmidt, *Seder ha-seliḥot*, according to the Polish rite, Jerusalem: 1965; according to the Lithuanian rite, Jerusalem: 1965.

[193]Goldschmidt, *Seder ha-kinot*, according to the Polish rite, Jerusalem: 1968.

[194]Goldschmidt, *Maḥzor la-yamim ha-nora'im*, according to all branches of the Ashkenazic rite, 2 volumes, Jerusalem: 1970.

[195]Goldschmidt, "Maimonides' Rite of Prayer according to an Oxford Manuscript," in *Studies of the Research Institute for Hebrew Poetry*, VII (1958), pp. 183-213.

[196]Goldschmidt, *Seder Rab ʿAmram Gaon*, Jerusalem: 1971.

[197]Cf., Goldschmidt, *Haggadah šel pesaḥ wetoledoteha* [henceforth: *Haggadah*], p. vii.

[198]See above, note 8, and below, note 349.

[199]See above, p. 116ff.

[200]Goldschmidt, *Haggadah*, p. 22.

[201]*Ibid.*, p. 24ff.

[202]*Ibid.*, p. 24.

[203]Cf., for example, Heinemann, *"Dawid ha-melek wehitparsut me ha-tehom (Ledarke mesiraton wisiratan šel ᵓaggadot)," Simon Halkin Festschrift,* Jerusalem: 1973, pp. 23-34; particularly pp. 25ff., 34. Heinemann is here dealing solely with *aggadic* passages of a free form, not with exegetical passages similar to the *beraitaᵓ* of the Four Sons. Passages of the latter type are dealt with to some extent by Jacob Neusner, *Development of a Legend: Studies on the Traditions Concerning Yohanan ben Zakkai*, Leiden: 1970, and *The Rabbinic Traditions About the Pharisees Before 70*, 3 vols., Leiden: 1971, but Neusner does not address himself directly and primarily to the methodological problem at hand.

[204]Goldschmidt, *Haggadah*, pp. 3, 17, 32.

[205]*Ibid.*, pp. 32-33, note 13; and p. 69.

[206]*Ibid.*

[207]*Ibid.*, pp. 16-17, 54.

[208]*Ibid.*, p. 54. Yet, "expansions" of this *Urtext* in very early Genizah fragments lead Goldschmidt to conclude that "already" in early times the text was not free of such additions.

[209]*Ibid.*, p. 65.

[210]*Ibid.*, p. 67, 108.

[211]*Ha-tefillah*, p. 47, and note 42 there; p. 152, note 55.

[212]*Tarbiz*, 30, pp. 407-9.

[213]*Ha-tefillah*, p. 47 (*Tarbiz*, 30, p. 409).

[214]*Tarbiz*, 30, p. 408; and cf., *Ha-tefillah*, p. 152, note 55.

[215]*Ha-tefillah*, p. 152.

[216]Goldschmidt, *Maḥzor*, I, Introduction, p. 18, note 18; and p. 22, note 23.

[217]The former is attested to in two Genizah fragments published by Jacob Mann in HUCA, II (1925), pp. 279, 325. In the first fragment, the *pesuqe dezimraᵓ* rubric concludes with *two*

(functionally interchangeable) benedictory formulae—both *yehaleluka* and *ʾillu finu.* *Yehaleluka* itself contains *two* concluding eulogy formulae here (cf., *Ha-tefillah*, p. 103). *Yištabaḥ* on the other hand, is still recited separately in the contemporary rites on weekdays as the concluding benediction of the *pesuqe dezimraʾ* rubric. Cf., Goldschmidt, *Haggadah*, p. 68; and *Mahzor*, Introduction, p. 22, note 23.

[218]The classic example of this process is the incorporation of *piyyuṭim* in the European rites, where poetic formulations of complete benedictions will be inserted into the standard formulations of those benedictions, with the resultant functional redundancy (cf., Goldschmidt, *Maḥzor*, Introduction, p. 17). Goldschmidt would also describe the present *yoṣer* benediction as a *conflation* of several originally interchangeable versions of the benediction (*Maḥzor*, Introduction, p. 23). Thus, the *piyyuṭ* *ʾel baruk*, should be viewed not as a poetic *addition*, but rather as a self-contained poetic version of the *yoṣer* benediction itself, which climaxes in the recitation of the *qeduššah*. He nonetheless cannot completely liberate himself from the philological model and continues to maintain that the "original version" was similar to Saʿadya's brief *yoṣer*. Cf., also, Spanier, "Dubletten in Gebetstexten," MGWJ, LXXXIII (1939), pp. 142-49, who also holds to the conflation theory, and applies it as well (with perhaps less justification) to the current Ashkenazic text of the Eighteen Benedictions. See below, p. 145ff.

[219]Goldschmidt, *Maḥzor*, Introduction, p. 15ff.

[220]*Ibid.,* Introduction, p. 18, note 18.

[221]*Ibid.,* Introduction, p. 17.

[222]*Ibid.,* Introduction, p. 15.

[223]*Ibid.,* Introduction, p. 16.

[224]Anton Baumstark, *Comparative Liturgy*, Oxford: 1958 [Baumstark, *Liturgie comparée: Principes et Méthodes pour l'étude historique des liturgies chrétiennes*, 3rd edition, revised by Dom Bernard Botte, O.S.B., Chevetogne-Paris: 1953].

[225]Botte, in *Comparative Liturgy*, p. viii, and note 2 there.

[226]Baumstark, *Comparative Liturgy*, p. 52. Cf., also, p. 92.

[227]*Ibid.,* p. 85, *et passim.*

[228]*Ibid.,* p. 31.

[229]*Ibid.,* pp. 16-19.

[230]*Ibid.,* pp. 19-23.

[231]*Ibid.,* p. 27.

[232]*Ibid.,* p. 3.

[233]*Ibid.,* pp. 31-32.

[234]Botte, in *Comparative Liturgy*, pp. viii-ix. Cf., also, *Ha-tefillah*, pp. 14-15.

235*Ha-tefillah*, p. 13.

236*Ibid.*, pp. 14-15.

237Baumstark, *op. cit.*, p. 11.

238Above, p. 111ff.

239Baumstark, *op. cit.*, p. 11, *et passim*.

240*Ibid.*, pp. 37-38. It would seem to be in place here to correct a mistranslation in the English edition of Baumstark's book, *loc. cit.* p. 38, lines 7-8, reads, ". . . declares that this practice is no longer considered as of obligation every day." For "no longer," read, "not yet." The French edition, p. 43, ". . . que cette pratique n'est pas encore considerée comme obligatoire chaque jour," is correct.

241Saᶜadyah omits Ps. 146. Cf., *Siddur Rab Saᶜadyah Gaon*, text, p. 33.

242Such an identification is made explicitly only in later documents, such as *Soferim* 17:11. Elbogen's reading of b. Shab. 118b, in *Gottesdienst,* p. 82, to which Baumstark refers, is based on the observation of Victor Aptowitzer, in *Ha-ṣṣofeh meᵓereṣ Hagar*, I, p. 85ff. (See note in Elbogen, *ad. loc.* [Hebrew, p. 440, note 2]), that Alfasi refers to these six Psalms in the context of this Talmud passage.' But Aptowitzer continues, "It is possible, however, that both the author of *Tractate Soferim* and Alfasi did not read thusly in their texts of the *gemaraᵓ*, but simply added their own explanations in conformity with the prevailing custom of their own periods, and such, in fact, is how R. Eliezer ben Joel Halevi understands Alfasi, viz., that this is only an explanatory gloss."

243Baumstark, *op. cit.,* p. 45. It *is* possible, however, that a special selection from the Hagiographa, most usually a Psalm, *was* read at one time at the Sabbath morning service after the reading from the Torah and the Prophets. The custom is alluded to in a number of the later *midrashim* and is attested to in a Karaite manuscript (cf., Ben Zion Wacholder, in Prologomenon to Jacob Mann, *The Bible as Read and Preached in the Old Synagogue*, Vol. I, Ktav Reprint, New York: 1971, p. XX, and note 29 there; p. LXIX). Such a custom is still retained in the Italian Rite, where the Psalm is recited as the Torah is being removed from the ark (cf., Goldschmidt, in Luzzatto, *Maboᵓ lemaḥzor bene romaᵓ*, pp. 95-98). None of these, however, constitute the *exact* parallel for which Baumstark is looking.

244Baumstark, *op. cit.,* p. 45. Cf., *Ha-tefillah*, pp. 156–57, and Chapter VI.

245Baumstark, *op. cit.,* pp. 49-50. His determination, p. 50, that "both the prayer of the *Jozer* as well as the many forms of the Christian Anaphoric prayer are the echo of a type of prayer which belongs to the worship of the post-exilic Temple. This euchological pattern also contained a survey of the whole history of the Patriarchs and of the People of Israel . . . ," closely resembles Liebreich's "Nehemiah" theory.

246For a more extensive discussion of the form-critical method, its history and its problems, cf., Klaus Koch, *Was ist Formgeschichte? Neue Wege der Bibelexegese*, Neukirchen-Vluyn: 1964 [*The Growth of the Biblical Tradition: The Form-Critical Method*, New York: 1969]; Rolf Knierem, "Old Testament Form Criticism Reconsidered," *Interpretation*, XXVII (1973), pp. 435-68; Martin J. Buss, "The Study of Forms," in John H. Hayes, ed., *Old Testament Form Criticism*, San Antonio: 1974.

247Christian Hermann Weisse, *Die evangelische Geschichte kritisch und philosophisch bearbeitet*, Leipzig: 1838.

248Julius Wellhausen, *Prologomenon to the History of Ancient Israel*, Cleveland: 1957 (reprinted).

249Hermann Gunkel, *Schöpfung und Chaos in Urzeit und Endzeit*, Göttingen: 1895.

250Gunkel, *Genesis übersetzt und erklärt (Göttingen Handkommentar zum Alten Testament*, I/1), Göttingen: 1901.

251Gunkel, *The Legends of Genesis*, Chicago: 1901 [*Die Sagen der Genesis*, Göttingen: 1901].

252*Ibid.*, pp. 124-25.

253Martin Dibelius, *Die Formgeschichte des Evangeliums*, Tübingen: 1919; 1933 [*From Tradition to Gospel*, New York: 1935].

254Dibelius, *From Tradition to Gospel* [henceforth: *Tradition*], pp. 3-4.

255*Ibid.*, p. 235.

256Cf., Gunkel, *Legends of Genesis*, p. 39; *The Psalms*, Philadelphia: 1967 [s.v. "Psalmen," *Die Religion in Geschichte und Gegenwart*, 2nd ed.,], p. 28; Dibelius, *Tradition*, p. 7.

257Dibelius, *Tradition*, pp. 7, 60.

258Cf., Gunkel, *Einleitung in die Psalmen* [henceforth: *Einleitung*], Göttingen: 1933, p. 10.

259Gunkel, *Legends of Genesis*, p. 40. Cf., with regard to the Psalms, *Einleitung*, pp. 4, 12.

260Dibelius, *Tradition*, p. 41.

261Gunkel, *Psalms*, p. 10. Gunkel describes the method more fully in *Einleitung*, p. 22ff.

262Gunkel, *Psalms*, p. 1ff.; *Einleitung*, pp. 4ff., *et passim*.

263Dibelius, *Tradition*, pp. 133ff., 16ff., *et passim*.

264Eduard Norden, *Agnostos Theos: Untersuchungen zur Formengeschichte religiöser Rede*, Leipzig: 1913.

265Dibelius, *Tradition*, p. 4. It would seem, in fact, that Heinemann's historical model, which stresses the *collective, folk* origins of the prayers as against their rabbinic "institution" from above, was influenced to a large extent by the significant emphasis which Dibelius places on this particular criterion. In effect, it constitutes a *justification* for the application of the form-critical method to the Jewish liturgy. See *Ha-tefillah*, p. 29ff., 151, *et passim*. In any case, Heinemann relies heavily on Dibelius in his account of the method. See pp. 9-10, and note 2 there, also p. 176, and note 1 there. Certain socio-psychological factors may have contributed to the formulation of Heinemann's model as well, viz., the overall drift away from "Prussian" authoritarianism in recent years (I owe this insight to my teacher, Dr. Jakob J. Petuchowski), and Heinemann's own earlier religious Zionist-socialist background.

266James Muilenberg, in his Introduction to Gunkel, *Psalms*, p. v. Gunkel's own formulation, *Einleitung*, p. 28, makes his process model even more explicit: ". . . ist doch jenes, *verhältnismässig unentwickeltes* [sic] *Altertum* in ganz anderer Weise vom Zwange der Sitte, auch in literarischen Dingen, abhängig, als wir es uns nur vorzustellen vormögen. . . . Dass sich manche gegenwärtigen Forscher . . . in diese Eigenart des Altertums und die daraus für unsere Forschung hervorgehenden Forderungen nicht haben finden können, ist einer der Hauptgründe, weshalb die Gattungsforschung bei ihnen so langsam Verständnis gefunden hat." (Italics mine.)

267Cf., Dibelius, *Tradition*, p. 10.

268Jacob Neusner, *Development of a Legend: Studies on the Tradition Concerning Yohanan ben Zakkai*, Leiden: 1970, p. xvi. Cf., Rudolf Bultmann, *The History of the Synoptic Tradition*, New York: 1963, p. 5.

269Cf., *ibid.*, pp. 189-90.

270Gunkel, *Einleitung*, pp. 24, 56, *et passim; Psalms*, p. 5.

271Sigmund Mowinckel, *Psalmenstudien*, 6 vols., Kristiania: 1921-24; *Offersang og Sangoffer*, Oslo: 1951 [*The Psalms in Israel's Worship*, 2 vols., New York-Nashville: 1962]. Cf., Gunkel, *Einleitung*, pp. 22, 81; and see below.

272Claus Westermann, *Das Loben Gottes in den Psalmen*, Göttingen: 1961 [*The Praise of God in the Psalms*, Richmond: 1965]; and see below.

273Cf., Dibelius, *Tradition,* pp. 54, 247, note 1.

274*Ha-tefillah*, p. 10.

275Liebreich objected to Heinemann's omission of the so-called prayers of affirmation, which all begin with the word ʾ*attah*. But cf., *Ha-tefillah*, p. 26, note 16; and above, p. 122. I am indebted to my teacher, Dr. Jakob J. Petuchowski, for this piece of information.

276Dibelius, *Tradition*, pp. 58-59; and cf., *Ha-tefillah*, pp. 10, 176ff.

277Gunkel, *Einleitung*, pp. 64, 66, *et passim*; and cf., particularly p. 397ff.

278Gunkel, *Psalms*, p. 5; *Einleitung*, pp. 12, 18.

279Cf., List of Literary Types and Technical Terms, in Psalms, pp. 40-41; also the Table of Contents, in *Einleitung*.

280Gunkel, *Einleitung*, p. 33ff. A very brief English *résumé* will be found in *Psalms*, pp. 10-13.

281*Ha-tefillah*, p. 147ff.

282Cf., also, *Ha-tefillah*, pp. 19-20, 55ff.

283Cf., Claus Westermann, *The Praise of God in the Psalms*, pp. 17-18.

284Gunkel, *Einleitung*, p. 397ff. An English *résumé* will be found in *Psalms*, pp. 36-39.

²⁸⁵Cf., Westermann, *op. cit.,* pp. 18ff., 152ff.; and Roland E. Murphy, "A New Classification of Literary Forms in the Psalms," *Catholic Biblical Quarterly,* 21 (1959), pp. 83-87. Westermann's criteria de-emphasize the sociological-topological *Sitz im Leben* and constitute a *modal* approach to categorization: "The 'categories' of the Psalms are not first of all literary or cultic in nature. They are this, of course, but it is not the essential element. They designate the basic modes of that which occurs when man turns to God with words: plea and praise. As these two basic modes of 'prayer' change and expand, the categories also change and expand" (*op. cit.,* p. 153). Such an approach, we should note, was applied to the Jewish liturgy by Spanier and criticized by Heinemann as too "simplistic." This underscores once again the basic problems inherent in the classification aspect of the form-critical method. To some extent, the choice of criteria for genre identification remains a subjective one, and depends upon the conceptual framework of the particular scholar.

²⁸⁶Such a tendency is in any case manifest in Gunkel's analysis of the "Hymns," *Einleitung,* p. 37: ". . . Alle diese genannten Formen der Einführung gehen im letzten Grunde auf die Grundform 'singet' zurück, von der sie augenscheinlich Abwandlungen sind. Als man müde geworden war, an dieser Stelle immer in der zweiten Person des Imperativs zu reden [!], hat man nach solchen neuen Formen gegriffen. Darum ist es nicht zu kühn, anzunehmen, dass das 'Halleluja', . . . die Urzelle [!] des Hymnensingens gewesen ist." Cf., *Psalms,* p. 11: "The basic form of the earliest Hymn, as well as the primitive core of the singing of the Hymn, is the word 'Hallelujah'. In later times this is still to be found as the acclamation of the congregation at the end (or at the beginning) of Hymns." This *Tendenz* may perhaps be a product of Gunkel's earlier philological training.

²⁸⁷See above, note 284.

²⁸⁸Gunkel, *Psalms,* p. 33.

²⁸⁹*Ibid.,* pp. 33, 26.

²⁹⁰*Ibid.*

²⁹¹*Ibid.,* p. 27.

²⁹²*Ibid.,* p. 28; and cf., *Einleitung,* pp. 29-30.

²⁹³Sigmund Mowinckel, *The Psalms in Israel's Worship,* p. 14.

²⁹⁴*Ibid.,* pp. 14-15. This also applies to the use of fixed phrases in rabbinic prayers.

²⁹⁵*Ibid.,* and cf., Sigmund Mowinckel, in "Psalm Criticism between 1900 and 1935," VT, 5 (1955), p. 15ff.

²⁹⁶The different nomenclature by which Gunkel and Dibelius refer to what is essentially the same methodological system would seem nonetheless to reflect a slight shift in emphasis between them. Dibelius' term *Formgeschichte* ("history of [literary] form"), conveys a greater interest in the historical process itself, which is reflected in the *Sitz im Leben* of the "constructive method," than does Gunkel's rather neutral term *Gattungsforschung* ("genre research"). In fact, Dibelius views the different genres in the Gospel materials as having developed *sequentially,* hence as containing the key to a proper understanding of the entire Gospel tradition in its historical development. The same cannot be said for Gunkel's categories which *by and large* do not reflect

such a sequential pattern. The exceptions, of course, would be the so-called "spiritual" Psalms and the "mixed types," which Gunkel regards as later developments.

[297]Cf., Dibelius, *Tradition*, pp. 9, 233ff.; and William R. Farmer, *The Synoptic Problem: A Critical Analysis*, New York. 1904, p. 17.

[298]Dibelius, *Tradition*, p. 10.

[299]*Ibid.*, p. 13.

[300]Cf., *ibid.*, p. 24ff.

[301]*Ibid.*, p. 287.

[302]Even on formal and stylistic grounds the distinction between Paradigm and Tale is not always as clear as Dibelius would like to see it. Rudolf Bultmann, for example, in *The History of the Synoptic Tradition*, New York: 1963 [*Die Geschichte der synoptischen Tradition*, Göttingen: 1921], had grouped all of the healing narratives, both "Paradigms" and "Tales," together as "miracle stories." Cf., Dibelius, *Tradition*, p. 54. Once again, we are confronted with the classification problem of the form-critical method. The "constructive method" of Dibelius has itself been criticized. Cf., Dibelius, p. 31, note 1.

[303]Dibelius, *Tradition*, p. 102.

[304]*Ibid.*, p. 63.

[305]*Ibid.*

[306]*Ibid.*, p. 193.

[307]*Ibid.*, p. 184ff.

[308]*Ibid.*, p. 182ff.

[309]*Ibid.*, p. 189. Cf., also, pp. 104, 114, 122, 204, 288f., 292.

[310]*Ibid.*, p. 245.

[311]Cf., *ibid.*, p. 28ff.

[312]*Ibid.*, p. 28. Dibelius, like Baumstark, makes use of the term "law" in this connection. While Dibelius is by no means as rigidly "deductive" as Baumstark, he nonetheless lays what is perhaps an undue amount of stress on the objectivity of his results.

[313]*Ibid.*, p. 28 *et passim*.

[314]*Ibid.*

[315]*Ibid.*, p. 136.

[316]Although "leading interest," it should be noted, is only one out of *several* possible criteria for classification and genre identification in Rabbinic literature.

[317]Note the affinity to the goal of the philological method which is expressed in this passage, in which "original Form" replaces "original text."

[318]Dibelius, *op. cit.,* pp. 141, 142.

[319]In addition to the use of form-criticism in the field of Jewish liturgy, the method recently has been applied, with some modifications and refinements, to the study of Rabbinic and legal and aggadic materials, most notably by Jacob Neusner, *Development of a Legend: Studies on the Traditions concerning Yohanan b. Zakkai,* Leiden: 1970; *The Rabbinic Traditions about the Pharisees before 70* (3 vols.) Leiden: 1971; *Eliezer ben Hyrcanus: The Tradition and the Man* (2 vols.), Leiden: 1973; *A History of the Mishnaic Law of Purities,* Parts I-XXII Leiden: 1974-1977. Cf., also, the application to materials in the Tannaitic Midrashim by Wayne Sibley Towner, *The Rabbinic "Enumeration of Scriptural Examples,"* Leiden: 1973; and Eugene Mihaly, "A Rabbinic Defense of the Election of Israel," HUCA, XXXV (1964), pp. 104-44.

[320]Arthur Spanier, "Zur Formengeschichte des altjüdischen Gebetes," MGWJ, LXXVIII (1934), pp. 438-47; "Stilkritisches zum jüdischen Gebet," MGWJ, LXXX (1936), pp. 339-50.

[321]In particular, the question of the origin of the liturgical *berakah* formula and its inclusion of the word *ʾattah,* which engenders a perplexing stylistic alternation between the second and third persons. Cf., Spanier, in MGWJ, LXXVIII, p. 442ff. Heinemann devotes a full chapter of his book to this problem, *Ha-tefillah,* p. 52ff.

[322]Spanier, "Dubletten in Gebetstexten," MGWJ, LXXXIII (1939), pp. 142-49.

[323]"Zur Formengeschichte des altjüdischen Gebetes," (1934), and "Stilkritisches zum jüdischen Gebet" (1936).

[324]"Stilkritisches zum jüdischen Gebet," and "Die erste Benediktion des Achtzehngebetes," MGWJ, LXXXI (1937), pp. 71-76.

[325]"Dubletten in Gebetstexten" (1939).

[326]*Ha-tefillah,* p. 10.

[327]Spanier, MGWJ, LXXVIII, pp. 438-39. The first approximation of such a classification is found in b. Ber. 34a, as Spanier points out, but the schema is not fully enunciated until the Geonic period, and later by the Franco-German Tosafists.

[328]Spanier, *loc. cit.,* pp. 442-45, holds that the word, *ʾattah* ("Thou"), in the opening liturgical *berakah* formula is secondary and that the *Er-Stil* was originally used in a consistent fashion in all *Preisgebete,* i.e., benedictions which begin with an opening liturgical *berakah* formula. Heinemann, *Ha-tefillah,* p. 53, agrees in principle, but is critical of the fact that Spanier does not attempt to account for the change. He also points to the the rigidity in Spanier's conception which stems from the latter's adherence to an "authoritarian" historical process model, viz., that the insertion of the word must at some time have been decreed from above while the rest of the formula remained too firmly fixed to be altered. Heinemann's own attempt to account for the change in (*Ha-tefillah,* pp. 59-66) style is not completely convincing, since some of his reasoning is circular and there are a number of internal contradictions.

[329]Spanier, *loc. cit.,* p. 446.

[330]Spanier, in MGWJ, LXXX, p. 343.

[331]Spanier, in MGWJ, LXXVIII, p. 445; and LXXX, p. 341.

[332]Spanier, in MGWJ, LXXVIII, pp. 446-47.

[333]An instructive comparison is with Heinemann's characterization of the *Bet Midrash* prayers, where exclusive use of the *Er-Stil* is intrinsically related to both the function and the topological-sociological *Sitz im Leben*. See *Ha-tefillah*, p. 158ff.

[334]Cf., Heinemann's criticism, *op. cit.*, p. 53. So, too, does Spanier's analysis of the *ki-ʾattah* style, viz., the "justification" or "rationale" clause following a petition, MGWJ, LXXX, p. 340ff., become a criterion for the identification of later insertions. Here, however, Spanier is standing on firmer ground, since the stylistic characteristic in question has a *functional* relation to its context. Nonetheless, this procedure runs the risk of degenerating into reductionism if it is applied too rigorously. We must not ignore the possibility of there being legitimate parallel structures in any prayer text. The same *caveat* is relevant to Spanier's identification of double readings in prayer texts, MGWJ, LXXXIII, p. 145ff.

[335]Spanier, in MGWJ, LXXX, p. 345. Cf., Baumstark, *Comparative Liturgy*, p. 11; and *Ha-tefillah*, pp. 85-86.

[336]Spanier, *loc. cit.*, p. 347.

[337]*Ibid.*, pp. 348-49.

[338]Heinemann, *op. cit.*, pp. 32, 86.

[339]Spanier, in MGWJ, LXXXI, pp. 72-73. According to Spanier, this would also account for the peculiar fact that the *ʾabot* benediction lacks the phrase, *melek haᶜolam*. He would view the present introductory formula as a *conflation* of the "original" form, *ʾelohenu weʾlohe ʾabotenu*, and the "later" liturgical *berakah* form, *baruk ʾattah ʾadonay*. Since the latter is "characteristic" of the *Preisgebet*, while the former "typifies" the *Bittgebet*, Spanier thinks he has found additional support for his contention that this benediction was originally a *Bittgebet*. The entire construction is baseless.

[340]Spanier here approximates the argument of Kohler, HUCA, I, p. 393, that the "original" *tefillah* must have been hymnic. See above, pp. 111-12, and our reservations there.

[341]Spanier, in MGWJ, LXXXI, p. 75, note 7: ". . . Aber die Rolle, die die palastinische Version in der Geschichte der Tefilla spielt, ist von Finkelstein sehr überschätzt worden: soviel ergibt sich . . . gerade auch aus der Heranziehung der äusserhalb unserer gesamten hebräischen Uberlieferung stehenden griechischen Version." Spanier's criticism of Finkelstein is justified, but its basis here is rather dubious.

[342]Spanier, in MGWJ, LXXXIII, p. 142.

[343]Spanier draws no distinction between Babylonia and Palestine in this respect. But Heinemann demonstrates conclusively that the Palestinian liturgy was never as fixed or as standardized as its Babylonian counterpart. See *Ha-tefillah*, pp. 182-83, *et passim*; and Hoffman, *Liturgical Responses*, etc., *passim*.

[344]Although the nature of these citations is problematic. See above, p. 103, and note 34 there.

³⁴⁵Cf., Goldschmidt, *Mahzor*, I, Introduction, p. 16, note 9, who refers to Spanier's article in constructing his own revised model.

³⁴⁶Spanier, in MGWJ, LXXXIII, pp. 146-47.

³⁴⁷*Ibid.*, p. 149.

³⁴⁸Jakob J. Petuchowski, in "A New Approach to Jewish Liturgy," *Judaism*, XV, 1 (1966), p. 120.

³⁴⁹Cf., D. Goldschmidt, *Mahzor layamim ha-nora²im*, Jerusalem: 1970, I, Introduction, p. 18, note 18; and p. 22, note 23: Louis Finkelstein, *Pharisaism in the Making: Selected Essays*, New York: 1972, pp. XIII-XV.

³⁵⁰*Ha-tefillah*, p. 9ff; 29ff.

³⁵¹*Ibid.*, pp. 9-10.

³⁵²See above, pp. 141–42.

³⁵³*Ha-tefillah*, p. 29ff., and cf., Petuchowski, *op. cit.*, p. 115.

³⁵⁴*Ha-tefillah*, p. 39ff.

³⁵⁵See below, p. 148.

³⁵⁶*Ha-tefillah*, p. 29ff.

³⁵⁷On this question, see Jacob Neusner, *A History of the Jews in Babylonia*, Leiden: 1965-1970, Vol. II, pp. 176-77; III, pp. 158-59, 167, 176-78, 235-38; IV, pp. 327-29; V, pp. 200-203 (and compare Neusner's understanding of R. Papa's dictum with that of Spanier, above, p. 145). Cf., also, the entries "Shema" and "Tefillah," in the index to Neusner, *Eliezer ben Hyrcanus*. In both instances he views the early Tannaim as defining something which previously had been left unspecified.

³⁵⁸See above, note 319.

³⁵⁹*Ha-tefillah*, p. 177.

³⁶⁰*Ibid.*

³⁶¹We would concur, however, with the opinion of Goldschmidt, *Mahzor*, I, Introduction, p. 29, note 8, that ᶜ*alenu*, for stylistic reasons, should not be viewed as a *bet midrash* prayer. Heinemann's suggestion, *op. cit.*, p. 174, that the local gatherings of the ²*anše* maᶜ*amad* constituted the original *Sitz im Leben* of this prayer seems *highly* speculative.

³⁶²Heinemann, *op. cit.*, p. 99ff. As we have. indicated previously, the results are not completely convincing.

³⁶³*Ibid.*, pp. 182-83.

³⁶⁴To a certain extent, the work has already been begun. See the very insightful Ph.D. thesis of Lawrence Hoffman, *Liturgical Responses*, etc.

365Cf., for example, Julian Morgenstern, "The Origin of the Synagogue," *Studi Orientalistici in onore di Giorgio Levi Della Vida*, II, pp. 192-201.

366Cf., for example, Ellis Rivkin, "Ben Sira and the Non-Existence of the Synagogue: A Study in Historical Method," *In the Time of Harvest: Essays in Honor of Abba Hillel Silver*, ed. Daniel Jeremy Silver, New York: 1963. pp. 320-54.

367Cf., for example, Elbogen, *Gottesdienst*, p. 233ff. [Hebrew, p. 178ff.].

368See Hoffman, *op. cit.*

369This problem is being dealt with in particular by Ezra Fleischer and Jefim Schirmann of the Research Institute for Hebrew Poetry at the Hebrew University in Jerusalem.

370The original version of this essay constituted part of a M.A.H.L. thesis written at Hebrew Union College-Jewish Institute of Religion, Cincinnati, under the supervision of Prof. Jakob J. Petuchowski. I wish to express my gratitude to Prof. Petuchowski for his wise counsel and unflagging support.

VI

According to Rabbi Y: A Palestinian Amoraic Form

GARY G. PORTON

UNIVERSITY OF ILLINOIS

I

For more than seventy years scholars of the Hebrew Bible have been aware of literary forms in Scripture. Since H. Gunkel's epoch-making commentary on Genesis,[1] the nature, structure, origin, and *Sitz-im-Leben* of these forms have been intensely studied. Similarly, M. Dibelius[2] and R. Bultmann[3] drew the attention of students of the New Testament to the existence of formulary patterns within that document. While form-criticism of the Hebrew and Greek Bibles has a long history of scholarship, the study of the forms found in the corpus of rabbinic materials has begun only recently. In 1943 A. Weiss published his studies on the literary units which comprise the Babylonian Talmud.[4] His subsequent investigations made scholars aware of the importance of set literary structures for the construction of the Babylonian *gemara*.[5] The logical implications of J. N. Epstein's introduction to the Mishnah[6] is that set patterns were used by the editor(s) of that basic Tannaitic document. It was not until J. Neusner published his studies on the traditions of Yohanan b. Zakkai[7] and the Pharisees before 70,[8] that the study of the literary forms found in rabbinic literature was set on firm ground. In these and other works[9] Neusner has isolated, described, and explained the various literary units found in Mishnah, Tosefta, and the two talmuds. He has been able to trace the history of these forms, to suggest how, when, and why they developed, and to explain why they were employed. Neusner has done for rabbinic literature what Gunkel, Dibelius, and Bultmann did for the Hebrew and Greek Bibles.

Following Neusner's lead, the present essay focuses on a form which occurs solely in one Amoraic text, the Palestinian Talmud. We shall describe the form, give examples of its proper use, show how a broken form leads to an incomprehensible *sugya*, and discuss the origin of the pattern.

173

II

We have entitled the form under discussion "according to Rabbi Y." Its characteristics are as follows:

A. Text
B. *ʿd kdwn kr* X (Until here the text follows the opinion of Rabbi X)
C. *kr* Y (But, what is the opinion of Rabbi Y)?[10]
D. *tny r* Y (Rabbi Y teaches)

The form occurs only in the Palestinian *gemara*.[11] So far as I am able to ascertain, the only rabbis who appear in C and D are Aqiba and Ishmael. When Frankel discusses the phrase *ʿd kdwn*, his examples all contain Ishmael and Aqiba.[12] J. Levy,[13] A. Kohut,[14] and M. Jastrow[15] do not discuss the form as such; rather, they mention a similar pattern which is used with biblical verses. Bacher merely refers to Frankel's discussions.[16] Although we have only a small number of studies done from the form-critical and literary-critical point of view which would allow for the isolation of this form within the traditions of other sages, none of these studies mentions this particular structure.[17] For these reasons I feel confident in stating that this pattern occurs exclusively with Ishmael and Aqiba.

We have isolated twenty-five examples of the use of this form. These *sugyot* are constructed as follows:

A. Text
B. *ʿd kdwn kr ʿaqybh* (Until here the text follows the opinion of Rabbi Aqiba)
C. *kr yšmʿ ʾl* (But what is the opinion of Rabbi Ishmael)?
D. *tny r yšmʿ ʾl* (Rabbi Ishmael teaches)

Aqiba's opinions are never stated directly. The text merely states that Aqiba agreed with a previous comment. Ishmael's words are attributed to him directly and are introduced by *tny*, which designates a Tannaitic tradition.

The pattern occurs in all the *sedarim* of the Palestinian Talmud; however, it is most prevalent in *Našim*. Of the twenty-five pericopae in which this form is used two appear in *Zeraʿim*,[18] seven occur in *Moʿed*,[19] ten are found in *Našim*,[20] and six are in *Neziqin*.[21] The form usually serves to compare the method of argumentation employed by Aqiba to that used by Ishmael. In the majority of passages, Ishmael's method is simpler and his proofs are clearer. The form also may function to compare the different exegetical principles of the two sages. In these cases, the rabbis agree on the point of law; they merely disagree over how one proves the point. The form also may be used to compare different interpretations of a biblical passage. The exegetical principles may be the same; however, the results reached are different. The rarest use of the form is when it brings together different legal opinions of Ishmael and Aqiba.

III

The following *sugyot* illustrate the proper use of the form, the problems in understanding a pericope when the form is broken, and the different patterns in which the same pericope can appear in different documents.

1. A. Mishnah: Fifteen women [who are closely related to the deceased, childless husband's brother] render their co-wives, and the co-wives of their co-wives and so on *ad infinitum* exempt from *ḥaliṣah*[22] and levirate marriage,[23] and these are they: his daughter, his daughter's daughter, his son's daughter, his wife's daughter, his wife's son's daughter, his wife's daughter's daughter, his mother-in-law, his mother-in-law's mother, his father-in-law's mother, his sister, his mother's sister, his wife's sister, the wife of his brother by the same mother, the wife of his brother who did not live at the same time as he, and his daughter-in-law. . . .

B. [The] Torah said: *And you shall not take a woman to her sister . . .* (Leviticus 18:18). [From this verse] I [can] only [learn about] her [that is, the sister]. From where [can I learn about] her co-wife? Scripture says: *For a rival (lṣrwr) (Ibid.).* [From the fact that *lṣrwr* is spelled in this matter and not in the shorter form, *lṣwr*, I can learn the prohibition against marrying] either her co-wife or her co-wife's co-wife.[24]

C. [From Leviticus 18:18] I [can] only [learn that one need not perform a levirate marriage with] the sister of one's wife. From where [can I learn that one need not perform a levirate marriage with the] rest of the forbidden relationships *(hᶜrywt)* [mentioned in Leviticus 18]?

D. R. Zeᶜorah[25] said in the name of R. Yosah b. Ḥaninah: "[One can learn about the rest of the forbidden relationships by means of an] *a fortiori* [argument].[26] Just as the sister of one's wife is permitted [to him] after [his wife has died, but who is a] prohibition with regard to levirate marriage, so the rest of the forbidden relationships that are not permitted [to marry him] after [his wife has died], how much the more is their prohibition [a prohibition with regard to levirate marriage]."

E. Just as this forbidden relationship [that of the wife's sister] exempts her co-wife [from the obligations of a levirate marriage], so also the rest of the forbidden relationships exempt their co-wives [from this obligation].

F. Until here the text follows the opinion of R. Aqiba.

G. [However,] according to R. Ishmael [how is the matter proved]?

H. R. Ishmael teaches: "[One must use this] *a fortiori* [argument]: Just as his wife's sister is a forbidden relationship specifically [mentioned in Leviticus 18] for which they are culpable for the punishment of "cutting off" [if they] intentionally [had intercourse] but for which [they are culpable] for a Sin-Offering [if they] unintentionally [had intercourse, and] she is prohibited from a levirate marriage, so also all the forbidden relationships for which they are culpable for the punishment of "cutting off" [if they] intentionally [had intercourse] but for which [they are culpable] for a Sin-Offering [if they] unintentionally [had intercourse are also] prohibited from [the requirement of a] levirate marriage.

(y. Yevamot 1:1; Venice 2b)

Comment: The *sugya* attempts to prove that the women mentioned in Leviticus 18 and their co-wives do not have to perform either a levirate marriage or the opposite rite, the *ḥaliṣah*. In D, Zeᶜorah in the name of Yosah proves that all the forbidden relationships mentioned in Leviticus 18 do not have to undergo a levirate marriage. D notes that a man may marry his wife's sister if his wife dies. However, his wife's sister is mentioned among the forbidden relationships in Leviticus 18:18, and she is exempt for the requirement of a levirate marriage. Therefore, *a fortiori* the rest of the women mentioned in Leviticus 18 who are never permitted to marry the man also are exempt from the requirement of a levirate marriage. E proves that the co-wives also do not have to undertake a levirate marriage: Since the wife's sister exempts her co-wives from the requirement of a levirate marriage, *a fortiori* that the rest of the women mentioned to Leviticus 18 exempt their co-wives and the co-wives of their co-wives *ad infinitum* from the requirement of a levirate marriage. The argument takes two steps, for E is dependent upon D. According to F, D-E, or E alone, follow the opinion of Aqiba.

H is Ishmael's proof that the forbidden relationships and their co-wives do not have to perform a levirate marriage. If one has sexual relations with his wife's sister, both are punished by cutting off or they have to bring a Sin-Offering. *A fortiori*, all the other relationships which have the same punishments are analogous with respect to a levirate marriage.

Ishmael and Aqiba agree on the point of law: The forbidden relationships found in Leviticus 18 and their co-wives do not have to perform levirate marriages. Since they are not required to undertake a levirate marriage, they do not need to perform the *ḥaliṣah*-ceremony which frees one from the obligation of contracting a levirate marriage. Both sages employ an *a fortiori* argument. The only difference between the sages is the wording of their respective arguments. Ishmael employs a one-step proof. The argument attributed to Aqiba involves two steps. The "according to Rabbi Y"-form compares the wording of the arguments used by the two sages.

We have some indication of the date of this pericope. Yosah b. Ḥaninah was a second generation Palestinian Amora.[28] This means that Zeᶜorah is probably Zeᶜorah I who was a third generation Amora.[29] Since F-H are dependent on D, this pericope cannot have been created before the third generation of the Amoraim.

2. A. Mishnah: [If] a man throws a writ of divorce to his wife while *(w)* she is in her house or in her courtyard, she is divorced. [If] he threw it to her [while she was] in his house or in his courtyard, even though he was with her in bed, she is not divorced; however, if [he threw it] into her bosom or into her basket, she is divorced.

B. It is written: [*He writes her a writ of divorce*] *and puts it into her hand* (Deuteronomy 24:1). [From this verse] I [can] only [learn that he should place the document] into her hand. From where [can I learn that he may throw it into] her garden or her courtyard? Scripture says: *And he shall put (Ibid.)* and [it says:] *And he shall put (Ibid. 24:3)*.

C. Until here the text follows the opinion of R. Aqiba.

D. [However,] according to R. Ishmael [how is the law derived]?

E. R. Ishmael teaches: "[It is written]: *And he took all his land from his hand as far as Arnon* (Numbers 21:26). But did he really take it from his hand? Rather, what does [the phrase] *from his hand* [mean? It means] from his control. Thus *(w)* her garden and her courtyard which are not used by a man for eating fruit [are therefore under her control. Because we have seen that *hand* means control in Numbers 21:26, we can conclude that *hand* in Deuteronomy 24:1 also means control; therefore, if he puts the writ of divorce into any area under her control, such as her garden or her courtyard, she is divorced].

(y. Gittin 8:1; Venice 49b)

Comment: Ishmael and Aqiba attempt to derive the law mentioned in the first clause of Mishnah from the Bible. They both agree that if a man throws a writ of divorce into his wife's courtyard or garden she is legally divorced. Aqiba's exegesis is based on the principle of "extension."[30] The phrase *and he shall put* appears twice in the same context; therefore, it must include more than merely the husband's putting it into her hand. From this repetition Aqiba derives the rule that the husband may divorce his wife by putting the document into her garden or her courtyard.

Ishmael employs a *gezarah shavah*[31] to prove his point. First he shows that *hand* in Numbers 21:26 means an area under one's control and not "hand" in the usual sense. He concludes that *hand* in Deuteronomy 24:1 must mean the same as *hand* in the verse from Numbers; therefore, if a man throws a writ of divorce into an area under his wife's control she is legally divorced.

Again Ishmael and Aqiba agree on the point of law. The form is used to juxtapose the exegetical arguments used by each sage in support of the law in Mishnah. Since Ishmael and Aqiba are the only rabbis named in this *sugya*, it is impossible to assign any date for its composition.

3. A. It is written: *For if your brother, a Hebrew man or a Hebrew woman is sold to you* [*he shall serve for six years; and the seventh year you shall let him go free*] (Deuteronomy 15:12).

B. A male Hebrew is compared to a female Hebrew. Just as a female Hebrew is acquired by money or by a document, so also a male Hebrew is acquired by money or by a document.

C. It is correct [to say that] she is acquired by money, for it is written: *Then shall she go out for nothing, without money* (Exodus 21:11) [which implies that she was acquired by money].[32]

D. But *(w)* from where [do we learn that she is acquired by] a document?

E. We learn that a female Hebrew [slave is acquired by a document by analogy with] a free Hebrew woman. And we learn that a male Hebrew [slave is acquired by a document by analogy with] a female Hebrew [slave].

F. Consequently a case may be illustrated by one itself defined only indirectly by analogy *(nmṣ' lmd mlmd.)*.[33]

G. Until here the text follows the opinion of R. Aqiba.

H. [who used the exegetical principle of] illustrating a case by one itself defined only indirectly by analogy *(ᶜd kdwn kr ᶜqybh dᵓyt lyh lmd mn hlmd)*.

I. [However,] according to R. Ishmael [how is the law derived],

J. for R. Ishmael does not use the exegetical principle of] illustrating a case by one itself defined only indirectly by analogy?

K. [But] it is found [that R. Ishmael once used this exegetical principle].[34]

L. R. Ismael teaches

M. concerning this matter: *whpšh mlh ḥpšy mḥwpšh.*[35]

N. In no [other] place does R. Ishmael use [the exegetical principle] of illustrating a case by one itself defined only indirectly by analogy; but here, R. Ishmael does use [this principle].

O. It is taught in the name of a certain sage *(tny lh bšm ḥkm):*

P. From where does R. Ishmael [learn that a male Hebrew slave is acquired by a document]?

Q. "[He learns it by means of a *gezarah shavah* with the words] *send* and *send.* Just as *send* is said elsewhere in conjunction with a document [in Deuteronomy 24:1 about a female, *when a man takes a wife and marries her, if then she finds no favor in his eyes because he has found some indecency in her, and he writes her a bill of divorce and puts it in her hand and sends her out of his house . . .*], also *send* which is said here [in Deuteronomy 15:12 about a male] must also be in conjunction with a document, [and if he is sent out with a document, he must be acquired by a document].

(y. Qiddushin 1:2; Venice 59a)

Comment: This *sugya* offers support for the claim that a male Hebrew slave can be acquired by a document or by money. Because there are no direct biblical supports for this law, the sages must use various exegetical principles. B states, on the basis of Deuteronomy 15:12, that the laws of acquisition of a male Hebrew slave may be derived by analogy with the laws of acquisition of a female Hebrew. C states that Exodus 21:11 proves that a female Hebrew slave is acquired by money; therefore, we may conclude that a male Hebrew slave also is acquired by money.

Because there is no biblical verse which states that a female Hebrew slave may be acquired by a document, this point must be derived by analogy with a free Hebrew woman who may be acquired as a wife by means of a document.[36] Thus, one case based on an analogy, the analogy of a free Hebrew woman and a female Hebrew slave, is used as the basis of a second analogy, the analogy of a male Hebrew slave and a female Hebrew slave. This argument and the exegetical principle employed is attributed to Aqiba.

Ishmael uses another exegetical method to prove that a male Hebrew slave can be acquired by a document. He notes that in Deuteronomy 24:1 the word *send* appears in conjunction with a document; therefore, we may conclude that the word *send* which appears in Deuteronomy 15:12 must also be in conjunction with a document. Ishmael employs only one analogy; the analogy of a male and female.

There are some stylistic problems with this *sugya.* I-L suggest that we have a pericope cast in the "according to Rabbi Y"-form. According to this form, H, J, K, and M-P should not appear. The fact that M-P intrudes into the normal formulary pattern may explain why M is obscure. If we omit M-P, the *sugya* makes perfect sense. It is important to note that the *sugya* becomes incomprehensible exactly at the point where the form is broken. David Frankel[37] and Jacob David of Slutzk[38] do not understand M and emend the text. Moses Margoliot's explanation of M is unclear and seems to go beyond the evidence of the text.[39]

It is probable that the *sugya* originally did not contain K or M-P. In other words, the text probably ended in the standard formulary pattern. These sections, which add nothing of importance to the exegetical arguments, seem to have been inserted to prove that at least once Ishmael did use the exegetical principle attributed to Aqiba. Since the point of the *sugya* should be that Ishmael and Aqiba had employed different exegetical principles and this point is made without K or M-P, these sections can be deleted.

4. A. Mishnah: He that comes upon a male or a beast [to have inter-course] and the woman who brings a beast [to have intercourse with it shall be punished by stoning. . . .]

B. From where [do we learn the] warning (ʾzhrh) not to come upon a male [to have intercourse with him? Scripture says:] *And with a male you shall not lie as with a woman* (Leviticus 18:22).

C. From where [do we learn about the punishment of] "cutting off"? [Scripture says:] *For whoever shall do any of these abominations shall be cut off* (*Ibid.* 18:29).

D. From where [do we learn about the] punishment (ʿwnš)? [Scripture says:] *And a man who lies with a male like a woman is an abomination, indeed both of them shall be put to death; their blood shall be upon them* (*Ibid.* 20:13).

E. You may learn [the meaning of] *their blood shall be upon them* [from the meaning of the phrase] *their blood shall be upon them* [in Leviticus 20:27: *A man or a woman who is a medium or a wizard shall be put to death; they shall be stoned with stones; their blood shall be upon them*. Just as the punishment is stoning in Leviticus 20:27, so too the punishment is stoning in Leviticus 20:13].

F. Until here [we have learned about the] one who lies [with another]. From where [do we learn about the one] with whom he laid?

G. [Scripture says:] *With a male you shall not lie (tškb) as with a woman.* Read, *shall not be lain with (tyškb)* [in the passive instead of *lie with (tškb)* in the active].

H. Until here the text follows the opinion of R. Aqiba.

I. [However,] according to R. Ishmael [how is the lesson learned]?

J. *Neither shall there be a male prostitute among the children of Israel.* (Deuteronomy 23:18)

(y. Sanhedrin 7:7; Venice 14:9, 28a)

Comment: B-E explain how we can derive the warning and the punishment for male homosexuals. F notes that B-E deal only with the one who had intercourse with another male; they do not treat the male who allowed the other male to have intercourse with him. We have two different methods of deriving the law concerning the consenting male. The opinion attributed to Aqiba is based on another reading of Leviticus 18:22. The word "to lie with" is read in the passive, "to be lain with;" therefore, the prohibitions concerning both males can be derived from the same verse. The proof attributed to Ishmael is much simpler. Ishmael merely cites Deuteronomy 23:18 which expressly forbids male prostitutes to exist among the Israelites.

The form is slightly broken, for *tny* R. Ishmael should begin J. The omission of this phrase, however, is not a radical departure from the standard form. Unlike the previous example in which a radical break in the form created an incomprehensible and awkward *sugya*, this minor omission had no effect on the meaning of the passage. The form is used to show the different methods by which Ishmael and Aqiba derived the law from the Bible that a male who permits another male to have intercourse with him is culpable for punishment.

5. A. Mishnah: He that comes upon a male or a beast [to have intercourse] and the woman who brings a beast [to have intercourse with it shall be punished by stoning. . . .]

D. From where [do we learn about] the male?

C. For our rabbis taught *(dtnw rbnn)*

D. *Man* (Leviticus 20:13) refers to a small male who lies with a male whether he is big or small; *as with a woman (Ibid.)* [Here] Scripture tells you that [this type of intercourse] is different from lying with a woman; [therefore, it is intercourse with a male].

E. Said Ishmael: "Behold, this comes to teach [about a male] but it is found to teach [about the punishment, for it says:] *Indeed they shall be put to death* [which means] by stoning.

F. You might say [that Scripture teaches either punishment] by stoning or [punishment] by any of the other means of death mentioned in the Torah. [However,] *their blood shall be upon them* is said here [in Leviticus 20:13] and *their blood shall be upon them* is said with reference to the medium and the wizard [in Leviticus 20:27]. Just as elsewhere [in Leviticus 20:27 this phrase refers to punishment by] stoning, so too here [in Leviticus 20:13 this phrase refers to punishment] by stoning.

G. We have learned about the punishment. From where [do we learn about the warning? Scripture says: *And with a male you shall not lie as with a woman; it is an abomination (Ibid.* 18:22).

H. "[From this verse] we learn about the warning not to lie with [another male]. From where [do we learn about] the warning not to be lain with? Scripture says: *Neither shall there be a male prostitute among the children of Israel* (Deuteronomy 23:18), and it says: *And there were also male prostitutes in the land. They did according to all the abominations of the nations which the Lord drove out before the children of Israel* (I Kings 14:24)"—the words of R. Ishmael.

I. R. Aqiba says: "This [argument of Ishmael] is not needed. Behold it says: *And a male shall not lie as with a woman.* Read: *shall not be lain with.*"

(b. Sanhedrin 54a-54b)

Comment: When we compare the Palestinian and the Babylonian versions of this *sugya*, it becomes evident that each was shaped according to the style of the respective documents. The Palestinian version brings proof texts for the warning, the punishment of "cutting off," the punishment, and the question of the consenting male. The order and style is found throughout the Palestinian version of Sanhedrin. In the Palestinian *gemara* the comments of Ishmael and Aqiba are cast in the "according to Rabbi Y"-form. In the Babylonian Talmud their comments are set in the form of a "words- of"-dispute,[40] a common pattern in the Babylonian *gemara*.

There are several differences between the two versions. Ishmael is introduced in E in the Babylonian account. Apparently, also F is to be attributed to him. F spells out the *gezarah shavah* which is only implicit in the Palestinian *gemara*, E. In H of the Babylonian *sugya*, Ishmael quotes two verses instead of the one verse he cites in J of the Palestinian Talmud. Since one verse was sufficient, it is possible that the editor of the Babylonian *sugya* has merely embellished Ishmael's saying.

While the two accounts are clearly related, it is impossible to prove dependence. They probably reflect a common source. Each editor (or set of editors) formed his *sugya* out of the existing materials.

6. A. *And if a man [lies with a beast, he shall surely be put to death]* (Leviticus 20:15).

B. We learn about the punishment [for one who] lies [with a beast]. From where [do we learn about the punishment for one who] consents to having [a beast] lie [with him]? Scripture says: *And all who lie with a beast shall surely be put to death* (Exodus 22:18).

C. If [this verse] does not apply to the case of one who lies with [a beast], apply it to the case of one who consents to having [a beast] lie [with him].

D. We learn the punishment of one who lies with [a beast] and the punishment of one who consents to having [a beast] lie [with him]. From where [do we learn] the warning? Scripture says: *And you shall not lie with any beast to defile yourself with it* (Leviticus 18:23).

E. We learn the warning not to lie [with a beast]. From where [do we learn] the warning not to consent to having [a beast] lie [with us]?

F. Scripture says: *There shall not be a male prostitute among the children of Israel* (Deuteronomy 23:18), and it says: *And there were also male prostitutes in the land* (I Kings 14:24)"—the words of R. Ishmael.

G. R. Aqiba says: "There is no need [for Ishmael's argument]. Behold, it says: *You shall not lie with.* Read: Shall not be lain with."

(Sifra 92c, ed., Weiss)

Comment: This *sugya* deals with the problem of having intercourse with animals. A–E deal with the subject at hand. The opinion attributed to Ishmael, F, does not discuss animals; rather, it discusses male prostitutes. In y. Sanhedrin 7:7 and b. Sanhedrin 54a–54b, Ishmael's comment and Aqiba's response appear in a discussion of male homosexuality. F–G seem more appropriate to that context than they do to the present one. Clearly F–G circulated as an independent unit, for they have been added together to an inappropriate discussion.

We find the statements of Ishmael and Aqiba cast in two formulary patterns. In the Palestinian Talmud they appear in the "according-to Rabbi Y"-form, and in Sifra and the Babylonian *gemara* they are cast in the "words-of"-dispute form. The evidence from Sifra, however, is ambiguous. In the codex Assemani LXVI we find the same passage as we find in the Babylonian *gemara* in place of the above account.[41] Since F–G do not belong in their present context, it is possible that this *sugya* has been influenced by the Babylonian *gemara*. The influence of the Babylonian Talmud is clearer in the codex Assemani. We can conclude, therefore, that the sayings of Ishmael and Aqiba were set in two forms: the "words of" dispute-form which appears in the Babylonian *gemara* and the "according to Rabbi Y"-form which occurs in the Palestinian Talmud. Each form is the one we would expect to find in the respective documents.

We have reviewed several pericopae set in the "according to Rabbi Y"-form. In the first two examples we found the proper formulary pattern. These passages compared Ishmael's methods of argumentation to those of Aqiba. In the first *sugya* they used the same exegetical principle; only the wording of their arguments differed. In the second example each employed a different method of exegesis. In the third pericope we found that the *sugya* became unclear exactly at the point at which the form was broken. This suggests a close correlation between the proper use of the form and the construction of a comprehensible passage. In the last three accounts we saw that the form in which a pericope was cast differed from one document to another. This suggests that the form and the content circulated separately. The accounts were too dissimilar to suggest that both were dependent upon a common single source; in their present state it was impossible to prove dependence between the two versions.

IV

Frankel suggests that the form under discussion is closely related to another pattern which often appears in the Palestinian *gemara*.[42]

A. What [is the meaning of the phrase] "he shall become unclean through them out of respect for the majority" [which appears above in the *gemara*]?

B. It is taught *(tny)*: [If] there were two twin roads one long but clean and one short but unclean [and] if the majority [of the people] walk on the long one, [you should also] walk on the long one. [But] if [they do] not [walk on the long one but walk on the short one you must also] walk on the short one out of respect for the majority.

C. Until here [the text discusses] the uncleanness [referred to in] their words (*ᶜd dkwn bṭwmᵓh šl dbryhm*).

D. Even the uncleanness of the words of Torah (*ᵓpylw ṭwmᵓh šhyᵓ mdbry twrh*).

(y. Ber. 3:1; Venice 6b)

Frankel states: "Its interpretation is until here we learn about the uncleanness of their words. What is the law of the uncleanness of Scripture?"[43]

If Frankel's interpretation is correct,[44] the similarity between the two forms is striking. One might conclude that our form is a development of this simple formulation. It is possible, however, that the forms have no real relationship. Since the sense of both constructions is dependent upon the plain meaning of *ᶜd kdwn*, it probably is claiming too much to say that our form is a development upon this simple structure.

As we have seen with regard to our first example, it is possible to establish an approximate date before which some *sugyot* cast in this form could not have been created. In seven of the twenty-five pericopae we find the names of sages other than Ishmael and Aqiba. The *sugyot* are structured so that the Ishmael-Aqiba-portion cannot be earlier than the sayings of the other masters. In y. Yevamot 1:1 we find Zeᶜorah[45] and Yosi b. Ḥaninah.[46] Yosi also appears in y. Yevamot 8:1 and y. Sanhedrin 7:5. Zeᶜorah occurs a second time in y. Sanhedrin 3:9. In y. Berakot 7:1 we find Samuel b. Naḥmani[47] quoting Yoḥanan. Yoḥanan and Habrayya[48] appear in y. Yevamot 10:6, and Haggai[49] is mentioned in y. Soṭah 8:1. Yosi b. Ḥaninah and Yoḥanan are second generation Amoraim. Ze[c]orah and Samuel b. Naḥmani flourished during the third generation of Amoraim, and Ḥaggai was a fourth generation sage. The earliest of these sages are Yoḥanan and Yosi. Since both men are consistently quoted by third generation Amoraim, we must conclude that the earliest any of these seven pericopae could have been created was during the third generation. Because Ḥaggai, a fourth generation Amora, also appears, we have limited evidence that the form was used during the fourth generation. Therefore, approximately twenty-four percent of the "according to Rabbi ·Y"—pericopae can be dated to the last decade of the third century and the first three decades of the fourth century of the common era.

The evidence further suggests that the form originated within the circle of Amoraim related to Yoḥanan. Although, as the following chart shows, the common denominator of the sages is Ḥanina b. Hama of Sepphoris, Yoḥanan and his followers seem to be the most important masters behind the creation of twenty-four percent of our *sugyot:*

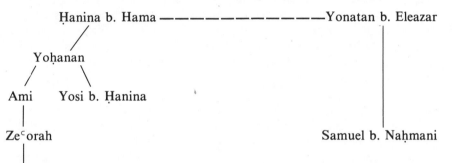

It is difficult to ascertain the locality in which these seven *sugyot* were created. Ḥanina stands behind the whole tradition, and was the leader of the academy in Sepphoris. Yoḥanan, however, seems to be more important than Ḥanina. Yoḥanan began his work in Sepphoris; however, he ended his career in Tiberias.[50] Since Samuel b. Naḥmani was also active in Tiberias,[51] we must conclude that these seven pericopae originated in Tiberias.

Yoḥanan's importance in the creation of the "according to Rabbi Y"-form which is used exclusively with Ishmael and Aqiba is paralleled by his importance in the Ishmaelean corpus which appears in the Palestinian *gemara* as a whole. Of the approximately one hundred twenty-one sayings of Ishmael which appear in the Palestinian Talmud, Yoḥanan quotes Ishmael in approximately seventeen pericopae.[52] Although Yoḥanan figures in only fourteen per cent of the Ishmaelean corpus, this is considerably more than any other sage. Yoḥanan's importance is difficult to explain. There is no obvious reason which accounts for his prominence. Because Yoḥanan quotes a wide variety of Tannaim in both the Palestinian and the Babylonian *gemarot*,[53] his importance in the Ishmaelean corpus may simply result from the fact that so few Amoraim or Tannaim quote Ishmael. In other words, Yohanan's prominence may be relative to the corpus as a whole and not a reflection of an absolute relationship between Yohanan and Ishmael's sayings.

The reasons which lie behind the creation of this form are obscure. The form itself, however, does allow us to make some suggestions as to these reasons. Aqiba and Ishmael appear in the same context thirty-four times in the Palestinian Talmud. In twenty-four of these pericopae, approximately seventy percent, the sayings of these two Tannaim are cast in the "according to Rabbi Y"-form. Thus, a primary function of the form is to juxtapose the sayings of these two masters. A unique feature of the pattern is that Aqiba's comments are never directly attributed to him; we never find, for example, "Aqiba says" or "Aqiba teaches." Ishmael's remarks, on the other hand, are almost always introduced by *tny*; that is, they are introduced by a term which indicates that a known Tannaitic statement follows.[54] Since we do find examples in the Palestinian *gemara* in which comments are attributed directly to Aqiba and Ishmael, this characteristic of our form gains importance. It appears that the form is used to juxtapose a "reliable" statement of Ishmael with a less "reliable" remark of Aqiba. Apparently Yohanan and his circle did not believe that one should use the standard dispute-form or debate-form[55] if the veracity of both traditions could not be established.

Thus far we have assigned a provenance to twenty-four percent of our *sugyot*. Can we place the remaining seventy-six percent in the same locality and within the same time period? We realize that extrapolating from twenty-four percent of our sources is risky; however, we suggest that there is some merit in such an endeavor. It is clear that we have a form which was rarely used. The fact that we have so few examples of this form argues against its being widely known and used by a large number of sages over a long period of time. We also saw a striking consistency in the names of those sages other than Ishmael and Aqiba who appear in our pericopae. There was absolutely no one who did not live in the second through the fourth generations in Tiberias. This also argues against a wide distribution of sages employing this form. Further, the form suggests that the sages using it were concerned primarily with the transmission of the sayings of Ishmael and Aqiba and that they were more certain about the authenticity of Ishmael's comment than they were of the remark attributed to Aqiba. This was unusual, for Aqiba was much more important than Ishmael and the former's traditions were much more widely known. We can conclude, with some reservation, that those *sugyot* cast in our form originated in Tiberias within the circle of Yohanan and his pupils.[56]

NOTES

[1]H. Gunkel, *Die Genesis* (Göttingen: 1901).

[2]M. Dibelius, *Die Formgeschichte des Evangeliums* (Tübingen: 1919).

[3]R. Bultmann, *Die Geschichte der synoptischen Tradition* (Göttingen: 1921).

[4]A. Weiss, *The Development of the Talmud as a Literary Unit* [Hebrew] (New York: 1943).

[5]A. Weiss, *Studies in the Literature of the Amoraim* [Hebrew] (New York: 1962). *The Talmud and its Development* [Hebrew] (New York: 1954). For excellent English summaries and evaluations of Weiss' works see S. Kanter, "Abraham Weiss: Source Criticism" and D. Goodblatt, "Abraham Weiss: The Search for Literary Forms" in J. Neusner (Ed.), *The Formation of the Babylonian Talmud* (Leiden: 1970), pp. 87-103.

[6]J. N. Epstein, *Introduction to the Text of the Mishnah* [Hebrew] (Tel Aviv: 1944). For an excellent summary and evaluation of Epstein's work see B. Bokser, "Jacob N. Epstein's *Introduction to the Text of the Mishnah*" and "Jacob N. Epstein on the Formation of the Mishnah" in J. Neusner (ed.), *The Modern Study of the Mishnah* (Leiden: 1973), pp. 13-55.

[7]J. Neusner, *Development of a Legend: Studies on the Traditions Concerning Yohanan ben Zakkai* (Leiden: 1970).

[8]J. Neusner, *The Rabbinic Traditions About the Pharisees Before 70* (Leiden: 1971).

[9]J. Neusner, *Eliezer b. Hyrcanus: The Traditions and the Man* (Leiden: 1973). *A History of the Mishnaic Law of Purities* (Leiden: 1974-1978).

[10]Frankel argues that C should be a question. He notes that often common words, such as "why" or "said" are missing from the text of the Palestinian *gemara*. Z. Frankel, *Einleitung in den jerusalemischen Talmud* (Breslau: 1870), p. 12a.

[11]The pattern $^c d\,kdwn\ldots k\ldots tny$ does not appear in any of the concordances to rabbinic literature published to date. B. Kosovsky, *Concordantiae Verborum Quae in Mechilta D'Rabbi Ismael Reperiuntur* (Jerusalem: 1965), II, p. 677. *Concordantiae Verborum Quae in Sifra aut Torat Kohanim Reperiuntur* (Jerusalem: 1967), XVIII, p. 52. C. Y. Kosovsky, *Concordantiae Verborum Quae in Sex Mishnae Ordinibus Reperiuntur* (Tel Aviv: 1957), III, p. 919.

[12]Frankel, *loc. cit.*

[13]J. Levy, *Wörterbuch über die Talmudim und Midraschim* (Darmstadt: 1963), II, p. 295.

[14]A. Kohut, *Aruch Completum Sive Lexicon Vocabula et Res, Quae in Libris Targumicis, Talmudicis et Midraschicis* (Vienna: 1884), II, pp. 200-201.

[15]M. Jastrow, *A Dictionary of the Targumim, the Talmud Babli and Yerushalmi, and the Midrashic Literature* (New York: 1971), p. 613a.

[16]W. Bacher, *Die exegetische Terminologie der judischen Traditionsliteratur* (Hildesheim: 1965), II, p. 147.

[17]A number of studies have been under the direction of Professor Neusner at Brown University which would have allowed us to isolate this form; however, the form has not been discovered to date. See W. S. Green, *The Traditions of Joshua ben Haninah*, S. Kanter, *Gamaliel of Yavneh*, C. Primus, *ᶜAqiba's Contribution to the Law 1: Zeraim*. These works are presently appearing in *Studies in Judaism in Late Antiquity* edited by Jacob Neusner and published by E. J. Brill of Leiden.

[18]y. ᶜOrlah 2:1, Venice 62a: y. Berakot 7:1, Venice 11a.

[19]y. Megillah 4:1, Venice 74d-75a; y. Shabbat 19:2, Venice 17a; y. Rosh Hashanah 3:5, Venice 58d; y. Ḥagigah 2:3, Venice 79a; y. Yoma 8:3, Venice 45a; y. Pesaḥim 9:1, Venice 36c; y. ᶜErubim 3:1, Venice 20c.

[20]y. Yevamot 6:2, Venice 7b; y. Yevamot 8:1, Venice 8c; y. Yevamot 10:6, Venice 11a; y. Yevamot 11:1, Venice 11d; y. Gittin 8:1, Venice 49b; y. Qiddushin 1:2, Venice 59a; y. Qiddushin 2:1, Venice 62a; y. Soṭah 8:1, Venice 22b; y. Qiddushin 1:2, Venice 59c; y. Nedarim 1:1, Venice 36c.

[21]y. Sanhedrin 7:5, Venice 14:5, 24c; y. Sanhedrin 3:9, Venice 9:10, 21c; y. Shevuᶜot 1:2, Venice 32d; y. Shevuᶜot 4:1, Venice 35b; y. Shevuᶜot 8:1, Venice 38c.

[22]*Ḥaliṣah* in the ceremony by which a woman declares she does not want to perform a levirate marriage with her dead husband's brother, Deuteronomy 25:9.

[23]The levirate marriage is that marriage a man must perform with his dead brother's wife if his brother died before conceiving a son; Deuteronomy 24:5ff.

[24]See comments of Moses Margoliot, *loc. cit.* and David Frankel *loc. cit.*

[25]This is the reading in the Venice and Leiden Mss. The printed editions of the text, however, read Zeᶜirah.

[26]*ql wḥwmr.*

[27]See comment of Moses Margoliot, *loc. cit.*

[28]Frankel, *op. cit.*, p. 102b. H. Strack, *Introduction to Talmud and Midrash* (New York: 1965), p. 123. A. Hymann, *History of the Tannaim and the Amoraim* [Hebrew] (Jerusalem: 1964) II, pp. 723-726.

[29]Frankel, *op. cit.*, pp. 77b-78b. Strack, *op. cit.*, pp. 125-126. Hymann, *op. cit.*, pp. 386-398.

[30]According to the traditional division of schools of biblical exegesis, Aqiba headed the one which was the more mystical. He based his interpretations on the appearance of certain words, the shapes of the letters, apparently needless repetition of words or phrases, and the like. These peculiarities of the Hebrew text suggest that one may either limit the meaning of the text or extend it. I. Gastfreund, *History of Rabbi ᶜAqiba* [Hebrew] (Lemberg: 1871). A. J. Heschel, *Theology of Ancient Judaism* [Hebrew] (London: 1962) I, pp. i-lix, 5-10. Strack, *op. cit.*, pp. 93-98, especially 98.

[31]Strack states: "*Gezerah Shawah*, literary: similar injunction or regulation. 'Inference by Analogy,' by virtue of which, because in two pentateuchal passages words occur which are similar

or have the identical connotation, both laws, however different they may be in themselves, are subject to the same regulations and applications." Strack, *op. cit.,* p. 94.

[32]See comment of Moses Margoliot, *loc. cit.*

[33]Jastrow, *op. cit.,* p. 712b.

[34]See comment of David Frankel, *loc. cit.*

[35]As it stands this phrase is meaningless.

[36]M. Qiddushin 1:1.

[37]Frankel suggests we read: *ʾškḥ tny r yšmᶜʾl lh mylt ḥpšy mḥwpšh.* He explains that this means that we find a *beraita* that Ishmael learns that a Hebrew slave is acquired by a document by analogy with a betrothed Canaanite handmaiden. See comment of David Frankel, *loc. cit.*

[38]Jacob David states that perhaps it is better to emend the text so that it reads *ʾškḥ tny r yšmᶜʾl lh mlh wḥpšy mḥwpšh.* It means that he employs a *gezarah shavah* on the basis of *ḥpšy* and *ḥwpšh.* See comment of Jacob David, *loc. cit.*

[39]Margoliot states that it is explicitly found that Ishmael employs the exegetical principle in question here. His *gezarot shavot* draw the analogy between a Hebrew slave and a female Hebrew slave. But he is forced to bring in verses which combine Ishmael's opinion here and the one cited in Q. See comment of Moses Margoliot, *loc. cit.*

[40]For a discussion of this form see J. Neusner, *The Rabbinic Traditions About the Pharisees Before 70* (Leiden: 1971), III, p. 7.

[41]L. Finkelstein, *Sifra or Torat Kohanim According to Codex Assemani LXVI* (New York: 1956), p. 379. No version of this *sugya* appears in Codex Vatican 31. *Torath Cohanim [Sifra] Seder Eliyahu Rabba and Zutta Codex Vatican 31* (Jerusalem: 1972).

[42]Frankel, *op. cit.,* p. 12a.

[43]*Ibid.*

[44]Compare with David Frankel's comment, *loc. cit.* and Moses Margoliot's comment, *loc. cit.*

[45]*Supra,* note 29.

[46]*Supra,* note 28.

[47]Frankel, *op. cit.,* pp. 126a-126b. Strack, *op. cit.,* p. 124. Hymann, *op. cit.,* III, pp. 1141-1145.

[48]Habrayya does not appear in any of the histories of the Tannaim or Amoraim. On Yoḥanan see Frankel, *op. cit.,* pp. 95b-97b. Strack, *op. cit.,* pp. 121-122. Hymann, *op. cit.,* pp. 653-672.

[49]Frankel, *op. cit.,* p. 80b. Strack, *op. cit.,* p. 128. Hymann, *op. cit.,* I, p. 409-410.

[50]*Supra,* note 48.

[51]*Supra,* note 47.

[52]For a discussion of the entire Ishmaelian corpus see G. Porton, *The Traditions of Rabbi Ishmael* (Leiden: 1976–) I-IV.

[53]See the partial list compiled by Hymann. Hymann, *op. cit.,* II, p. 658.

[54]Jastrow, *op. cit.,* p. 1681b. Bacher, *op. cit.,* I, pp. 238-240.

[55]Neusner, *Rabbinic Traditions,* III, pp. 16-23.

[56]My teacher Jacob Neusner kindly read the several drafts of this paper and made many important comments. As I noted above, any study into rabbinic literary forms owes a direct debt to the work of Professor Neusner; therefore, much more of his than the specific comments he made on this paper appear here. I also wish to thank my teacher and colleague W. R. Schoedel for his help in the preparation of this essay. Professors William S. Green and Baruch Bokser read the drafts of this paper and made many valuable comments. Professor Bokser drew my attention to the works of Bacher and Frankel.

VII

Biblical and Rabbinic Contributions to an Understanding of the Slave

DEAN A. MILLER

UNIVERSITY OF ROCHESTER

Few human categories and activities identifiable in the premodern world carry as many emotive and psychological affects in and around them as the slave and the institution of slavery. That a gulf of centuries separates the investigator from the culture does not lessen the likelihood of explicit or implicit moral judgment. The student of Mesopotamian or Mediterranean slave-systems, then, finds at least some of the subjective restraints operating upon him which have traditionally affected, and still affect, the study of 18th or 19th century American slave-holding societies.[1] Even if he can create the empathic link which allows him simply to register, as the ancients did, the presence of the unfree in their societies as a natural and unquestioned phenomenon, this absolute difference between that time and this must work upon him. As a historian, one may say—and believe—that the drudging, bentbacked workers who dragged out their shortened and grimy lives through the earlier stages of the Industrial Revolution were in worse case than any but the lowest mine-slave or galley-oarsman of two or three millenia ago. Still, reading the cuneiform inscription or its translation which says, baldly, that man X brought man Y—or encountering M. I. Finley's acute interpretation of the utility of Greek slavery: that the *polis* which went farthest toward the equitable distribution of political power, and which built the most creative civilization in the ancient world, was also the most firmly based on slave labor—one is inclined to wince.[2]

Penetrating the psycho-social mystery of the *owned* human being still may be deflected by emotional affect, then. The deflection may be toward the indefatigable multiplication of examples, the listing of variations within a slave-owning society without any attempt at analytic comment: *the* slave is personal, municipal, agricultural, married, forbidden to marry, half-free, a monster, an employee. The enumerator then figuratively throws up his hands, and from all of this no reader can do much more than guess at the answer to the question: what is "the slave?" What indelible mark is set upon him—upon the unfree—in the archaic mind, or is there such a mark?

Another deflection causes the analyst to void or evade the question of moral estrangement by positing an explanation for slavery which sweeps everything—every differentiation and variation—aside with the clumsy (but morally neutral) sword of economic determinism: the slave is an economic counter, a resource, a lowest-level proto-proletarian. Or, in a more rigidly ideological or metahistorical sense, slave-labor is identified as the central element in a "mode of production" which characterizes and underlies a macrohistorical zone or segment.

What I have here termed "deflection" seems to evade the moral, judgmental attitudes of our own society and, in doing so, also becomes opaque or resistant to the *archaic* or pre-modern identification of the nature of the slave. For ancient societies not only see no immorality in the institution of slavery, but transfer the moral problem—contained in the unavoidable puzzle of the human being fallen into absolute, inhuman dependence on others—to an identification which accompanies the act of exploitation, or social and economic use: the identification of the slave as an ambiguous—at once morally suspect and magically potent—intrusion, a dislocation in the natural order. What I mean to suggest below is the addition of a "deep" dimension in the psycho-social analysis of slavery, a connective with theories of human social perception which place the unfree into a specific category of "otherness," threat, and power.

In respect to the oldest civilizations from which our Western inheritance is drawn, the slave is already present at the creation. Woven into the fabric of society, on almost all levels, he or she moves, as possessor, worker, and actor, certainly human—and yet always the *tertium quid*, between man and non-man. Researchers have, with some effort, produced categories of analysis which connect this variety of unfree labor to other types of economic activity: the situation in law, the familial rights or lack of them, the methods by which a human being is made dependent or freed from that dependence. Here I propose to separate certain examples, out of the multiplicity of problems surrounding the unfree, in order to illuminate in microcosm the possibilities of understanding and misunderstanding the "essence" of slavery.

The use of the term *tertium quid* in fact points the way into the complex of powers in which the slave is involved. The anthropological studies of Victor Turner and Mary Douglas, and E. R. Leach's refinement of Lévi-Strauss' structural theories, have described the powers of the liminar, mediator, or interstitial being: the occupant of the tabooed zone *between categories*.[3] The slave is not and cannot be perceived as a full or normal being, because he is less than subordinate, he is owned. He falls into the zone between the human state and other, opposite states whose characteristics may be said to be mixed into his—the animal (especially the "beast of burden"), the child (the dependent non-adult) or even the monster (the *anomaly* as metaphor or as nightmare). He is an interstitial character *par excellence*, and as such projects, or has projected onto him, the potency of his state. He is part of the homologic

Gestalt which includes so many "powerful ones" in the archaic perceptive field, and his powers: dangerous, negative, contaminative—dark, in most senses of that word—explain much about societal patterns of behavior and definition concerning the slave.

This concept of the liminal potentiality of the slave may be brought to bear on three fragments of evidence taken from slaveowning societies of the ancient Near East:

(a) The Hebrew slave, according to Ex. 21:6 and Deut. 15:17, is transferred from provisional to permanently dependent status through the following effectuating ritual:

> Then his master shall bring him unto the judges; he shall also bring him to the door, or unto the door post; and his master shall bore his ear through with an awl; and he shall serve him forever.

> Then thou shalt take an awl, and thrust it through his ear into the door, and he shall be thy servant forever. And also unto thy maid-servant thou shall do likewise.

What is this ritual's significance? The two key elements are: the insistence on the placement of the "binding" ceremony at the doorway of the master's house, and the piercing of the ear (even, as some translations seem to suggest, if the awl used by the master does not in fact affix the slave to the doorpost). The doorpost/doorway, I believe, easily can be construed here within the complex of threshold magic: this place is the fully identifiable *signum* of the House (and of the Master of the House) where the House means not nourishing safety (for this sign is the hearth or the granary) but protective, separable identity.[4] At the doorway the inward conserving forces of the protective shelter meet the external exotic-chaotic. And, the slave is caught between inside and outside, and there is made to stand—possibly, in another extension of the complex, where *his* apotropaic-prophylactic force—negative force—stands as an additional guard against the exterior powers (as, in another instance, excluded or tabooed individuals—the leprous or insane in Medieval Europe—are held "in the wall" for purposes both of segregation and to utilize, it would seem, their unconscious potentiality to protect those within the wall.)[5]

The slave's ear is pierced. According to Mendelsohn, piercing may have been followed by the marking of the slave with a seal or tag; a visible sign (Sumerian *abbuttum*) of servile status and the rights of ownership, similar both to the slave-collar of some societies, and the mutilation of the slave's body (by branding, tattooing, or cutting) practiced by other slaveholding groups.[6] Given, however, that the indicator of *complete* (as differentiated from provisional or proto-servile) slave status in the Near East is most often a cutting of the hair ("frontal" hair is often specified), the attention to the slave's ear may be explained by analogy.[7] The rights of the master over slave are given, in another Near Eastern context, as: the right to beat, to cut the hair, to bruise, to pierce or bore the ear.[8] These rights seem to combine a more or less strictly punitive aspect—the violation of the slave's body by blows, which he or she cannot legitimately resist or ask restitution for—with a further "marking," by the cutting of hair or the piercing of the ear.

Head-hair as a repository of sexual identity and personality has been thoroughly examined by E. R. Leach.[9] From the Medieval European or Hindu monk's tonsure to the mourning ceremonial of the Trobriand Islanders, innumerable cultures display their sensitivity to symbolic identity of head and genitalia, of head-hair and sexual personality. And it is precisely in this area, the tabooed zone of sexual power, that the slave attracts the most serious social derogation. In this perceptive field, the male slave, having no clear right to pass on his *nomen* (for he has none) is thus free from social constraint; he is considered as an unfettered, even animal, predative sexual force. No power (no power in society, no *caput* in the Roman legal definition) in this respect signifies an extreme power: the negative extreme from acceptable, controlled, socialized sexuality constrained within the familial structure.[10] The female slave enters this unconstrained zone as passive rather than active: also detached from the formularies of social bargaining and familial exchange, she is simply available.[11] What this availability of slave women meant in terms of the inner dynamics of the family, we will probably never know; but we can guess that unfettered sexual opportunity in this case as well gave rise to beliefs of unnatural or extreme ultrapotent female sexuality.

The ceremony of the piercing of the ear, then, signifies the attempt by the slave-owner to curtail and control this sexual energy; to castrate, in the most general and least Freudian sense of symbolic castration. The "head" and thus the sexual potencies of the unfree are marked and mutilated as well as being brought under control and duress. If the slave's ear is further signed with a tag or tablet, as may have been the case, the continued guardianship of the owner over the slave's sexual personality is marked as surely as is his physical control .over the slave's work, residence, and other aspects of his or her life.

The response of the developing rabbinate to the parts of Scripture dealing with the "passage" to total slavery is especially illustrative of the conscious or unconscious antagonism of this rationalistic tradition to the magical (or tabooed sexual) substrate in this Scripture. As Urbach notes in his lengthy study of the laws regarding slavery, Yohanan ben Zakkai (in the first century A.D., the attribution is later) described the boring of the ear as a punishment for one who had (a) "heard the Commandment"—forbidding theft—and disobeyed, or (b) had heard the "other words"—God's declaration to the Hebrews that they must consider themselves all *His* slaves, and could have no human master—and also disobeyed. It is also of interest that Yohanan perceives two origins for slavery: either a man sells himself, because of poverty, or is sold "by the court" to indemnify the victims of his theft.[12]

The rabbinical exegesis of the two passages thus imputes to the "punishment" of the boring of the ear a logical cause: the offending ear, a receptor of the Word, had ignored either of two divine messages. Unfortunately for this explanation, the slave whose ear is bored as a mark of total servility is seen in other, and earlier, Near Eastern cultures. This "punishment" is not restricted to Jews under the Commandments; more, the non-Hebrew sources contain no hint of such a rational (or "verbal") explanation for the boring of the ear. The rabbinical argument *ex verbo Dei* must be regarded as a gloss—and a very late gloss—explaining a practice borrowed from other Near Eastern cultures. In fact, in the complicated skein of argument over details of slavery woven by the rabbinate, additional evidence appears for the loss of sexual identity implicit in the ritual of ear-marking. Differentiating between the self-enslaved and the court-enslaved individual, the author of an anonymous *baraita* states: first, that the self-enslaved does *not* have the ear bored; the court-enslaved does. And the master of the self-enslaved "has not the right to assign him a Canaanite or gentile handmaid (as a concubine)" while the master of the court-enslaved has this right.[13] No clearer evidence of the significance of the bored ear could be found: residual or partial sexual identity = no marking of the ear; subtraction of sexual identity, potentiality, and choice = the bored ear.

(b) A second fragment of evidence which describes, on one level, a basic socio-economic relationship, states that a slave, in several related Near Eastern societies of the third to first millenia B.C., must be "checked" before final purchase to make sure that he or she is free of either of two conditions: leprosy and epilepsy.[14] Here again our common ("economic") sense may or may not tell us what was going on in the minds of the redactors of archaic law codes, as they reflected the values of their society. These two afflictions certainly have a surface resemblance—in medical terms both are sufficiently traumatic maladies, incapacitating to a degree (though we recall that ancient "leprosy" was an unsightly skin condition, not comparable to the modern disease).[15] We may know the archaic sensitiveness and antipathy towards, especially, the leper as unclean. Yet as afflicted conditions or traumata epilepsy and leprosy are, objectively considered, not at all alike. What the ancient world termed leprosy was immediately and dramatically apparent; epilepsy, on the other hand, was a dysfunction which displayed no specific symptoms until the "fit" or seizure occurred, and in fact the testing or quarantine period allotted in (Sumerian) law to detect it was a month or more.[16] So, one condition was betrayed by immediately visible stigmata; one was essentially hidden, potential. What, in the archaic mind, drew the two together?

The detection of severe disabilities obviously appealed to the pragmatic sense of the presumptive purchaser. He would not wish to buy a slave who, as an "unclean" individual, would be excluded from certain duties or who, as an epileptic, would be even less useful, depending on what tasks were set him. But again, why these ailments specifically? Certainly other diseases or dysfunctions would affect the slave's usefulness—diseases which might weaken him, infections or contagions which might be passed on to others. Presumably, because these two diseases have a more than physical aetiology even if a general archaic theory of disease made it always caused by an intervention of demonic forces: both were evidences of extraordinary, supernatural attention paid to the sufferer. Leprosy was a result of fault, sometimes identified more specifically as sin—an inner uncleanness made external—while, in the case of epilepsy, there as a "descent of the god," perhaps random, un-looked for, but evoking terror and pity and marking off the sufferer or recipient as a vessel of other, inhuman and superpotent, forces.[17]

To recapitulate, in the archaic perception-field the unfree individual is already in the dangerous marginal or *liminal* world; the ambipolarities (human/property; man/animal; person/non-person) of his or her very existence make up a complex of powerfully negative, contaminative forces. A slave who bears the stigmata of leprosy, or who is revealed as an epileptic, is a container of forces additionally contaminative and potent, a carrier of powers beyond the acceptable range, and we can guess that no slave-owner cared to deal with these super-liminal powers.

Since we are seeking to penetrate to the "deep" causative base under an archaic society's reactions to its unfree category, we might take the problem one step further: is specific attention paid to a slave's "uncontaminated" physical condition because the forbidden diseases pertain to a status to which he cannot by definition aspire, or because he is to be peculiarly susceptible to these traumata? Leprosy (or "leprosy") is presumably an exterior sign of an interior, or at least separately considered, uncleanness or state of sin. Must not the unclean individual be free to commit the sin or be guilty of the uncleanness—i.e., be, in religious terms, a valid or capable personality? We must say: an animal cannot sin. Does a slave have the capability of committing acts defined as polluting?

In the case of epilepsy, the dysfunction pressed upon the individual might be perceived in a similar fashion, as an interaction between the affected individual and a divine power, producing a secret, *potential* affliction, in the pattern of other mysterious seizures, trances, possessions by the god of a more or less permanent nature. The question here again is: can a slave be subject to such divine attention? In either instance, we might posit the reaction of the archaic mind to be that the afflicted individual was being worked on by forces in a way which was not conformable to his or her slave status—and the logical extension of this is, that the afflicted individual could not, in fact, be a slave at all, but a complete—free—personality. But if this were so, the only way to resolve the anomaly would have been to release the slave, revealed as a free individual by divine intervention.

However, there is no evidence cited by Mendelsohn which separates the slave from the cultus—quite the contrary. And there is certainly no indication that a slave revealed as a leper or an epileptic was freed. The slave, then, was tested because of his liminal state, and his possible betrayal of *other* evidences of ambiguous status. The slave as touched by the gods in one sense—for so his loss of freedom or absence of freedom was seen—was even more liable to betray his ambiguity in another form. This may appear to be scholasticism or Devil's Advocacy, but the ramifications of the archaic perception of liminality are still not completely understood, nor all the possible formulations open to us.

We may see that, in dealing with the socio-economic patterns which express the actualities of slave life, care must be taken not to conceal the indelible character of the unfree. The slave, male or female, was a liminal or interstitial individual in society and, as such, was subject to, and expressed, certain potencies which separated him or her from the free. These potencies were most likely to appear when the slave "passed"—moved from semi-dependent to totally dependent status (as in the Hebrew example above) or was transferred from one owner to another.

The act of *passage* in fact raised the liminal potentiality of the slave to yet another level of threat or power, illustrated as:

(a) Hebrew case:

(b) Babylonian-Assyrian case:

PASSAGE (+LIMINALITY)

In the Hebrew instance the individual moves from a "grey" area of modified or pre-servile status into "black"—purely servile and additionally danger-ous —status across, in this case, the literal *limen* or threshold itself. In the Babylonian-Assyrian instance the full slave is checked *en passage* for addi-tional tabooed potencies before reassuming his already sufficiently danger-ous servile status.

In each case a pragmatic aspect is clear: the owner marks or identifies his property, or is concerned that a disability or ailment will not reduce the utility of his property. In each case, as well, the liminal-magical character-istic of the slave is dealt with: his powers, especially his sexual powers, are brought under control; or an unacceptable increase in the numenal "voltage" which he carries is guarded against.

(c) A third example; from the vita of a distinguished rabbinical figure:

When Hanina ben Dosa came to study with Rabban Yohanan ben Zakkai in Arav, it happened that Yohanan's son was deathly sick. He said to him, "Hanina my son, seek mercy for him that he may live." Hanina put his head between his knees, and prayed for mercy, and the boy lived. Rabban Yohanan ben Zakkai said to him, "If ben Zakkai were to throw his head down between his knees all day long, none would pay attention to him." Yohanan's wife then said to him, "And is Hanina greater than you?" "No," he replied, "but he is like a slave ($^c bd$) before the King, and I am like a (minister, *śr*) before the King. [10]

In the true rabbinic tradition (or the popular view of that tradition) this tale might be variously interpreted. Responding to his wife's singularly ill-considered but very human question of her husband ("is Hanina greater than you?") the latter explains that *he*—Yohanan—has no power in the matter of his son's healing, for he is as a "minister" in his relationship to the King-God, while Hanina is a "slave." Is he thereby derogating Hanina? Perhaps so, although since his son's healing depended from the second man's appeal, Yohanan would have appeared particularly ungrateful.

The wariness with which the "rationalist" rabbinate viewed magical interventions and the whole area of irrational powers may again be noted here, but more to the point are the powers Yohanan attached to the term "slave," as contrasted to his own powers.[19] A "slave" to the King—i.e., to God—Hanina was obviously not unfree in the ordinary sense—was able to do that which Yohanan, the "minister," could not do: ask for and receive mercy for the son of Yohanan, which was in fact a miraculous intervention. Why was this miracle possible? We might say first that a slave *qua* slave could not ask for justice—the partner of mercy—because a slave is felt to have no juridical character in the ordinary sense, being obscured in and by the judicial character of the master.[20] Therefore a "slave" in the metaphoric sense also cannot ask for justice—the rational balancing of legal desiderata, characters, and goals—but only for irrational intervention: for causeless mercy.

Undoubtedly this perception was in Yohanan's explanation, but more pertinent is the characterization of the slave as *magician*—intervenor in the magical line—which is implicit in that explanation.

Hanina, the "slave of God," has a direct relationship with the Royal Deity which has as its analog the relationship of Subject to King, except that in this instance the "slave" is, in a word, "super-subject," a *totally dependent*—in metaphoric terms—individual. Dependence in this case does not mean hierarchic ranking, but that link between lowest and highest which is magical-irrational in nature.

This matter may become clearer if one considers the opposition that Yohanan extends as a response to his importunate, and one may say archetypal, wife, whose desire it is to salve his dignity and with it, her own. Yohanan places himself as a "minister" in respect to God as King. Now, as I among others have stated elsewhere, of the doubled powers of the true King only the magisterial or juridical power—*Mitra*l power, in Dumézil's term—may be delegated: to a member of the bureaucracy, an official of the rational hierarchy, a *minister*, in other words.[21] Mercy—the power of miraculous intervention, on the Varunal side of the royal-divine character—is kept by the

King, and may not be delegated. But presumably it may be called out, or on, by the lowliest: the slave-magician.

The irrational powers of Hanina as "slave" follow the line of other connections between divinity, kingship, and the categories below them. The power of the sword may be delegated, the power of the miracle not. Yohanan correctly identifies his own potency: as belonging to the sphere of rationality, of analytic cognition. But a "slave"—a magician, an individual defined as intervening in the magical or Varunal line—saved his son. Obviously not all slaves are magicians, but in the ambiguous definition of complete subjection is always the capability of directing the power latent in the liminal aspect, where "lowest" appeals to, and is answered by, "highest."

The slave-master relationship, in the ancient Near East as in other slave-holding cultures, is undoubtedly one which, on one level, falls back on the monopoly of legal power—of open and legitimated force—by the master, to the end that the slave's labor and talents are exploited for the benefit of the master. However, the very definition of a superiority-dependence relationship reveals in the slave potentialities which are suspect, potentialities at the other end of the continuum of power from the area of legalized force, and which the master attempts to control.

Put in another way, the slave-master relationship has been characterized as "violence-prone." The master can legally offer violence to his slave, and the presumption is that he—the master—fears a retributive violence in return. This may be. But what can be described as open retribution by slave against master is, in terms of the numbers of the unfree in ancient slave-systems, quite rare. The punishments prescribed for an act openly directed against the master are, of course, terrible. I suspect, however, that the comparative rarity of open violence—individual or mass—directed by slave against master is explained by the "un-manning" of the slave: a state of consciously felt separation from the effective options available to the free man. But what *is* available to the slave is the working out of those powers specific to his state: powers belonging to the *limen*, to the interstitial area. These are secret powers, powers which spring from the hidden realms where magic and sorcery abide. These powers *may* be invoked by the slave, but they are *definitely* feared by the master.

In examining the archaic thought-world in its perception of the slave, then, Occam's Razor still bites: unnecessarily convoluted explanations of cause or aetiology should give way before simpler explanations. But in the archaic mind, psychic-magical aspects combine in perfect comfort with practical economic functions.

NOTES

[1] I am indebted to Miss Gail Thomas, a doctoral candidate in the Department of History, University of Rochester, for aid given me in this study.

[2] M. I. Finley, "Was Classical Civilization Based on Slavery?" in M. I. Finley, ed., *Slavery in Classical Antiquity: Views and Controversies* (Cambridge, 1960), p. 72.

[3] Victor Turner, *The Ritual Process: Structure and Anti-structure* (Chicago, 1969); Mary Douglas, *Purity and Danger: An Analysis of Concepts of Purity and Taboo* (London, 1966); E. R. Leach, "Anthropological Aspects of Language: Animal Categories and Verbal Abuse," in P. Maranda, ed., *Mythology* (Penguin, Baltimore, Md. 1973), esp. pp. 47-50.

[4] On threshold magic: see A. van Gennep, *The Rites of Passage*, trans. M. Vizedom and G. I. Caffee (Chicago, 1960), s.v. "portal rituals"; also H. Wagenvoort, *Roman Dynamism: Studies in Ancient Roman Thought, Language, and Custom* (Oxford, 1947), pp. 156, 161.

[5] Michel Foucault, *Madness and Civilization: A History of Insanity in the Age of Reason*, transl. R. Howard (New York, 1965), pp. 9, 11.

[6] I. Mendelsohn, *Slavery in the Ancient Near East. A Comparative Study of Slavery in Babylonia, Assyria, Syria and Palestine from the Middle of the Third Millennium to the End of the First Millennium* (New York, 1949); p. 49.

[7] Mendelsohn, *Slavery*, pp. 9, 20, 21ff., 28-29.

[8] In Assyria: Mendelsohn, *Slavery*, pp. 28-29.

[9] E. R. Leach, "Magical Hair," (Curl Bequest Prize Essay, 1957), *Journal of the Royal Anthropological Institute* (1959); pp. 147-164.

[10] Wagenvoort, *Roman Dynamism* p. 24.

[11] For the varieties and permutations of Near Eastern slave marriage, see Mendelsohn, *Slavery*, pp. 10-14, 52-7, 72-5, 84f., 87, 104f., 122, 142, 147.

[12] E. E. Urbach, "The Laws Regarding Slavery as a Source for Social History of the Period of the Second Temple, the Mishnah and Talmud," *Papers of the Institute of Jewish Studies*, London vol. 1 (Jerusalem, 1964), p. 10.

[13] *Ibid.*, p. 9.

[14] Mendelsohn, *Slavery*, pp. 9, 38, 40: in Sumerian, Babylonian (Hammurabic) and Assyrian codes.

[15] K. P. C. A. Gramberg, "'Leprosy' and the Bible," *The Bible Translator*, 11 (1960): 10-23; J. L. Swellengrebel, "'Leprosy' and the Bible," *Ibid.*, 69-79; D. H. Wallington, "'Leprosy' and the Bible: Conclusion," *The Bible Translator* 12 (1961), pp. 75-79. See also J. Neusner, *The Idea of Purity in Ancient Judaism* (Leiden, 1973).

[16]Mendelsohn, *Slavery*, p. 38.

[17]Neusner, *Idea of Purity*, pp. 114, 116-17; for epilepsy, Karl Sudhoff, *Aerztliches aus griechischen Papyrus-Urkunden* (Leipzig, 1909), pp. 142ff. (noting that epilepsy, in Greek, is θεία νόσος: "the divine sickness." See also O. Temken, *The Falling Sickness, A History of Epilepsy from the Greeks to the Beginnings of Modern Neurology* (Baltimore, Md., 1945).

[18]From J. Neusner, *A Life of Rabban Yohanan ben Zakkai, Ca. 1-80, C.E.* (Leiden, 1962): the translation is Neusner's with the exception that Neusner gives *śr* as "prince." The cluster of meanings attached to the term suggests that it denotes one who is "great, but less than a king." *śr* can mean "prince," "captain" or "chief." The modern rendering, "minister" is appropriate to these meanings and does not misrepresent the use of the term in the passage. See Francis Brown, S. R. Driver, and Charles A. Briggs, *A Hebrew and English Lexicon of the Old Testament* (Oxford, 1966), p. 978; Marcus Jastrow, *A Dictionary of the Targumim, the Talmud Babli and Jerushalmi, and the Midrashic Literature* (New York, 1950), p. 1627; Reuben Alcalay, *The Complete Hebrew-English Dictionary* (Hartford, 1965), cl. 2715. Whether Hanina the Wonderworker was in fact a disciple of Yohanan, by the way, is neither affirmed nor denied here.

[19]See above, p. 192.

[20]The non-juridical character or lack of *nomen* or *caput* of the slave is stronger in other legal traditions such as the Roman, but is sufficiently marked in the ancient Near East: see Mendelsohn, *Slavery*, 34ff.

[21]G. Dumézil, *Mitra-Varuna, essai sur deux représentations indo-européennes de la soveraineté* (Paris, 1948); see D. Miller, "Royauté et ambiguité sexuelle," *Annales E.S.C.* (Nos. 3 et 4, Mai-Aout 1971): pp. 648-649, with citation to J. A. Wilson, "Authority and Law in Ancient Egypt," in S. Eisenstadt, ed., *The Decline of Empires* (Englewood Cliffs, New Jersey) (1967), p. 15.

VIII

The Impact of the Dead Sea Scrolls on Jewish Studies During the Last Twenty-Five Years

GEZA VERMES

UNIVERSITY OF OXFORD

During the nineteenth century, the "Jewish Science" (*jüdische Wissenschaft*) introduced a new scholarly slant to the study of Judaism.[1] Nevertheless, although the pioneering efforts of Zunz, Fränkel, Graetz and Geiger, followed by the great achievements of the golden generation of the turn of the century—the generation of Bacher and Blau, Büchler and Goldziher, Kaufmann and Krauss, the two Löws and Marmorstein, not forgetting also the occasional non-Hungarians such as Abrahams, Lauterbach and Israel Lévi, and of course Solomon Schechter—resulted in a genuine renewal of Jewish studies, it would be correct however to add that this fell far short of the total upheaval to which the Bible itself was subjected at that time. Jewish scholars of the 1850-1950 period certainly managed, in the main, to free themselves from pure traditionalism, and to apply to rabbinic literature modern methods of research, yet for various reasons, and despite the loud protest of ultra-conservatives that the contrary was the case, the movement they initiated was in fact not revolutionary.

In part, this is to be attributed to an absence of archaeological finds in the domain of Rabbinica. The acquisition by Western scholars of the contents of the Cairo Geniza came nearest to such a discovery; but although its importance is undeniably great, it never succeeded in firing academic enthusiasm, let alone that of laymen, so much so that at the present time, nearly eight decades after Schechter's visit to Fustat, the main (Cambridge) collection of Geniza fragments still waits to be fully catalogued, evaluated and published.

Another more subtle reason has to do with an unwillingness, by the experts best qualified to do so, to shake the foundations of post-biblical Judaism. This is not the moment to psychoanalyse them, nor am I qualified to perform such a task; suffice it to say that this lack of critical inclination is in keeping with an apathy affecting the *Wissenschaft des Judentums* that is

responsible for the failure, after more than a century, to produce a truly
critical edition of either the Palestinian or the Babylonian Talmud, or even of
the complete Mishnah. Furthermore, I need not remind you that our
dictionaries and grammars are antiquated, that concordances are either non
existent or incomplete, and mostly based on non-critical texts. Admittedly,
the great men of the nineteenth century and those of the pre-Holocaust era in
the twentieth, required no such tools since they knew the whole of the rabbinic
literature inside out, and by heart. Who, apart from the Kasowskys (pater et
filius), would have wasted his time in the pre-computer age in compiling
inventories of words and phrases when everything could be quoted from
memory? (And what did it matter if now and again the references were within
a folio or two from the actual passage?) The various sorts of criticism—Gat-
tungsgeschichte,   Formgeschichte,   Traditionsgeschichte,   Redaktions-
geschichte—had scarcely begun to be applied to biblical studies, and certainly
not to Judaica: the master-pieces of that blessed era, Bacher's works on
Haggadah and Büchler's attempts at historiography, thoroughly informed
and brilliant though they are as far as traditional lore is concerned,
intentionally or unconsciously avoid the fundamental questions of historical
criticism, particularly those relating to the antecedents and derivation in the
Second Temple period of the system often referred to in the past as
"normative Judaism."

It would of course be unforgivable to ignore the steps taken towards
widening the horizon of Jewish studies by drawing on the auxiliary resources
of classical philology, Roman law, patristic Bible interpretation and straight
New Testament research, as Samuel Krauss,[2] Jean Juster,[3] Louis Ginzberg,[4]
and Claude Montefiore[5] endeavoured to do with greater or lesser success.
Nonetheless, I venture to suggest that among most spokesmen of the
Wissenschaft des Judentums—the extreme liberals excepted—it is possible to
detect an instinctive apologetical tendency that seeks scientific proof to
support traditionally held views.

This was this kind of scholarly world, one unaccustomed to real
novelties, that was suddenly faced with the unprecedented phenomenon of
Hebrew and Aramaic documents dating to the intertestamental era. Between
1947 and 1956, eleven caves on the northwestern shore of the Dead Sea gave
the lie to the axiom that no document written on the perishable material could
survive in Palestine and disgorged an enormous quantity of leather and
papyrus manuscripts and fragments, some large, some tiny, as well as a few
ostraca and hoards of coins. The longest of the rolls, the Temple Scroll, did
not surface until after the Six-Day-War in 1967. All these, and additional
finds, dating to the first and early second centuries A.D., made at Murabbaᶜat,
Naḥal Ḥever and Nahal Zeᵓelim, as well as in the fortress of Masada, have
altered beyond recognition our documentation regarding the Judaism of that
period.

How did the academic world of biblical and post-biblical Jewish research react to this most exciting event?

On the superficial level, there was immediate and almost universal acclaim. The archaeologists and Hebraists who acted as negotiators, advisers and excavators, or as decipherers and editors—Sukenik, de Vaux, Albright and Millar Burrows with his team—used only superlatives in describing the Scrolls as the most ancient and the most important in existence, their discovery as the most significant ever made in biblical archaeology, and everything connected with them as sensational, and indeed epoch-making. Yet the jubilation was more apparent than real. Apart from the scholars already mentioned, who were involved willy-nilly because they happened to be in Jerusalem at the crucial moment—Albright was not, but he was consulted explicitly as the American oracle on all matters pertaining to Palestinian archaeology—most established authorities opted for a wait-and-see attitude. Only a few specialists of international reputation ventured bravely into the Qumran labyrinth: André Dupont-Sommer in France[6] and H. H. Rowley in this country.[7] The already elderly, but still adventurous, Paul Kahle also joined in,[8]—without making any noticeable mark on the issue: and the sadly missed Professor G. R., later Sir Godfrey, Driver contributed in 1951 a booklet which is now best forgotten.[9] The one expert in Judaica to throw himself headlong into the argument, that peculiar genius Solomon Zeitlin, declared even before seeing the smallest photograph of the tiniest fragment:

> Although I have not seen these manuscripts and have not the right to pass judgment, I have my doubts about them. I know that during the Second Commonwealth the Jews did not write commentaries on biblical books.[10]

A little later, he became dogmatic:

> As to the *Commentary to the Book of Habakkuk* . . . far from being an ancient book, it clearly belongs to the Middle Ages. It is axiomatic that the Jews did not write commentaries on the prophetic book during the period of the Second Commonwealth.[11]

Zeitlin remained faithful to his original intuition, and flooded JQR (edited by him) with ink, if not vitriol, in its defence. His only inconsequential move came in 1950 when, in spite of a formal declaration of intent, "The Hebrew Scrolls: Once more and finally"[12] he did not stop but continued his anti-Qumran crusade. But of the early well-known protagonists, Dupont-Sommer alone made a lasting impression on the literary and historical study of the Scrolls.[13] Apart from him, the foundations of Qumran research were laid mainly by a new generation of scholars, the young men of twenty-five years ago, untried but eager for adventure.

In 1952, I was preparing for publication my doctrinal thesis on "The Historical Framework of the Dead Sea Scrolls" and travelled to Israel to look at the originals. I was refused access to them by the ailing Sukenik.[14] So, with the connivance of a consul in Jerusalem who furnished me with false papers, I changed my identity, and passing through the Mandelbaum Gate (in the consular car) went to spend a month at the Ecole Biblique et Archéologique Française. There I found two scholars (both roughly my contemporaries and famous names today) working on the fragments collected in Cave 1, and studying the new bits and pieces brought by the Beduin to the Palestine Archaeological Museum in cardboard boxes of every size: the Frenchman Jean Dominique Barthélemy, and that most brilliant editor of Qumran material, the Pole, Joseph Milik. Then, in 1953, F. M. Cross—now the leading Scrolls expert in the United States—began his association with the manuscripts from the Judaean Desert; and at the same time a man in his thirties, whose studies had been interrupted by service in the Israeli army, became his father's pupil once again and started his Ph.D. work on, appropriately, the War Scroll. His name was Yigael Yadin.

If I tell this story, it is not only because of the common middle-aged tendency to reminisce, but to point out that the fact that none of us had reputations to risk or lose, or previously advanced theories to defend, turned out to be a distinct advantage. Freedom to move, without the blinkers of prejudice one way or another, and without ties, was absolutely essential if quick progress were to be made in an extremely complex and sensitive area of knowledge.

The first struggle over the authenticity and dating of the Scrolls was soon settled: the discovery of the caves and their contents and the successive stages of the excavation of the Qumran site removed by the mid-50s all reasonable doubt in that respect. It was almost unanimously agreed that the documents were to be assigned to the last couple of centuries of the Second Temple. This conclusion reached chiefly on palaeographical and archaeological grounds, was further indirectly confirmed by the subsequent finds at Masada and in the hiding-places of the Bar Kokhba period.

I. TRANSMISSION OF THE TEXT OF THE BIBLE

The sudden emergence of a large corpus of Hebrew and Aramaic texts, many centuries older than anything previously known except the Nash Papyrus, had far-reaching implications in most areas of Jewish history and culture. To begin with, it completely revolutionised—and I am using the term on purpose—our understanding of the history of the biblical text itself. The eleven Qumran caves have revealed scrolls and fragments belonging to all the books of the Hebrew Scriptures, apart from Esther, antedating by over a millennium the earliest Masoretic codices. Clearly, textual criticism will benefit enormously from these documents (especially when Cross and Patrick Skehan release the Cave 4 material), but since our Association is not primarily concerned with the evaluation of the Scrolls from a text-critical viewpoint, I will dwell, instead, on that aspect of the biblical manuscripts which possesses a wider historical significance.

The Qumran Scrolls of the Old Testament represent several textual or recensional traditions and not just a single one. Some biblical books testify to the *textus receptus* of the later Masoretic tradition; others especially the books of Samuel and Jeremiah and the chronology of Kings, echo the Hebrew underlying the Greek Bible; others still correspond to the Samaritan version. To grasp the meaning of this multiplicity, we must bear in mind that it is found in a religious community quick to react in the domain of precision in belief and practice, yet apparently quite happy with a mosaic of textual traditions. It had been the common assumption before Qumran that the canon of the Hebrew Bible was finally established at Yavneh at the very end of the first century. The Scrolls now show that the rabbis assembled there under the leadership of Yohanan ben Zakkai and Gamaliel II had also to decree which single type of text should count henceforward as sacred.

As I have already noted, the text which became the official (proto-) Masoretic text was not a new creation: it was one of the three main types current at Qumran. In other words, when religious authority proceeded to unify the plurality of textual traditions, it canonised one of the existing varieties more or less *in toto* rather than create, as modern biblical scholars often do, a new version with the help of what seems to them to be the best reading found in any of the competing recensions. Whichever method was chosen to achieve a unique canonical text, the basic fact remains that plurality came before an authoritatively imposed unity.

But is there no flaw in this argument? Might not the undeniable plurality at Qumran be attributed to the "unorthodox" position of a sect? After all, it is possible to surmise—though, no doubt, without hard evidence to back it— that in the "right" (non-sectarian) circles of Judaism—say among the Pharisees—the sole authority of the (proto-) Masoretic text was never challenged. And the existence of such a text at the time in question is now at least in part vindicated by the Scrolls themselves.

In theory, this would be a perfectly logical attitude. Yet quite apart from whether the notions of orthodoxy and heterodoxy are applicable in the sense implied here during the existence of the Second Temple, the thesis just outlined seems to run against a snag not properly emphasized so far.

Frank Cross, when analysing the variants in the Samuel fragments discovered in Cave 4, noticed that their Hebrew reflects the Semitic substratum of the Greek Samuel, more precisely the so-called Lucianic recension, and that the same type of text recurs again and again in the relevant Greek extracts contained in the *Antiquities* of Josephus. Even more extraordinary, in several passages where Samuel and 1 Chronicles overlap, the Masoretic version of Chronicles reproduces, not the Masoretic Samuel, but the 4Q-proto-Lucianic variety.[15] In Cross's own words:

> The agreement between the text of Chronicles and 4QSam[a] is most significant. It makes clear how that the text of the Deuteronomic history used by the Chronicler toward 400 B.C. was by no means identical with the received text.[16]

Set within our frame of reference, this means that when the final compilation of Chronicles was under way, parallel textual traditions were already in existence, and that they were all employed by the ultimate redactor of this biblical work. It would doubtless be inadvisable in the present state of our information to go as far as to suggest that the 4Q type is actually the oldest (and most genuine?) text of the Bible, a text which at a later stage came to be superseded for reasons impossible to guess, by the proto-Masoretic version. Be this as it may, the paradox deserves to be repeated: the Masoretic compiler of 1 Chronicles quotes, at times, 1-2 Samuel from a non-Masoretic form of the Hebrew text.

In brief, Qumran has disclosed that even in the field of the transmission of the Biblical text itself we have to reckon not with a single chain of tradition, but with a multiplicity of parallel sources. If fully substantiated, this finding will mark a major break-through not only in textual criticism, but also in Jewish intellectual and religious history.

II. APOCRYPHA AND PSEUDEPIGRAPHA

Although, in principle, the Apocrypha and Pseudepigrapha are eminently part of the literature of Judaism, before Qumran they were rarely conceived of as properly belonging to the realm of Jewish studies. There were two main reasons for this lack of recognition, one linguistic, the other dogmatic. Concerning the former, none of the compositions classified under the dual heading of Apocrypha and Pseudepigrapha was available in Hebrew or Aramaic until relatively recently. True, a large part of Ecclesiasticus could be read in Hebrew, and a section of the Testament of Levi in Aramaic, thanks to the Cairo Geniza; nevertheless, when we spoke of the Apocrypha, we instinctively associated them with the Greek language, while the Pseudepigrapha evoked the variegated philogical spectrum of Greek, Latin, Syriac and Ethiopic.

The dogmatic reason for keeping this literature in a position apart is that the Tannaim held them to be *sepharim hizonim*, books beyond the pale of religious influence and not meriting to be preserved. In fact, their survival is due to the interest and respect shown to them, not in Jewish, but in Christian circles.

The Scrolls, needless to say, have fundamentally altered this state of affairs. Not only have they confirmed that the already familiar Hebrew Ben

Sira, and Aramaic Testament of Levi, belonged to Jewish antiquity and not to the Middle Ages—as we all know, further Hebrew remains of Ecclesiasticus were discovered at Masada, too—but they have also provided fragments of the Hebrew and Aramaic originals of Tobit, Jubilees, the Testament of Naphtali and especially of Enoch, not to mention previously unknown works of a similar nature. Thus, Apocrypha and Pseudepigrapha have become demonstrably, and not just hypothetically, Jewish literature, and have had to be accommodated as such. Together with the Qumran Community's own compositions, they have suddenly appeared, not as a secondary and negligible phenomenon, but as clear evidence of Palestinian Jewry's rich intellectual creativity in the multi-party system of the pre-Destruction era. The reduction to unity of religious inspirations which the masters of the Tannaitic age achieved, from Yohanan ben Zakkai to Judah ha-Nasi, was necessitated by the conditions in which Judaism was re-organized, and by the way it responded to the needs and pressures of that period of crisis.

The Aramaic Books of Enoch of Qumran Cave 4, prepared for edition by J. T. Milik and at present in the process of production by the Clarendon Press in Oxford, are likely to form the *pièce de résistance* in the pseudepigraphic material from the Dead Sea especially when read in conjunction with M. A. Knibb's new edition of the Ethiopic text, scheduled to appear in 1976. The publication of this work is bound to affect the ideas hitherto in vogue concerning the most important Pseudepigraphon. As you are all aware, the section of the Similitudes (chaps. 37-72), known also as Book II, is unattested at Qumran, although Book I is represented fragmentarily by five manuscripts, Book III by four, Book IV by five, and even Book V by one manuscript. This means among many other things, that the famous Enochic "Son of Man" about whom New Testament scholars have speculated so much, appears to be missing from the pre-70 text of the Aramaic Enoch. Milik now advances the theory that the Similitudes were written in the third century, and his arguments will have to be weighed with the greatest care, although on the basis of literary contacts and doctrinal features I myself would be inclined to date it to the last quarter of the first century.

The pseudepigraphic collection from Cave 4 suggests that Aramaic was extensively used during the earliest phase of non-biblical writing activity, and that the revival of Hebrew as normal vehicle came only somewhat later. In a not too distant future it may perhaps be possible to argue that Aramaic was the original language of works such as Tobit and Daniel, surviving bilingually, and that Hebrew is the translation?

At present, the corpus of Pseudepigrapha, so marvellously and competently edited by R. H. Charles some sixty years ago, needs a complete reworking. To my knowledge, three projects are afoot. The first, directed by H. F. D. Sparks, was launched in the fifties, but is still not ready for the printer. The other, a fresh American initiative sponsored by the Society of Biblical Literature and planned as a companion volume to Doubleday's

Jerusalem Bible is, as the publisher's jargon goes, "in active preparation," thanks to the efforts of the energetic secretary of the enterprise, James H. Charlesworth of Duke University. The various works to be included have by now been allocated to an international team of scholars. Meanwhile, a German venture directed by W. G. Kümmel, and planned to consist in five volumes, has taken the lead by starting publication in the form of fascicles.[17] We can await, therefore, a true revival, essentially due to the impetus of Qumran, in this crucial corner of inter-testamental Jewish literature.

III. PALESTINIAN JEWISH HISTORY AND CULTURE

Another area in which the Dead Sea Scrolls discoveries are exercising some influence is that of the history and culture of the Jews in Palestine in Late Antiquity. Admittedly none of the Dead Sea Scrolls is a historical document in the strict sense of the word, and the little information we have concerning persons and events and, in general, of the past of the Community, derives from Qumran Bible interpretation. Nonetheless, it must be emphasized that we now possess the literature of a Palestinian group (I try to avoid if I can the term "sect" which is so misleading), a literature written by its members for internal use (and not for Hellenistic consumption as in the case of Philo and Josephus), in Hebrew and Aramaic. What is more, this literature survives in documents dating to the epoch of the Community's actual existence. These are facts unparalleled in Jewish religious history during those centuries. I hardly need to remind you that no works of the Sadducees have been preserved, and all we know of them derives, with the exception of the brief notices of Josephus and occasional hints in the New Testament, from accounts of controversies reported not by themselves, but by their opponents, the Pharisees. Moreover, neither these accounts, nor those in which the Pharisees describe their own teachings and practices, have reached us in a direct Pharisaic formulation; they are available only in the considerably later rabbinic compilations of Mishnah, Tosephta, Midrash and Talmud. If, to complete the picture, I may be allowed to treat the Gospels as Jewish literature of the first century, they can be said to be close in time to the events they relate, but they are extant only in Greek, whereas the language of the chief characters of the story, and even more so their concepts and whole civilization, were Jewish and Aramaic-Hebraic.

An assessment of the Scrolls from the point of view of Jewish history in its broadest sense still largely remains to be done. Some small progress, I hope, has been made in this direction by the revisers of the first volume of Schürer's *History of the Jewish People*,[18] and more is to come in volume II dealing with Jewish institutions. To name only the most obvious topics, Temple, Priests, Levites, worship, biblical exegesis, will bear the noticeable imprint of the Scrolls. It goes without saying that no discussion of the Second War against Rome can now be conducted competently without recourse to the evidence disclosed by the caves of Murabbaᶜat and Naḥal Ḥever.[19] But, I repeat, much is still to be achieved, including a fresh evaluation of the secondary evidence contained in rabbinic literature relating to the period down to Bar Kokhba.

Talmudic experts will be welcomed as partners in a collective task, and as participants in an effort to integrate the sources, *all* the sources, of Jewish culture. Their expertise will complement usefully the specialised knowledge of biblical, inter-testamental and New Testament scholars, and of students of the Graeco-Roman and Parthian-Persian worlds. Perhaps here, too, some optimism is warranted. In the 1950s some of the leading spokesmen of Jewish studies briefly pointed the way. I should like to name Saul Lieberman[20] and Naftali Wieder,[21] and that all-rounder Chaim Rabin.[22] But their example has not always been followed. E. E. Urbach's major work, *The Sages: Their Concepts and Beliefs*,[23] is so construed that in seven-hundred Hebrew pages there is little room for reference to non-rabbinic documents. Enoch and the Testaments obtain three quotations each; the Book of Jubilees four; and the Dead Sea Scrolls, or more precisely the Scrolls of the sect from the Judaean Desert, come on top with nine mentions (of which three are general allusions). S. Safrai has not even Urbach's excuse that the Second Temple period is outside his scope, for it is on the opening page of a volume entitled, *The Jewish People in the First Century*, and in a chapter dealing with "The Sources" that he writes:

> Books . . . belonging to a Jewish sect or sects whose headquarters were at Qumran . . . did not become part of Jewish tradition and, like the Apocrypha, will not be discussed directly here.[24]

But there are signs of increasing awareness of the importance of the Dead Sea manuscripts and other non-Talmudic documents among Judaica experts, especially in the writings of the younger generation of practitioners of Jewish studies such as Jacob Neusner[25] in the United States and Bernard Jackson[26] in this country. The new style of scholarship attempts to amalgamate the various sources reflecting Jewish customs, and adopts the sophisticated techniques evolved by biblical and New Testament experts, and by that fine race of proven scholars, the students of classical antiquity. I hope and pray that many more, old and young, will join in in a grand venture of exploration of the entire field of post-biblical Judaism. They will have a special contribution to make to the study of the halakhic literature from the Dead Sea, particularly when the Temple Scroll, the most voluminous and possibly the most important source, is published. In the meantime, I would like to stress two issues meriting careful scrutiny. The first concerns the discovery of written religious rules at Qumran. How does this affect the commonly held view that halakhah was, by definition, an oral discipline? Secondly, the Damascus Rule, and if the preliminary reports are correct, the Temple Scroll, are collections of extra biblical laws arranged according to subject matter. This suggests that the tendency that resulted, after the compilations by Aqiba and Meir, in Yehudah ha-Nasi's Mishnah, was already active long before the destruction of the Second Temple.

IV. HAGGADAH AND RELIGIOUS THOUGHT

I have left to the end the field of haggadic scriptural exegesis in its Qumran connections. The subject has been investigated by many, including myself,[27] so I will restrict my exposition to a few random observations.

1. Haggadah in the Scrolls employs the main techniques of rabbinic haggadah and is directed towards similar ends: clarification, supplementation, and apologetic or polemical argument.

2. Qumran exegesis either precedes Jubilees (as the Genesis Apocryphon may well do), or stands between this second century B.C. re-writing of the Genesis story and the midrash embedded in rabbinic literature. It displays many similarities to the latter but is at the same time closely connected with the Bible interpretation appearing in Josephus, the Pseudepigrapha and the New Testament. Consequently the Scrolls constitute a valuable yard-stick for the study of the development of exegesis among Palestinian Jews.

3. In this domain, the Qumran *pesher*, or fulfilment interpretation of real or presumed prophecy, occupies pride of place. In addition to its intrinsic importance, it is as I have already pointed out, our principal source for the Community's history. The Qumran exegetes saw in the words of the prophets predictions referring ultimately to events marking the destiny of their own movement.

4. The close links between the Dead Sea *pesher* and the use of the Hebrew Bible in the New Testament have been noticed since the early days of Qumran research. As is well known, the first generation of Jewish-Christian writers sought to explain and justify or defend their beliefs by appealing, through a special interpretation, to Old Testament oracles. The Scrolls have revealed themselves as a brilliant parallel to this central feature of the Gospels. Nevertheless, the eschatological vantage-point suggesting that ancient prediction applies to contemporary event is not exclusively a Qumran and New Testament monopoly: it occurs sporadically in rabbinic literature as well, and is traceable to the most recent book incorporated into the Palestinian canon, that of Daniel.

In chapter 11, verse 30 the author implies that the humiliation of Antiochus Epiphanes (the King of the North) before Alexandria, brought about by the intervention of the (Roman navy "the ships of Kittim"), was simply the fulfilment of a prophecy of Balaam in Numbers 24:24. The words of Numbers 24:17, "A star shall come forth out of Jacob," were used by Aqiba to accredit Simeon ben Kosiba as the royal Messiah. In another context, Yohanan ben Zakkai is said to have announced the imminent rise of Vespasian to the imperial throne by quoting Isaiah 10:34, "And Lebanon shall fall by a mighty one." To the contemporaries of the midrashist the sense was crystal clear: when Yohanan surrendered himself to the Roman general, forseeing the futility of any further resistance, he remembered that Lebanon was a symbol of the Sanctuary, and Mighty one, a synonym for a king. So since Vespasian was to destroy the Temple, but first had to be proclaimed king, Yohanan, as we read in the Midrash, greeted him in good Latin, Vive Domine Imperator—Long live my lord, the emperor! The Habakkuk Commentary contains a similar exegesis identifying the Lebanon mentioned by the prophet with the Council of the Community because it tacitly assumes that the Jerusalem Temple has lost its holy status and is superseded by the Community's supreme institution, the Council, until the seventh year of the eschatological war.[28]

The point on which I will end this survey is at first sight of minor importance. One day, some seven or eight years ago, a graduate student of mine came to me and timidly suggested that he'd found something odd in Codex Neofiti. I looked at the passage in question in a photostat copy—this was before the publication by Díez Macho of the volume on Genesis—and immediately realized what he meant. At that point, rather pleased with ourselves, we nearly collided in the corridor of the Oriental Institute with John Barns, our late professor of Egyptology. "What are you two so jolly about?"—he asked. "We've discovered a new angel," I said. Barns laughed. "You should send him to the Church of England," he told me. "She needs all the help she can get."

Whether or not this angel is available for such onerous additional duties, I don't know, but the passage in which he reveals himself certainly throws a little more light on the intricate bond between Targum, Midrash, Pseudepigrapha and the Scrolls.[29]

The section I have in mind is Genesis 32:25-32, the story of Jacob's struggle with a mysterious and anonymous opponent, a struggle that in spite of the patriarch's injury, finished in a draw, and also in the change of his name to Israel.

In Neofiti, the rival is described and named. He is an angel by the name of Sariel, and appears "in the likeness of a man." But he is not an ordinary angel; he is a prince in charge of the heavenly choirs.

> Let me go . . . for the time has come for the angels on high to praise and I am the chief of those who praise.

Later on, when Jacob is re-named Israel, Sariel adds the following justification:

> For you have conducted yourself as a prince with angels from before the Lord and with men, and have prevailed against them.

A few interpretative comments may be called for.

Jewish tradition since Hosea 12:5 sees in the heavenly Wrestler an angel. Targumic exegesis, moreover, is unanimous in portraying him as a celestial choirmaster. The same view is expressed in the late first century midrashic composition, Pseudo-Philo's Book of Biblical Antiquities (18:6). However, none of these sources know him as Sariel, and to my best knowledge, no angel called by this name ever appears in rabbinic literature.

In the Pseudepigrapha, we find a Sariel among the fallen angels in 1 Enoch (6:8). In the Greek version of the same book (20:1-8), Michael, Gabriel, Raphael, Uriel, Raguel, Remiel and Sariel are given as the seven chief angels. Yet before claiming this text to be a satisfactory parallel to Neofiti's Sariel, we have to admit that in the Ethiopic text Saraqael is substituted for Sariel.[30]

Instead of these uncertainties, the Scrolls furnish us with a firm pointer. The Qumran War Rule (9:12-15), in its description of the four battle formations called "towers," each consisting of three hundred men equipped with shields and spears, mentions that they are to be under the protection of the four archangels, and that every soldier is to bear the name of the heavenly protector of his unit inscribed on his shield.

> On all the shields of the towers they shall write: on the first Michael; on the second Gabriel; on the third Sariel; on the fourth Raphael.

So at Qumran, Sariel becomes one of the four chief angels, replacing Uriel, the traditional fourth archangel in the Greek Enoch and in midrashic literature (Cf. Num. R. 2:10; Pes. R. 46:3). He also appears in an Aramaic fragment of 4Q Enoch 9:1: "Michael, Sariel, Raphael and Gabriel."[31]

Now to find the missing unit in this puzzle, the known elements of which are: Mysterious wrestler (Gen.) = angel (Hos.) = heavenly choirmaster (Palest. Targums) = Sariel (Neof.) = one of the four archangels (Qumran)—I must add the parallel appearing in the Similitudes of Enoch (40:9; 54:6; 71:8; 71:9). Here, the fourth chief angel is neither Uriel, nor Sariel, but Phanuel. But since this name is dependent on the Peniel/Penuel of Genesis 32, the designation by Jacob-Israel of the place where he struggled with the angel, it would appear that in the circles represented by the Similitudes of Enoch, Qumran and the Neofiti variety of the Palestinian Targum, the angelic adversary of Jacob was recognized as one of the four celestial princes, and called alternatively as Sariel or Phanuel.

As for the etymology of Israel, Neofiti explains it, not from the root שׂרה (to struggle) as modern scholars do; nor from שׂרר (to be strong), implied by the Septuagint (ἐνισχύειν) and the Syriac version, but from שׂרר (to rule, to act as a prince). All the other Targumic recensions (אתרבב, רב), as well as Aquila and Symmachus (ἄρχειν), represent the same understanding of the title, Israel.

It is noteworthy that when the Damascus Rule 6:5-6 seeks to expound the phrase, "the penitents of Israel," it identifies them as those whom God (אל) has called princes (שׂרים).

Is it merely by chance that Qumran and Codex Neofiti go hand in hand in disclosing, and finding an answer to, a Jewish doctrinal issue? I think not. In fact, I am inclined to believe that this conjunction of Scrolls, Pseudepigrapha and rabbinic literature prefigures many more "happy coincidences."

I would like to conclude by expressing the hope that the final quarter of this century will be as fortunate as the last one in uncovering new vistas, and in deepening our understanding of inter-testamental and rabbinic Judaism, and that the members of our new-born Association will distinguish themselves in every one of the many branches of Jewish studies.[32]

NOTES

[1]This paper was delivered as the first presidential address at the founding meeting of the British Association for Jewish Studies in London on 1st January 1975.

[2]*Griechische und lateinische Lehnwörter in Talmud, Midrasch und Targum* I-II (1898-99).

[3]*Les Juifs dans l'empire romain* I-II (1914).

[4]*Die Haggada bei den Kirchenvätern* I-II (1899-1900).

[5]*The Synoptic Gospels* I-II (1909, ²1927).

[6]*Aperçus préliminaires sur les manuscrits de la Mer Morte* (1950); *Nouveaux aperçus sur les manuscrits de la Mer Morte* (1953).

[7]*The Zadokite Fragments and the Dead Sea Scrolls* (1952).

[8]*Die hebräischen Handschriften aus der Höhle* (1951).

[9]*The Hebrew Scrolls from the Neighbourhood of Jericho and the Dead Sea* (1951).

[10]"The Hoax of the Slavonic Josephus," JQR 39 (1948), p. 180.

[11]"A commentary on the Book of Habakkuk. Important Discovery or Hoax?," JQR 39 (1949), pp. 236-37.

[12]JQR 41 (1950), p. 1.

[13]See in particular, *The Essene Writings from Qumran* (1961).

[14]I took my scholarly revenge by deciphering, translating and publishing a Hodayoth photograph which he mistakenly allowed the London society journal, *The Sphere*, to print on 18 February 1950. See G. Vermes, *Les manuscrits du désert de Juda* (²1954), pp. 193-94.

[15]F. M. Cross, "The History of the Biblical Text in the Light of the Discoveries in the Judaean Desert," HTR 57 (1964), pp. 292-97.

[16]*Ibid.*, p. 294.

[17]The general title is *Jüdische Schriften aus hellenistisch-römischer Zeit* the first fascicle of which appeared in 1973.

[18]Emil Schürer, *The History of the Jewish People in the Age of Jesus Christ* I. Revised and edited by Geza Vermes and Fergus Millar. Literary Editor: Pamela Vermes. Organizing Editor: Matthew Black, F.B.A. (1973).

[19]See, e.g., *ibid.*, pp. 534-57.

[20]"Light on the Cave Scrolls from Rabbinic Sources," PAAJR 20 (1951), pp. 395-404.

[21]"The Habakkuk Scroll and the Targum," JJS 4 (1953), pp. 14-18; "The 'Law-Interpreter' of the Sect of the Dead Sea Scrolls: the Second Moses," *ibid.*, pp. 158-75.

[22]*The Zadokite Documents* (1954); *Qumran Studies* (1957).

[23]The Hebrew edition appeared in 1969. A two-volume English translation was published in 1975.

[24]*Op. cit.* (1974), p. 1.

[25]Among his numerous publications, I would like to single out *The Rabbinic Traditions about the Pharisees before 70* I-III (1971) and *The Idea of Purity in Ancient Judaism* (1973).

[26]*Theft in Early Jewish Law* (1972) and his *Essays in Jewish and Comparative Legal History* (1975).

[27]Cf. *Scripture and Tradition in Judaism. Haggadic Studies* (1961, [2]1973); *Post-Biblical Jewish Studies* (1975).

[28]See *Scripture and Tradition*, pp. 32-35, 165-66.

[29]Cf. G. Vermes, "The Archangel Sariel. A Targumic Parallel to the Dead Sea Scrolls," *Christianity, Judaism and other Greco-Roman Cults: Studies for Morton Smith at Sixty*, ed. by J. Neusner III (1975), pp. 159-66.

[30]Suriel, prince of the Presence in b. Ber. 51a is probably a conflation of Uriel and Sariel. The latter is mentioned twice as overseer of the camps in the sixth heaven in *Sefer ha-Razim*, ed. M. Margolioth (1966), pp. 104-5. (Information supplied by Dr. P. S. Alexander).

[31]Cf. J. T. Milik, "Problemes de la littérature hénochique à la lumière des fragments araméens de Qumrân," HTR 64 (1971), p. 346.

[32]During the discussion which followed the paper, a number of valuable suggestions were made, some of which have been introduced into the present text. I am particularly indebted to Professor Edward Ullendorff, of the School of Oriental and African Studies (London), Dr. M. A. Knibb of King's College (London), Dr. Emanuel Tov of the Hebrew University (Jerusalem) and Dr. Philip Alexander of the Department of Near Eastern Studies (Manchester) for their helpful criticisms and comments.

IX

The Use of the Later Rabbinic Evidence for the Study of First-Century Pharisaism

JACOB NEUSNER

BROWN UNIVERSITY

The character of Judaism in the first century emerged, for the next nine-teen centuries, solely from sources preserved by Christianity, beginning, of course, with the New Testament itself, but, among the more enlightened, including works of the Apocrypha and Pseudepigrapha as well. Even though books purporting to describe "Judaism" or "Late Judaism" and omitting all reference to the sources preserved by Judaism do appear, it is now nearly a century that scholars have concurred in the importance of referring, in the description of Judaism of the first century, to the entire range of ancient documents which allude to the Judaism of that period, explicitly including the rabbinic literature. The shift from neglect of, to careful attention to, the rabbinic sources surely was complete by the time of Schürer. Important revisions by twentieth-century scholars of first-century Judaism[1] merely confirmed that the Judaic sources of first-century Judaism would now be permitted to have their say.

But this shift has brought with it a distortion of the evidence no less marked than that effected by utter neglect of the matter. For in turning to the rabbinic sources of first-century Judaism, New Testament scholars quite naturally have defined the scholarly program to suit the principal concerns of New Testament studies. Both the questions they bring to the rabbinic literature and the historical-epistemological suppositions in accord with which they read that literature quite naturally emerge from their prior and more important interest, which in the main has been in the character and teachings of Jesus.[2] The Jewish scholars of the rabbinic literature, moreover, eagerly respond to precisely these same matters. Their larger purpose, to make a place for the study of the rabbinic literature in the wider world of culture and its institutions, is well served by talking to begin with about what everyone else is discussing. So the New Testament scholars turn to the rabbinic literature for information on first-century Palestinian Judaism, that form of Judaism in which nascent Christianity took shape, and the rabbinic scholars of the rabbinic literature present themselves as able to provide exactly that information.

To illustrate the consequences of this felicitous union of interests, we consider one matter of the phrasing of the issue of historical knowledge and one matter of historical fact or substance.

As to the former, the single most compelling question before New Testament scholars is whether or not sayings attributed to Jesus were said by him and stories told about him are true. The importance of the answers to the living faith is self-evident. But if scholarship is primarily for historical purposes, then we must wonder whether with reference to any other figure of late antiquity we ask so intensively about the veracity of *ipsissima verba*.[3] I cannot recall, for example, so vivid an interest in the historical Socrates or the historical ᶜAqiba[4] as we find in the historical Jesus. I also cannot find in studies of other important figures of antiquity so deep a sense of systematic skepticism. To state matters simply: when we study Socrates or ᶜAqiba, less is doubted, but much less is affirmed. If, as we have for Jesus, we had for ᶜAqiba diverse traditions deriving from people who were contemporaries and written down within a half-century of his death, we who regard ᶜAqiba as a principal voice in nascent Rabbinic Judaism should be satisfied that we can do a fair amount of history of Judaism. We work as best we can with what we have, as I shall explain. So we doubt less than the New Testament scholars have taught us we ought, but we learn to claim much less concrete biographical information about ᶜAqiba than the New Testament scholars of Jesus want to have. So we affirm less than New Testament scholars seek to affirm. The result for the study of that form of first-century Judaism revealed by the later rabbinic writings is a poorly framed argument. For the issue of whether or not ᶜAqiba really said what is attributed to him is seen as decisive. But this is hardly the right question because the character of the literature which preserves materials attributed to ᶜAqiba is not such as to suggest that we have anything like *ipsissima verba*. The earlier and more reliable rabbinic sources present virtually all sayings attributed to individuals in language so obviously patterned and stereotyped that it is impossible to maintain that one person at some one time said this unique thing. On the contrary, much that is attributed preserves the gist of an opinion without even the pretense that the opinion is stated in precisely the language said by the individual to whom it is attributed. In the earlier rabbinic compilations, moreover, the subjects on which all authorities are permitted to speak to begin with are defined not by the idiosyncratic interests of the individual, but by the exceedingly well defined program of the document itself. There are no random topics; all things are carefully redacted in accord with a clear-cut plan. So even the range of topics on which individuals speak is going to be the work of quite distinct, and much later, figures than said individuals.[5] It follows that rabbinic biography is not so important for the study of Judaism as biography of Jesus is for the study of Christianity, and the rabbinic sources in any case are hardly so valuable for biography as are the Gospels and Apocryphal Gospels for that same purpose.[6]

The substantive matter to which I alluded is excessive emphasis upon the character of messianism and sectarianism in the study of first-century Judaism, to the exclusion of other themes of equal importance. Because of their quite proper interest in the sorts of messianic expectations by which the life and teachings of Jesus were interpreted, and because of their correct view of Palestinian Christiantiy of the first century as a sect within Judaism, New Testament scholars have asked the rabbinic literature to tell them about Jewish messianism and the Jewish sects of that period. To be sure the New Testament scholars have brought the same research-program to the Essene Library of Qumran, with results which to my mind are by no means uninteresting. But that eschatological sect with its *moreh haṣedeq*—its reliable teacher—illuminates the Pharisaism of the period before 70 as much as it does the Christianity of the period before 70.[7] For its part, the sect was profoundly committed to a *halakhic* way of living, took with intense seriousness the requirement of cultic purity at meals outside of the cult, and in other ways conformed to the paradigm of life-in-accord-with-Torah to which, for its part, Pharisaism also conformed. Accordingly, to study the Dead Sea Scrolls and Christian origins without also addressing the issue of the Dead Sea Scrolls and Judaic origins is to lay improper emphasis, with consequent distortions of interpretation, on what by its own testimony was important to the Essene community of Qumran itself. The powerful impulse to stress the messianic character of the reliable teacher, of course, is natural but susceptible of the same effect of distortion.

To the rabbinic sources the issues of messianism are addressed with equal force, as though the rabbinic sources had much to tell us about that matter, and as if what they had to tell us demonstrably was shaped in and probably derived from the first century. But the rabbinic sayings about messianism present a complex problem of interpretation in their own context, which is hardly that of the first century to begin with.[8]

And, finally, the New Testament agendum, with its paramount interest in sectarianism, has neglected the issues of the description of the normative Judaism of first-century Palestine, which, viewed without theological bias, is hardly Essene, Christian, Pharisaic, or Sadducean, since, on the face of it, these are sects. Surely the religion of the Jewish part of the country as a whole requires description in its own terms. To treat Pharisaism as "Orthodoxy" or "the normative religion" as is commonly done is not merely anachronism. It is anachronism for a peculiarly polemical-apologetic purpose, and must be dismissed so that scholars may do their work without needless diversion.

To recapitulate the argument to this point: When scholarship of the New Testament and scholarship of the rabbinic literature agreed that the latter would be asked to contribute to the work of the former, the study of the rabbinic literature paid a heavy price. Attitudes of mind and questions of investigation came to be imposed upon the historical study of rabbinic sources which are wholly congruent neither to the character of those sources nor to their principal concerns. As I said, the processes of formulation and transmission of the rabbinic literature, both oral and written, simply do not make provision for the preservation of *ipsissima verba*. To ask whether or not we have *ipsissima verba,* therefore, is to allow the literature to say what it does not have, but to prevent it from saying what it does know.[9] As is clear, the same attitude of mind introduces into the methodological debates on the rabbinic literature issues which have no natural place therein, so that the "conservatives" allege in the twentieth century what they cannot demonstrate anyone even claimed in the third or fourth or fifth centuries, or, at any rate, claimed in the way in which they now choose to phrase matters. It has become an article of faith among the "conservative" scholars of the rabbinic literature that whatever was assigned to ᶜAqiba was really said by him, whatever is told in fables about him really happened. Didactic and homiletic literature then is not distinguished from the legal literature, and fables are forced to serve as histories. The whole corpus of sources is homogenized as critical historical writing and then given in paraphrase, as though the conception of unbiased reporting of what really happened were available in the first century. This profound misunderstanding of the character and claims of the evidence is the direct result of the motive for which the evidence is examined. I think the false stress, moreover, upon topics such as sectarianism and messianism, upon which the rabbinic literature hardly centers its discourse, similarly exemplifies the state of affairs which prevails when the issues of the "outsiders," that is, a tangentially relevant field, are adopted by the "insiders,"[10] and when all parties concur, for diverse reasons to be sure, that what they agree upon shall then and thenceforward be deemed to be truth.

Let us now consider the result of this common agreement as it is stated by scholars of Judaism. The prevailing position on the results of the use of the rabbinical, and all other, sources for the study of first-century Judaism is as follows:

> At the time of Jesus there was one "Jewish nation" or "people" of which all Jews everywhere were members. This one people had one religion which was "orthodox" Judaism. Of this one religion the correct representatives were the Pharisees, who were followed by the overwhelming majority of the people; other sects were minor. The religion of the Pharisees in Jesus' time is revealed with substantial accuracy in the rabbinic literature of two or three centuries later. This religion is the true and direct descendant of the Old Testament; Christianity was a deviant. At the time of Jesus, Jews were almost the whole of the Palestinian population and the true people of the country, the rest were aliens (usually "Greeks"). Therefore the revolts against Rome in Palestine were wars of the one Jewish people for national independence from foreign tyranny and were supported by the vast majority of the population. Their leaders (sprung from the Zealots, founded by Judas of Galilee) were national

heroes. Outside Palestine, however, the Jews were a non-political, innocent people, mainly intent on observing their peculiar laws. The hostility to them throughout the diaspora was wholly due to gentile misunderstanding and malignity, and these, compounded by Christian propaganda (notably in the Gospels), have been the causes of all the persecutions of all the subsequent centuries.[11]

This summary of the prevailing position attends to a wide range of issues. Let me deal, once more, with only one methodological question and one substantive matter.

It seems to me self-evident that sources deriving from the early third, fourth or fifth centuries first have to be read as testimonies to the prevailing viewpoints of those centuries, and only with very great reserve as evidence of the viewpoints of, or on, the earlier periods, to which they may or may not even claim to refer. Obviously, no one will claim that a fifth century source by definition tells us nothing whatsoever about the first century. That proposition is as absurd as the one which maintains that everything said in the fifth century source about the state of affairs in the first century must be adopted as historical fact, with the obvious exclusion of a few incredible details such as miracles.[12] But the question that requires attention, as I said, is why, to begin with, we should be asked to require the materials of the Talmuds to address matters clearly of peripheral interest to the Talmuds themselves. And why should the Talmuds be subjected to tests of historical veracity, not about the matters about which they may be presumed to be well-informed, that is, the topics under discussion in the Talmuds themselves, but about matters introduced on the fringes of the Talmuds' own inquiry? This self-evidently brings to mind the observation that the issues of interest to New Testament scholarship and those about which the rabbinic literature is capable of testifying have yet to be brought into alignment.

As to a substantive issue: even if the religion of the Pharisees in Jesus' time were revealed with substantial accuracy in the later rabbinic literature, the claim that that religion is the true and direct descendant of the Old Testament (with Christianity as deviant!) is exceedingly difficult to understand. The blatantly apologetic character of such a claim would impress the School of Matthew, with its interest in illustrating Scripture out of the life of Jesus. But it seems to me to have no place whatsoever in historical scholarship today. For it is part of the theological apologetic that there is a linear history of Judaism, which leaps from the Old Testament directly to the rabbinic literature, that is, to Mishnah and beyond, without attending to the literary and religious events of the period between, let us say, Ezra and Judah the Patriarch, except so far as these literary and religious events stand within the limits of the rabbinic literature. Accounts of the Judaism of ancient times which pay slight attention, for example, to the evidence of the Dead Sea scrolls, Targumim, Apocrypha, the relevant Pseudepigrapha, let alone the Gospels and other pertinent materials, testify to the notion that the acceptable sources for history of Judaism are the normative sources of Judaic theology.[13] That notion is correct for theological inquiry and false for history.

But let us go a step further and ask, what is it that we claim when we state that Pharisaism is "the true heir of the Old Testament" (however we deal with others who make the same claim)? It seems to me a rather sizable allegation, given the diversity of the Scriptural materials themselves. Precisely which Scriptures of the Old Testament are supposed, then, to be authentically and accurately carried forward? The repertoire of the School of Matthew is well known. What is the normative florilegium of acceptable Scriptures in behalf of which the claim of continuity by Mishnah is laid down? Is it "everything"? Self-evidently not, since sizable stretches of Scripture elicit little or no attention in the rabbinic writings. So it is some one thing or a carefully selected group of materials which are accurately and authentically carried forward. It follows that the claim correctly to interpret and therefore carry forward and embody the biblical imperatives is secondary to the claim correctly to *select* those imperatives which Scripture itself selects for transmission and perpetuation. This of course is nonsense. Scripture by definition has selected nothing and transmitted everything! That is, even if Mishna-Tosefta accurately carries forward and develops the purity-laws of Leviticus 12—15, as I believe I have demonstrated that it does,[14] it does not prove that the entire process to begin with is not eisegetical. On the contrary, all exegesis, however "historically-accurate," begins in a prior act of eisegesis, which is committed by the very selection, or choice, of those Scriptures to be subjected to exegesis. If for the moment we concede that the laws of the menstruant as represented by Mishnah-tractate Niddah and those of the Zab or Zabah as represented by Mishnah-tractate Zabim accurately develop what Scripture has laid down, so that the laws of the Mishnah in these areas rest wholly within and upon the foundations laid down by Scripture, we still cannot claim to have demonstrated that the Mishnah is the fulfillment and completion of Scripture—except in these areas. And what Scripture says on this subject it says principally to the authorities of Mishnah. It says nothing of the sort to other groups who read the same Scripture but selected other passages as important for interpretation.[15] It follows that the claim that Pharisaism is the direct descendant of the Old Testament is true only from the persepective of Pharisaism. Once its interests and emphases have been defined, then, but only then, is the issue of accurate interpretation of Scripture relevant. First comes the selection, then comes the recourse to Scripture not merely for prooftexts—one form of eisegesis, but also for accurate information, which, I argue, is another, more subtle, form of eisegesis in itself.

The later rabbinic evidence for the study of first-century Pharisaism cannot be dealt with item by item atomistically, as if the diverse documents in which evidence is found had no interests and integrity of their own. It also should not be dealt with whole, as if the evidence derived wholly from a single source, period, set of tradents, or group of redactors. The evidence is diverse, specifically because it is compiled in diverse documents, Mishnah, Tosefta, several strata of the Palestinian and Babylonian Talmuds, collections of *midrashim,* some early, some late, even medieval, all with their as-yet-to-be-discerned tendencies and interests. If a document such as Sifra shapes all its materials into a single formal and thematic structure to make a single point, which is that the true source of law is revelation, not reason, then prior to the use of any of Sifra's materials must be the question of how Sifra has shaped, and has not shaped, what it presents to serve its purpose.[16] And the same consideration affects each and every document. It also should be addressed to strata within documents, tradents, redactors of diverse conglomerates of materials. This work has yet to be done. That is why I find such futility in arguments about why this story or that saying assigned to a first-century figure is or is not to be believed and taken as accurate evidence of things done or said in the first century. The arguments as presently phrased are altogether too abstract. They lack concrete reality for the working historian. It is argued that we must believe as true everything which we cannot show to be false. Then what is that truth which we must believe? Is it that Hillel or ᶜAqiba really said something? But what is it that I am required to believe they said, in a pericope in which all that is assigned to them will be *liable* or *exempt, unclean* or *clean?* The matter can be reduced to a series of ever more absurd propositions, each requiring still greater acts of faith than the foregoing. But the whole seems to me beside the point.

Let me now phrase matters as I think they should be seen. I offer two propositions, one of method, one of substance.

As to method: the rabbinical literature is no more uniform in point of historical origin and literary character than are the books of the New Testament or of the Old Testament. Like both, the diverse writings grouped together as "rabbinical literature" form a varied library, produced over a long period of time. It follows that the ways in which the materials of rabbinic literature are going to serve to illuminate the periods of which they speak before the time of their own, various moments of redaction, are going to be diverse. It is true that the various moments of redaction are going to be diverse. It is true that the various documents tend to employ the same names, e.g., Hillel, ᶜAqiba, Eliezer and Joshua, and the like. But we should not be well served if we assume that everything put into the mouth of Hillel or ᶜAqiba by any rabbinic document, whenever or wherever it was compiled and redacted, belongs there. Such a supposition requires us to include as authentically first- and second-century sayings the whole of the Zohar, for example. If we are to follow Zohar, however, then we must suppose that in the first and second century ideas and issues were under discussion which we otherwise first encounter a thousand years later. This seems not very likely.

We further cannot ignore the much-proven fact that the materials attributed to a given first-century authority do vary not only in concrete opinion but in overall character from one document to the next. For example, what Mishnah-Tosefta wants to have us believe about Tarfon or Eliezer and what the Babylonian and Palestinian Midrashic compilations want us to believe about them have virtually nothing in common—scarcely a single shared *theme,* let alone a concrete, specific idea or allegation, whether legal or theological.[17] That fact leads us to suspect, as I said, that diverse documents have their concrete and specific points of interest and concern, things that they in particular want to address. The accuracy of their attributions is of less consequence to them than it is to us.

We have, therefore, to begin our inquiry by isolating some one document and analyzing its data in the context of the unfolding of its problem, not ours. What Mishnah, the earliest rabbinic document and therefore the one with which all work must commence, has to tell us about the first century, however, is a consequence of what it wants to say about the sacred and the profane. It has a large message, a vigorous polemic, an urgent apologetic, which it proposes to lay forth. Everything is subordinated to the polemic and apologetic which define and account for both Mishnah's literary character and its contents. It follows that once we treat the several documents with due deference to their distinctive character, we enter into the world constructed by said documents. We may then take the closely related methodological step forward: to lay forth a series of probabilities as to what is less likely, and more likely, to constitute a veracious report of first-century ideas and events.

Treating Mishnah (with its supplement, Tosefta) as the beginning of the matter, we have to ask how we may assess these relative probabilities. The answer is to ask (1) whether what is attributed to an authority assumed to have lived before 70 is prior in logic to what is attributed to an authority assumed to have lived after 70, (2) whether what is attributed to the one intersects with what is attributed to the other, and (3) whether what is attributed to the latter depends upon and develops what is attributed to the former. If these three conditions—chronological sequence, intersection, and logical sequence—are met, then we have reason to believe that what is assigned to the authority before 70 in substance (*only*) is prior to what is assigned to the authority afterward. It then will follow that we have established a credible sequence of ideas in a document which took shape nearly two hundred years after the events and men of whom it claims to speak. But that is the sole fact we have in our hands.[18] To assume that Mishnah's authorities who are supposed to have flourished before 70 were Pharisees is reasonable, even likely, but as yet unproved. Only two figures who occur in Mishnah are mentioned in extra-Mishnaic literature as Pharisees. These are Gamaliel I, whom Acts 22:3 knows as a Pharisee, and Simeon b. Gamaliel, to whom Josephus refers as a Pharisee.[19] The other sources of the period know nothing of all those other people mentioned in Mishnah as having thrived before 70 and assumed by us to have been Pharisees. My own inclination is to extrapolate from the known—Gamaliel and his son, Simeon—to the unknown.[20] The methodological point thus is very simple. We cannot settle merely by decree that everything attributed to ᶜAqiba in all documents actually was said by him, nor will abstract arguments settle the matter. What must be done is the hard work of close literary-critical analysis, followed by the even harder work of fresh exegesis, then the systematic assessment of how what is attributed to ᶜAqiba fits into the larger sequence of what is attributed to everyone else, before and after ᶜAqiba, down to the end of Mishnah.

The substantive result will not be entirely satisfying for New Testament scholars whose principal interest in the rabbinic literature is in finding assistance for the exegesis and historical study of New Testament literature. For what begins now to emerge is a picture of a kind of piety which simply is quite different from that represented by the Gospels, an expression of a Judaic ontology entirely distinct from that operative in the Judaism of what is assigned to Jesus. What we learn about the Pharisees therefore is at the foundation simply not very relevant to the small-scale and atomistic exegesis of the New Testament and its history. For what the Pharisees evidently stood for is an ontological conception, a set of ultimate concerns, distinct from, but not necessarily in conflict with, that of the earliest church of Jerusalem. It will follow, alas, that the two sets of materials—the New Testament and the rabbinic literature—really cannot say much to one another in matters of detail. To be sure, those who are interested in the History of Religions and in the history of Judaism find the two sets of writings exceedingly interesting, but that is because of a quite fresh and large-scale perspective.[21] What is this center of interest for Pharisaism?

If we draw together the Mishnah's data which apparently tell us something about the character of the Pharisees before 70, these data form the picture of a group of people who form a commensal group, whose rules relate principally to conditions for eating together in a state of cultic cleanness.[22] This result conforms to the Synoptics' chief points about the Pharisees, which concern their observance of certain rites in general, and their stress on preserving cleanness when eating ordinary meals in particular. But the other two sources on the Pharisees, the Gospels and Josephus, report traits about the Pharisees as a group of which Mishnah-Tosefta's pre-70 figures know remarkably little. Josephus' references to what Pharisees did and who Pharisees were in the first century are not rich. But he does know Simeon b. Gamaliel as a Pharisee in the leadership of the Temple council, just as Paul in Acts knows about Gamaliel as a Pharisee in the Temple council. So Josephus and the Gospels know about the Pharisees as a political group and not merely a pietistic sect. True, in other rabbinic documents we do find a number of stories about the Pharisees as a political group, but on closer examination, these stories appear to derive from that same source from which Josephus drew a fair measure of his narratives about the Pharisees (as distinct from of the source of his descriptions of the Pharisees).[23] Even if we believed every word the Babylonian and Palestinian Talmuds have to tell us about all those "sages" who flourished before 70 and who, we assume, are Pharisees, we should not have a substantial picture of the role of the Pharisees in the life of the country. In the main the rabbinic picture sets the Pharisees into juxtaposition with, and opposition to, the Sadducees, and phrases the issues of partisan dispute in terms of the calendar and purity rules of the cult (matters in which we know the Pharisees as portrayed by the rabbinic literature were particularly interested), and not in terms of the conduct of public affairs, such as should have interested people who took a place in the council of the Temple. It follws that the rabbinic evidence for the study of first-century Pharisaism presents a rather distinctive view of the sect, not wholly congruent with the picture of a rather more political group deriving from the other two principal sources.

Let me conclude by defining this Pharisaic ontology which stands at the center of the rabbinic picture of the first-century Pharisees.

The Pharisaic stress on eating food suitable for the cult and eating it in conditions of cultic cleanness means that, for their system of piety, the central metaphor is the cult, by analogy to which what is clean is deemed clean, and what is unclean, unclean. That analogy is inevitable, given the system's ontological conviction that regularity, permanence, recurrence, and perpetual activity define what is normal and delimit life from non-life. For the ontology in this context is ultimately realized in that permanent, recurrent, and perfect world created by the cult and extending its lines of structure and order from the center which is the cult to the periphery formed by the setting of holy Land and People. Just as food is permissible to the Israelite when it is acceptable for the altar, so conditions for eating it are defined by the circumstances of cultic cleanness. Just as the Land is contaminated by sexual misbehavior within and upon the Land, so the cult—reverting to what is at the center of the circle—is contaminated, and, therefore, so is the Israelite bed at home. Just as the people are potentially agents of contamination through sexual misdeed and culinary misstep, so the cult and the Land may be endangered by the people and may also be sanctified by them. And all the elements, Land, People, and cult, are to be holy because God is holy, God, who brought the people from Egypt, ordained the cult, and owns the Land. If the cult is at the center, therefore, it is only because it serves as the supreme exemplification of the pervasive analogy, the umbilicus of the metaphor. That which is compared is comparable to that which is beyond compare, which is the holiness of the Holy One. Served by Israel at the cult in the Land and with the products of the Land, the Holy One above is the paradigm and model for the whole and integrated world of life below; life below is modeled against the Holy One above. The cult therefore is at the center of the Pharisaic metaphor because the cult is the nexus, the pivot at which the axis is located between heaven and earth. All things always revolve endlessly around that axis, the enduring system on earth not testifying to, but attested by, the eternal one in heaven. Such a system, it goes without saying, has no place for disruptive historical events, which produce only disintegration and disorder.

When we turn to the central ontological affirmation of the Gospels, it is the very disruptive and disintegrative, profoundly historical and even world-historical, moment described therein. What is remarkable is not the stories and sayings of Jesus, in the main commonplaces for ancient Judaism, but the passion and the resurrection, on the one side, and Paul's reflection on the meaning of the cross, on the other. These are what make Christianity an essentially distinctive and fresh mode of Judaic piety. And they begin in an ontology quite distinct from that of the cult, an ontology which centers, as I just said, on a profoundly disruptive historical event, one which has shattered all that has been regular and orderly. So far as history stands at the center of being, so that the messiah and the conclusion of history form the focus of interest, the ontological conception of Christianity scarcely intersects with that of Pharisaism. So, I think it is clear, the two kinds of piety, the one with its effort to replicate eternity and perpetual order, the other with its interest in the end of an old order and the beginning of a new age of history, scarcely come into contact with one another. They speak of different things to different people. In concluding, I stress that the rabbinic evidence for first-century Pharisaism is apt, in time to come, to yield a more complex and detailed picture than that which I have sketched. But it seems unlikely that the main outlines will be greatly revised. For Mishnah-Tosefta and its continuators in the Talmuds stand for that same ontological principle, the permanence and recurrence of the sacred in time and beyond time, which I believe forms the deepest foundation for the Pharisaic ontology as well.[24]

NOTES

[1] I refer to the works of my teacher, Morton Smith, Montefiore and Loewe, Moore, Danby, Davies, Ginzberg, Urbach and Zeitlin. The works of these illustrious scholars are too well known to require specification.

[2] The comparison of various paradigms or types of Judaic religious structures has scarcely been undertaken, as we shall note below. Indeed, one of the curious lacunae is the failure to attempt the comparative study of religions using these interesting, yet essentially distinct, sets of data.

[3] Let alone *magnalia Christi*! I do not understand why people ask about *ipsissima verba* but seem less interested in whether or not the stories of things Jesus *did* are equally true. The distinction between the one and the other seems to me to require examination, particularly in light of Morton Smith, *Jesus the Magician* (New York, 1978: Harper & Row), which shows that the character of the reports of wonder-working deeds is at least as commonplace in antiquity as is the content of the principal ethical teachings a commonplace for Judaism.

[4] To be sure, the reason is that, when the scholars of Judaism come to the Talmudic stories, they simply take them all at face value as fact. Louis Finkelstein, *Aqiba: Scholar, Saint, Martyr* (1936. Repr., New York: 1962) and Jacob Neusner, *A Life of Yohanan ben Zakkai* (Leiden, 1962. Second edition, completely revised, 1970) are indistinguishable in this regard.

[5] See especially William Scott Green, "What's in a Name? The Problematic of Rabbinic 'Biography'" above, pp. 77–96.

[6] I am amazed at the neglect of the apocryphal Gospels of Jesus, as though the canonical ones were historical and the apocryphal ones not. An important correction in this state of affairs is in Morton Smith, *op. cit.,* who makes extensive reference to apocryphal Gospels. My distinguished colleague, Professor Stephen Gero, moreover has given seminars at Brown University on the apocryphal Gospels.

[7] See my *History of the Mishnaic Law of Purities.* XXII. *The Mishnaic System of Uncleanness: Its Context and History* (Leiden, 1977), pp. 24–109.

[8] The most interesting materials are not even attributed to authorities before the third century, although sayings on the character of the Messianic age are assigned, also, to first-century figures. But the history of Messianic thought has to be investigated not solely through reference to Talmudic sayings, on a much broader scale. Merely collecting sayings and stringing them together without rigorous thought on their interrelationships and even on the structural potentiality of the topic as a whole hardly add up to the sort of history we require for this idea.

[9] The result will be the construction of a scholarly agendum along lines important to Christian theological inquiry but not congruent to the character of the rabbinic literature itself. This emerges both in G. F. Moore, *Judaism* (1927. Repr., Cambridge, 1954) and Ephraim Urbach, *The Sages: Their Concepts and Beliefs* (Jerusalem, 1975. English translation: Israel Abrahams). In this regard, one can hardly fault C. G. Montefiore and H. Loewe, *Rabbinic Anthology* (1938. Repr., Philadelphia, 1959), for arranging sayings and stories as an anthology, rather than as a work of autonomous scholarship. Their categories and results and those of Moore and Urbach hardly differ in material ways.

[10]For a much richer account of this curious problem in learning, see Robert K. Merton, *The Sociology of Science. Theoretical and Empirical Investigations.* Edited and with Introduction by Norman W. Storer (Chicago and London, 1973), pp. 99-138.

[11]Summary by Morton Smith in his review of S. Safrai and M. Stern, eds., *Compendia Rerum Iudaicarum ad Novum Testamentum. Section One. The Jewish People in the First Century. Historical Geography, Political History, Social, Cultural, and Religious Life and Institutions* (Philadelphia, 1974), in *Anglican Theological Review,* 58, 1976, pp. 112-14. Smith concludes, "All the statements in this position are probably false, and most are demonstrably so." Israeli scholarship in this area is totally out of touch, and, as this statement seems clearly to suggest, is an exercise in contemporary religio-political apologetics, not history.

[12]But distinguishing fact from fiction is not accomplished merely by declaring something "historical" and something else "unlikely," let alone by capriciously and unsystematically accepting as "historical" one set of stories while rejecting some other. Yet, it must be said, in works such as those edited by Safrai and Stern, nearly everything is declared to have "the ring of truth" or to be "obviously historical." I cannot find a single systematic statement of the meaning of such judgments.

[13]Urbach's *Sages* is only the most recent instance, but it is the most blatant one.

[14]See in particular my *History of the Mishnaic Law of Purities.* VII. *Negaim. Sifra,* XV-XVI. *Niddah,* and XVIII. *Zabim.* This proposition is systematically worked out in reference to those three tractates.

[15]As I tried, in work for my *Purities,* to find materials from other Jewish sources of ancient times, I was consistently frustrated to discover that, in the main, no one else in ancient Judaism seemed terribly interested in the subject matter, let alone the pertinent Scriptural verses, so central to Mishnah in this area.

[16]See *Purities.* VII. *Negaim. Sifra,* where this is systematically spelled out and instantiated.

[17]This has been proved in the following systematic works on sayings attributed to first-century authorities by the sequence of rabbinic compilations: Gary G. Porton, *The Traditions of Rabbi Ishmael* (Leiden, 1976-   ) Vols. I-IV; Tzvee Zahavy, *Eleazar ben Azariah* (Missoula, 1977: Scholars Press for Brown Judaic Studies); Jack Lightstone, *Yose the Galilean,* William Scott Green, *Joshua ben Hananiah,* Shamai Kanter, *Gamaliel of Yavneh,* and Joel Gereboff, *Tarfon* (all in press at Leiden for publication in 1978 and 1979); and in my *Eliezer ben Hyrcanus: The Tradition and the Man* (Leiden, 1973).

[18]See "The History of Earlier Rabbinic Judaism: Some New Approaches," *History of Religions* 16, 3, February, 1977, pp. 216-36.

[19]*Life* 190ff., 216.

[20]That is, since the chains of authority of M. Abot 1:1 and M. Hagigah 2:2, we find Gamaliel and Simeon b. Gamaliel, it seems to me others on those chains also are apt to have been Pharisees like them. But I find this an ever-less-secure assumption.

[21]That is to say, comparative study of religions is to be undertaken in these intersecting groups, which must, however, be permitted to stand in all their distinctiveness and integrity upon their own essentially separate, if contiguous, territories.

[22]See my *Rabbinic Traditions about the Pharisees before 70* (Leiden, 1971). But it must be stressed this does not exhaust the totality of relevant material, nor are the Pharisees to be represented solely as a table-fellowship sect.

[23]Professor Shaye Cohen, Jewish Theological Seminary of America, is presently working on the problem of materials shared by Josephus and rabbinic documents.

[24]The critical comments of my teacher, Morton Smith, are gratefully acknowledged. This paper was presented at the 500th Anniversary Celebration of Tübingen University, Germany. It also was delivered as a lecture at the Free University of Berlin; University of Cologne; Kings College, University of London; Oxford University and the University of Manchester.

SOURCE INDEX

OLD TESTAMENT

NEW TESTAMENT

MISHNAH

TOSEFTA

PALESTINIAN TALMUD

OTHER ANCIENT SOURCES

LITURGICAL TERMS AND FORMULAE

GENERAL INDEX